D0257889

To Colin Trusler

With sincere good wishes

David Dreman

April 1993

TRANSFORMING COMPANY CULTURE

Getting your company from where you are now to where you want to be

TRANSFORMING COMPANY CULTURE

Getting your company from where you are now to where you want to be

David Drennan

McGRAW-HILL BOOK COMPANY

London · New York · St Louis · San Francisco · Auckland · Bogotá
Caracas · Hamburg · Lisbon · Madrid · Mexico · Milan · Montreal
New Delhi · Panama · Paris · San Juan · São Paulo · Singapore
Sydney · Tokyo · Toronto

Published by
McGRAW-HILL Book Company Europe
Shoppenhangers Road, Maidenhead, Berkshire, SL6 2QL, England
Telephone 0628 23432
Fax 0628 35895

British Library Cataloguing in Publication Data

Drennan, David
  Transforming Company Culture : Getting
  Your Company from Where You are Now to
  Where You Want to be
  I. Title
  658.4

  ISBN 0–07–707660–5

Library of Congress Cataloging-in-Publication Data

Drennan, David,
    Transforming company culture : getting your company from where you
  are now to where you want to be / David Drennan.
        p.   cm.
    Includes bibliographical references and index.
    ISBN 0-07-707660-5
    1. Corporate culture.   2. Industrial management.   I. Title.
  HD58.7.D74   1992
  658.4′063 – dc20   92–9046
                                                                         CIP

Copyright © 1992 McGraw-Hill International (UK) Limited. All rights
reserved. No part of this publication may be reproduced, stored in a retrieval
system, or transmitted, in any form or by any means, electronic, mechanical,
photocopying, recording, or otherwise, without the prior permission of
McGraw-Hill International (UK) Limited.

1234 CUP 9432

Typeset by Cambridge Composing (UK) Ltd
Printed and Bound in Great Britain by Hartnolls Limited, Bodmin, Cornwall.

Contents

profit-sharing – Rewarding employees imaginatively
– Getting everyone to search out excellence – The
power of visible recognition – Publish and make
heroes – Celebrate success – Look for opportunities
to celebrate success – Distinctive ways of celebrating
success – Making people feel good about their work –
Back to the fundamentals – Key points summary

Lack of top management control – Middle
management resistance – Employee resistance –
Lack of 'structure shift' – Training problems –
Problems of company size – Lack of persistence –
Key points summary

The distinguishing factors – Kwik-Fit – Mars
Confectionery – Linn Products – Key points
Summary

Foreword

'No man puts his foot into the same river twice' wrote Heraclitus some 2500 years ago as he sought to explain the nature of change. Society and institutions are in a process of continuous change but now the stream seems faster and the eddies and cross-currents more frequent. Industrial, commercial and public bodies are being influenced by the increasing challenges of national and international competition, of the environment and society, of customer standards and fashion, of employee values and the prospect of different governments with differing policies. 'The way in which we do things around here', the general definition of company culture, is under challenge, sometimes as a result of crisis, sometimes as a result of a deliberate plan.

There is general agreement that business organizations need to create an environment of continuous planned change to meet the competition expected in the last decade of the twentieth century, but how is this to be done without losing that which is good and effective within organizations? How can one avoid 'throwing out the baby with the bath water' and at another extreme how can one meet the accusation 'the more it changes, the more it remains the same thing'? How can management continue to maintain the support of employees faced with the need to meet annual targets and at the same time remodel the organization to prepare for the implementation of new strategies, when both groups feel threatened by the speed, nature and 'chaos' of the demands?

It has been my privilege to have been associated with great cultural changes in the past few years. In the UK National Health Service (NHS) I was given the task of beginning the changes in management culture which still continue. These were initiated by the Griffiths Report and the introduction of General Management to replace the consensus style which previously existed in the Health Service. This process was continued under the 1989 White Paper which seeks to introduce, amongst other things, the concept of an internal market in the Health Service.

More recently in IBM, a company which has a nationally, indeed internationally, known culture, a revolution has begun since the organization needs to change itself from a hierarchical, centralized structure to an institution where delegation and empowerment of the manager and employee are the hallmark of the management style. It shares this new approach with many other large organizations. Indeed one is impressed by the apparent similarity of actions which are occurring in major companies throughout the United Kingdom and the United States. Culturally the vocabulary is the same. Delegation, 'small is beautiful', delayering or removing management levels, the importance of a team as well as the individual, empowerment, market driven quality, the rediscovering of the customer are all trends which characterize the new cultures being created in large and medium sized organizations.

Changing a culture is not easy. When employees have been brought up in a particular tradition, they may find it difficult to recognize the need for and scope of the changes required. All the mechanisms which David Drennan describes so admirably are needed to accomplish change: good and constant communications, management training, measurements, objective setting and feedback on achievement and failures, employee involvement, incentives and so on. But by themselves they are not enough. Indeed, changing the attitudes of managers and employees, while constituting the vital step in developing and implementing new strategies will not, by itself, achieve the desired objectives.

Personnel managers with organizational development responsibilities sometimes fall into the error of believing attitude change is in itself enough. It is not. There frequently has to be physical change in the organization structure in order for it to reflect the new values otherwise it will not be able to deliver. In the computer industry this has meant the switch from geographic structures with branches serving all customers, within their local area, to industry-based branches where distant customers of like interest, product and needs can be provided with the solutions which are required to meet their special or unique problems.

In addition, the very administrative process by which a company operates are the result of its historical culture and themselves need to be reviewed and revised. A simple example is the number of signatures required for an approval for any particular action by management. If the organization preaches delegation and yet maintains a system which requests six or seven sign-offs then the culture can hardly change. Expressed at a higher level, if the national or international headquarters retains substantial reserved powers or, even worse, commits unpredictable interferences from time to time, then the attempt to create delegation or empowerment will have no credibility.

So organization structure and administrative process has to mirror the changes in attitudes and actions which are being carried through. Clearly the overall strategy must be seen to be sound. A new vocabulary has grown up around this topic over the past five or six years, the need for a vision, for critical success factors and so on, but clearly a strategy for the business which is thought to be wrong and which does not pay off will not result in a change of culture. Much has been made by researchers of the success of organizations in changing their behaviour and culture and the use of management techniques in order to achieve this but this has to be seen against a background of a choice of a strategy which is perceived and accepted as the correct way to go. This is much easier to plan than to implement since it frequently involves very painful decisions. For example, the recognition by a company that it should not be in manufacturing and that it should concentrate on being 'free to buy and sell other organizations' products is certainly one which will be resisted by the manufacturing management and staff who will not be won over in any way!' Yet many organizations have had to make this step to survive and change their culture from that of manufacture to marketing.

David Drennan is well aware of these points since his book is not that of an academic but of a practitioner who has called upon his own experience in one of the best managed companies in the world as well as drawing upon his consultancy knowledge and the work of other leading authorities on this topic. In reading his work I admire the authenticity and quality of the various approaches which he puts forward, agree with almost all of its content and, reflecting on my own experience, wish that this book had been written a number of years ago so that I could have made full use of its valuable lessons. I also admire its clarity, and the summaries of the various chapters which make for speedy revision and recall. It is easily read, full of good advice and guidance and should become part of the established literature on this important topic which will continue to dominate management thinking for many years to come.

Sir Leonard Peach
Director of Personnel and Corporate Affairs
IBM United Kingdom Limited

To Dee

My invaluable critic,
wife,
and best friend

1

What 'culture' is

WHAT WE MEAN BY CULTURE

Whatever company 'culture' may mean to you now, it will have a specific meaning throughout this book. Culture equals *'how things are done around here'*.

That simple, enveloping phrase is made up of a number of elements. Over a period of time in any company people develop particular ways of handling the recurrent work of the organization, and gradually this becomes the 'accepted' way of doing things. The methods that work tend to get repeated, supervisors make them into procedures and then teach them to their subordinates and new staff. Staff use the procedures because they are the 'safe' way of doing things, the way of keeping themselves in good odour with their boss. By repetition these ways of doing things become habits, and that is what culture is: the *habits* that have grown up over time and become part of the organization's personality.

Organizations have personalities just like people; they have *attitudes* just like people. 'Attitude' normally describes a person's life position, that is, how they normally react to the world they live in. They may be generally happy and outgoing, for example, or withdrawn and reclusive; they may be energetic or lethargic, aggressive or compliant. Company attitudes show in how they handle their business: they may be a rough and ready 'let's get the job done' type of company, or one which is rather bureaucratic and likes to do things 'strictly by the book'. They show, too, in how they treat their customers, their suppliers and their employees. Indeed, the attitudes of the company's employees are also part of their culture, and may have largely developed in response to their treatment by the company over the years.

That is why culture is also what is *typical* of the organization. The people in the company feel they know what the company is *likely* to do in any given situation. They say things like: 'That is not how we would do it here', or 'What we would do in a case like this is . . .'. They seem to know how the business is likely to act and react, and that understanding helps them fit their behaviour to that of the organization. On the other hand, they do not necessarily like everything the company does, so when they hear negative stories they may say: 'That's just typical of us'. The good and the bad are all part of the culture.

The word 'culture' can of course mean quite different things in other contexts. 'Cultured', for example, can mean sophisticated in taste, interested in the arts, urbane in manners, and so on, but this is not the meaning we are discussing in this book. We are dealing here with the traditions and style of an organization which have grown up over the years and have gradually become its natural 'way of doing things'. Members of the organization have absorbed the atmosphere and procedures of the company into their everyday habits until they almost do not realize they are doing it. When you ask, 'Why do you do that?', they reply: 'We've always done it that way'.

When new members of staff join they soon get absorbed into the existing way of doing things. Right from their first days supervisors show them 'how we do things here' and their colleagues quickly teach them the ropes. Naturally, new employees want to be accepted – they are anxious to please and to fit in. As a result, they readily conform to the behaviour that is *expected*, and, expectations, as we will see later, have a powerful influence in getting both new and existing employees to conform, i.e. to perpetuate the existing culture.

In your organization you may have a proper induction procedure already installed, but the standards of behaviour laid out in your Personnel Practices Manual are not necessarily your real expectations or your real culture. Your real culture is what employees see their fellow workers do and what they find *their managers accept*. A young manager told me that some years ago he joined a household name engineering company as a turner machinist. He was put to work machining a particular production part on his first morning. At about 10.30 am he was working on his third part when he was approached by his section shop steward who asked him what he was doing. He was abruptly informed that 'We only do three of these a day'. Because his supervisor had told him no different the new man then spent the rest of the day visiting the tool store, wandering off to the toilet, sweeping up round his machine and 'cutting fresh air'. The company did not get what he was capable of, but what they expected. The new employee fitted into the company culture right from his very first day. The culture of a business is not formed by what management preach or publish, but by what they accept in practice.

To sum up: *culture is 'how things are done around here'*. It is what is *typical* of the organization, the *habits*, the prevailing *attitudes*, the grown-up pattern of *accepted* and *expected* behaviour.

CULTURE IS CHANGEABLE

Managers and executives often say that what they need in their companies is 'a complete change of attitude'. Generally, they mean on the part of their employees, of course, rather than themselves. But one thing is for sure: if nothing changes in the procedures of the company, its organization, or the attitudes of its management, employee attitudes will not change either. Employee attitudes are largely a product of the environment in which they work. The conditions external to the company have their influence, of course. If unemployment rises and jobs become hard to get in the area, for example, employees may temporarily become more amenable and co-operative. But the environment which has most influence on employee attitudes is the one *inside the business*. That is why the power to change company culture lies largely in the hands of management.

The task is not easy, however. It takes vision, commitment and determination. Without that combination it will not happen, and it certainly will not last. The culture of your business did not grow up overnight, and it will not be changed overnight either. It takes time, and patience. Just as the current behaviours in the business only become habits by repetition over time, so it will take time for the new behaviours to become the new habits. But the journey can take you into completely new territory, to levels of performance you did not even dream about when you started out. It can herald a whole change of era. And that is what this book is about: the crucial factors which can help you *transform company culture*.

2

Where culture comes from

Before you launch out on a major culture change programme, it is as well to understand the causal factors and the influence they each have had in shaping the culture you have now. There are many subtle influences which affect the development of company culture, but we identify here 12 of the most important.

INFLUENCE OF A DOMINANT LEADER

With the authority to make decisions affecting virtually every person in the organization, a strong-minded chief executive can clearly exert a powerful influence in shaping a company's culture over a period of time. This power is even greater if he is also the owner and founder of the business. Such a man was Forrest Mars senior.

Forrest was a man of clear vision and strong views right from the outset. He had learned his trade in the confectionery business run by his father Frank in Chicago, but could not wait to do things his way. With some money in his pocket he made his way to Europe, and started making Mars bars in Slough in England in 1932. One of his key ideas was to make good confectionery with a low unit price which would sell in big volume. In fact, the Mars bar is now one of the biggest selling brands in the world. When Mr Mars expanded into pet food and rice, he again employed the same formula: low coupon, high volume. And that philosophy still governs the company today.

He hated to have anything other than products he could be proud of. On one occasion, his pet food company planned to introduce a new cornflake-like product called Bonzo. They built the manufacturing plant and he went to see it. When he saw the product they were producing he ordered the manager to stop production immediately. The following morning the directors were assembled in the boardroom each facing two bowls, one filled with cornflakes and the other with Bonzo. 'Let's see you eat it,' he said, 'which one would you buy?' The plant was dismantled that very day.

He expected above average performance from his people but was willing to pay above average in return. Forrest Mars felt you have to pay well both to get good people and to retain them. They will give you well above average performance in the good times and in the leaner times are just the kind of people you need to get you out of trouble. One of his favourite questions when he visited his plants was: 'Are you paying your people enough?'. Today Mars employees still enjoy a package of pay and benefits for their work which is well above the average: in fact they religiously conduct pay surveys to make sure it stays that way.

Way back in the 1930s Mars was a single status company. Everyone was called an 'associate'; they were all paid weekly, they all clocked in, and got 10 per cent more pay every day if they clocked in on time. Everyone, including the MD, ate in the same cafeteria, used the same toilets, was provided with working clothes, and was called by their first name: a very unusual situation in England at that time. And the same policies carry on today, 60 years later, in Mars plants all round the world. In addition, Forrest Mars was a stickler for 'open door' communication at every level in the business. On one occasion he is reported to have kicked in the closed door of a personnel director's office and then arranged for maintenance men to remove it completely just to make the point. Naturally, that message soon reverberated round the business! Today there is no danger of managers' doors being closed, because there are none. Everyone works in completely open-plan offices.

Forrest Mars senior long ago gave up executive authority in running the business to his sons John and Forrest, but his influence remains. They and their managers continue and add to the policies first set in motion several decades ago, but they have stood the test of time and continue to shape the business today. Dominant leaders do not always have such a positive influence, however. They can enjoy the decision-making power so much that they become intoxicated by it. It is ego-gratifying to see managers jumping to your orders, to use the muscle of position to cut through procedures, to make arbitrary changes just because you say so. But giving orders is not necessarily being effective.

It was in sheer frustration that the chief executive of a Midlands engineering company sought consultant help to improve his manufacturing productivity. However, the consultant soon discovered that the chief was a man of dominant personality who ran his managers ragged in getting production out and customers' orders met. He was in the habit of prowling around the production areas, questioning storemen, querying supervisors on the charts on their walls or the figures on their desks, and barking orders wherever he thought they were necessary. Everyone ran scared of 'Malcolm'.

Having carried out his own investigations, the consultant decided to get the key production managers together for an intensive off-site workshop. On subjects such as programme changes, meeting customer delivery dates and using their time, the managers at the workshop began to prioritize the actions that they could all take which had the biggest potential for improvement. One of the recurring issues was 'interference by Malcolm' . . . but who was going to tell him? At the end of the three-day session 'Malcolm' attended to hear the conclusions. He was in fact very impressed with some of the constructive and ingenious ideas they had come up with. With the consultant's help they were also able to tell him that *he* was actually one of their biggest problems. That came as a bit of a shock, but as an experiment he contracted to let them run things for three weeks with no interference from him. During the following three weeks productivity was 13 per cent higher than ever before.

Chief executives of this type are often so impressed by their own superior knowledge and energy that it never strikes them that in productivity terms they could be their company's biggest liability. Curiously enough, their own managers, despite being repeatedly exasperated by their sweeping and arbitrary decisions, are often very admiring of their chief's tireless energy, his memory for detail, and clarity of decision-making. In this case, 'Malcolm' would often be contacted on the phone by important customers and make off-the-top-of-the-head promises to them there and then just to keep them happy . . . and to show that he was the type of person who could get things done. He then sent out his orders via his production controller, generally causing serious disruption to already tight production schedules. When production managers protested to the controller he would simply say: 'You had better go and see Malcolm about it'. As 'Malcolm' could often involve his managers in a loud and public scene, few would take the risk. But for years when they failed to make schedule at the end of the month 'Malcolm' just assumed it was another demonstration of his junior managers' general incompetence.

So, strong leaders can certainly affect a company's 'way of doing things'. But 'dominance' is not the key factor. The culture that 'Malcolm' created lasts only as long as his presence in the company. When a new man takes over all that changes. The culture that Forrest Mars established continues way beyond his working lifetime. Because of its basic simplicity and common sense, succeeding managers and leaders of the business not only continue with it, they add to it and develop it. Over the years it digs its way into the company's psyche and becomes part of its personality. And that is one of the distinctions between culture and style: culture stands the test of time; it continues beyond the working lifetime even of the founder.

COMPANY HISTORY AND TRADITION

Tradition dies hard, they say. But why is it so? People prefer structure to their lives, to have a known framework within which to work so that they can adapt their behaviour to manage their environment successfully. When they know how things are they do not have to keep developing new behaviours, the tried and tested patterns will handle all the known and familiar situations. As a result, there is comfort in structure, comfort in a well-known environment. Even when the environment has its unpleasant features, at least you know how it is, and just what to do. Better the devil you know. . . . Anxiety arises when there is the prospect of a major change in the environment. People get upset if they think their routine is going to be disturbed, if they have to learn a whole new set of behaviours just to cope with the new situation. People prefer stability. So, tradition dies hard.

And tradition plays a large part in shaping the culture of many industries. The scotch whisky business is one such industry. Many of the companies grew up as independent family businesses who guarded their recipes and quality jealously. Some years ago I was engaged to do some work for Teacher's, a company with a world-known name. Most whiskies are blended products, and while at the company I discovered that every morning at 10 o'clock the directors conducted a tasting of the single whiskies which were later to be used in producing Teacher's Whisky. Their purpose, I was told, was to ensure that Teacher's always retained its distinctive flavour, that it remained the same this week as it was last week, as it had last year and 10 years ago. This daily tradition, designed to prevent creeping change, had its effect throughout the business. Matters changed slowly, and only after the most serious consideration. The old ways that had served the business well were not to be overturned lightly. On the contrary, there was value in stability.

A good sprinkling of senior managers had previous backgrounds as officers in the armed services; their tradition of working in stable organization structures where honour and authority were foundation values suited the industry very well. The industry was also one where traditionally margins were high, where markets were stable and one could count on steady growth year on year. No great crisis was likely to spring on managers in the whisky business. In these conditions company life assumed a comfortable and gentlemanly character. Pre-lunch drinks and fine dining rooms were commonplace. Life was pleasant and predictable. The habits and traditions which grew up over the years still affect the culture of the business today.

On the other hand, some industries – like the docks – had tough, cut-throat traditions. Again, the nature of the work and the conditions in which it was done had much to do with how the culture developed. Take the port of the Tees on the northeast coast of England as an example. In the 1960s work was allocated twice a day, at 6 am and at midday. Dockers assembled in what looked like cattle pens and foremen simply made their personal choice from the pleading men holding up their union cards. Accusations of favouritism and dockers slipping secret presents of cigarettes and the like to foremen were commonplace. If you did not work that day, because there were not many ships in dock or you did not get chosen by the foreman, you simply did not get paid. The system was much resented.

For years the dockers operated a work allocation hierarchy, nominating stevedores as 'number 1 men', 'number 2s' and 'number 3s'. Number 1s got first choice of any work available with number 2s and number 3s getting only what was left, in turn. Casual workers with no number categorization got only the dregs or nothing at all. As a result pay varied hugely between number 1s and number 3s, while the uneven arrival of ships would mean huge pay packets one week followed by nothing the next week. It was a feast or famine existence. Conditions of work could also be primitive, with the wind often blowing a gale, generally the crudest of toilet facilties, and conditions in the ships themselves frequently smelly, unhygienic and dangerous.

Goodwill between dockers and management was not of the highest, to say the least, with each side often bending the rules and minor disputes breaking out with regularity. The dockers' unions took up militant positions with management and in an attempt to preserve jobs insisted often on blatant overmanning. Such are the traditional positions that grow up over time and they can be hard to shift without some major structural change in the industry. But just such a structural change did come along. In 1968, following the Devlin Report, dockers were engaged on new contract conditions. In return for registration with the National Dock Labour Board, they became entitled to a minimum weekly wage whether work was available or not, and a guarantee of no redundancy. When dockers on the Tees voted on the deal it was overwhelmingly accepted. But since they were now all engaged on the same contract, they also chose to vote on whether the number 1, 2 and 3 men categorization ought to continue. Naturally, the larger numbers of 2s and 3s voted the number 1s down. *Force majeure* had wiped out a long tradition overnight.

History and tradition can be a major factor in the culture of many organizations. People in the business remember how it was and have long memories. As in the docks, fathers pass on their views and advice to their sons and thus habits and tradition are perpetuated. The ways which have kept employees safe and secure throughout the past are not lightly given up. Long entrenched attitudes are hard to shift. It took major legislation to bring changes to the docks. For the management of private companies it takes determination, patience and a clear long-term plan.

TECHNOLOGY, PRODUCTS AND SERVICES

The nature of any business – its kind of technology, products or services – often has a prime influence in shaping its culture, on 'how they do things round here'. In the West Yorkshire town of Castleford the major local employer is Hickson (formerly Hickson and Welch). Hickson is a chemical manufacturer who treats the safety of its operations very seriously. It has to: many of the chemicals are dangerous so great care and precision is required in their handling and processing. Castleford residents know this, too. Hickson is one of some 300 companies in the UK who have to inform all residents within a radius of one kilometre of the procedures to adopt in the event of a major accident at the plant. As you walk round the plant you realize how important the matter of safety is to all employees; whatever might happen, remedial actions are well known and documented. Safety warning signals are built into every process. If urgent action is needed employees know where to get help. Because of its importance to the company's operations, sensitivity to safe working practices has simply become part of the company's culture.

By contrast, even though safety is of first importance in the building industry, the accident record is not good. This is partly because of the large number of small builders and contractors in the industry whose standards on safety vary enormously. It is often accepted that building sites cannot be tidy places because of the nature of the work. As a result sites are often muddy, with off-cuts, equipment and debris lying everywhere in higgledy-piggledy fashion. It can be a real obstacle course trying to visit work in progress, jumping ditches, picking one's way between discarded bricks and metal straps, dodging the mud, avoiding objects falling from above, etc. It all may look terribly untidy and even dangerous to the outsider, but those who work in the industry simply do not notice it any more. 'It has always been that way ever since I've been in the industry,' they say. It has just become the habitual way of doing things, part of the culture.

On the other hand, changes in technology, or discovery of more efficient methods can make old skills redundant and radically change or even eliminate a whole part of a company's culture. For many years Whitbreads, the brewers, would engage hop-pickers from London and elsewhere to gather the hop harvest each year at their farms in Kent. Postcards would be sent out to the regulars who would 'emigrate' with their families and chattels for the duration of the harvest. They came mostly by train bringing their pets, pillows and musical instruments, knowing they would be in for some hard work, but knowing they would earn a few shillings and have some sing-songs and good times with friends they had not seen since last year. It was part of the Whitbread scene, all part of the culture. But gradually hop-picking machines took over. Eventually they became so sophisticated and efficient that there was no economic point in continuing with the human hop-picker tradition. So technology changed a whole section of the company's culture.

So it is in every business. The work they do, the products or services they deliver to customers obviously have a major effect on the shape of their culture. As technology develops people regret the passing of old skills. The younger people who eagerly take on board the new technologies will later in their turn regret the passing need for their old skills. That is how it is with culture. It provides a comforting framework of structure and continuity while adapting gradually over time to absorb the new, giving both continuity and renewal.

THE INDUSTRY AND ITS COMPETITION

For some industries, such as consumer electronics, rapid change and constant product innovations by competitors is normal and has simply become part of the culture. We can see the effects in our own experience. You may like the television you bought two years ago from your local dealer and decide to have another. Almost inevitably you can't find that model any more: it has been superseded, and has even more bells and whistles than before. The electronics manufacturing companies know that is now the name of the game. So their marketing and research people keenly watch the competition, and keep coming up with innovations and gimmicks of their own to keep the competition on the hop. Similarly, production managers and trainers realize that constant training and retraining of their product assemblers is now part of the scene. Employees know, too, that product changes are to be expected and repeated retraining for them is 'just how things are around here now'.

In other industries, where the pattern of work has for years remained largely unaltered, where the businesses are large and have enjoyed near monopoly conditions, changing their culture has become a much more traumatic process. The UK Conservative Government's drive to introduce competition to many nationally owned companies via privatization, and to demand better profit performance from those scheduled to be privatized, sent shock waves through these businesses. British Steel, under the direction of Sir Ian McGregor, paid a heavy price in disruption, suffering and violence to move from a loss-making, lethargic monolith to a profit-making, competitive business. McGregor insisted that capacity and numbers employed had to be reduced significantly. There was huge opposition by Unions and politicians, bitter complaints about lack of concern for whole communities, and in 1980 an acrimonious three-month strike with constant publicity of the affair on radio, on national television and in the press. In the end, separation terms for those choosing redundancy were generous by any standards, with total manning falling from 186 000 in 1979 to some 52 000 in 1989. During that period the time to produce a tonne of steel dropped from 14.3 man hours to less than 5, and a loss of £1784 million in 1979 became a profit of £733 million in 1989. Most managements do not have the stomach for such dramatic and gut-wrenching changes, but when survival is at stake teeth-gritting resolve can often be the response.

Where survival is not at stake, the company's market is largely assured, the business is large, and practices have dug deep habit-forming grooves, moving the culture of a business in a positive direction can be a huge and frustrating task. The British Royal Mail is a case in point. Separated from British Telecom in a privatization process in 1984, the company has struggled to improve customer satisfaction in terms of perform-ance ever since. The public continually complain about the rising cost of postage, the Post Office Users' National Council repeatedly offer evidence of their failures and inattention to customer needs, while the consumers' magazine *Which?* conduct regular trials to demonstrate how they are failing to meet their own 'Quality of Service' targets. With modest staff pay, high people turnover, many middle managers and staff with long service and ingrained habits, it is a tough assignment to move the attitudes and motivation of a business employing some 200 000 people. Meanwhile, there is a great proliferation of businesses stealing Post Office business by offering more expen-sive but guaranteed delivery services.

CUSTOMERS

Companies who depend for the bulk of their business on one major customer tend to listen very intently to their needs. Their motivation and responsiveness are greatly enhanced by the customer's unspoken power of life and death. As a result the style and culture of their business is greatly influenced by the style of the client. Marks and Spencer, who manufacture none of their own products, often have such a relationship with their suppliers. This is not to say their relationship is not generally constructive and a positive influence for develop-ment. Indeed they work directly with their suppliers in their premises to produce the high and consistent quality they demand, or to install the type of equipment and procedures which will keep them as a consistent and reliable supplier. Inevitably their company style bears evidence of Marks and Spencer influence.

Customers shape business culture in other ways of course. In service industries, for example, where front-line staff are meeting large numbers of customers face to face every day, and where clients can simply move their business if they do not like what they get, customers loom large in the company's consciousness. In some cases, customer needs and satisfaction have become the very *raison d'être* of the company's philosophy. An outstanding example has to be the Stew Leonard Dairy located in Norwalk, Connecticut. Stew listens to his customers so well he sells nearly ten times as much per square foot as the average US supermarket. He has a large complaints and suggestions box which he loves to open since it gives him endless opportunities to do what the customers like. Stew says: 'There's no magic about this. We simply listen to the customers and *do what they say*.' He has cast in granite outside his store the company's simple mission statement. It goes:

> Rule 1 The customer is always right.
> Rule 2 If the customer is wrong, see Rule 1.

The total focus and culture of the business has become uniquely the company's customers and their satisfaction.

COMPANY EXPECTATIONS

A company's expectations have a large influence on how its employees behave. For example, a new employee coming from a job with a run-of-the-mill retail shop will match the Stew Leonard high standards within the first few weeks of joining. That is because it is very much what is *expected*. The selection and induction process makes the standards clear, and when they see every other employee striving to meet them they soon join in and become part of the team.

The urge to conform to expectations is a powerful driver of employee behaviour. Why it is so is due to its origins way back in early childhood. Parents teach their children what is acceptable behaviour by praising and encouraging the behaviour they want to see, and by discouraging or punishing what they do not want to see. They in fact create for their children a kind of OK Box, where behaviour inside the Box is OK and accepted, and behaviour outside the Box is NOT OK and actively discouraged. Over time behaviour inside the Box becomes strongly associated with affection, love and security. On the other hand, NOT OK behaviour is associated with scolding, pain, punishment and what Freud said was the worst form of punishment – rejection. The child soon learns that the only way to stay loved and secure is to stay within the OK Box, to meet their parents' expectations.

That same drive, to meet the expectations of the person in authority, remains active at work. Managers are in fact *in loco parentis*. They create an OK Box at work: they create the ongoing culture of the business, the 'how things are done around here'. That is why companies need to look jealously to three critical factors in shaping and maintaining the culture of their own businesses.

Firstly, employees' expectations are largely formed in the first three weeks of joining a business. It is during that time that they learn what actually goes on. That is why the induction process – making clear your expectations right from the start – is a crucially important time. If there is no planned induction, or it is done disinterestedly, employees immediately get the impression that the company does not worry too much about its standards, that any reasonable behaviour will be OK. It will then be no wonder if they, like the others, do not try all that hard.

Secondly, the standards the front-line manager spells out have to match exactly the expectations created at the induction stage. If the manager implies that that was all just a bit of window-dressing, or he sees it really as a bit of a waste of time, then the employee will obviously treat the process with some disdain. If, on the other hand, the manager follows on and describes just what is expected in his area, in detail, then very early the new employee's expectations will be reinforced and they will immediately try to please, i.e. to get the approval and acceptance associated with performing in the OK Box.

Thirdly, the actions of the employee's fellow-workers have to match the standards spelled out at induction and by the manager. If they do not, the new employee will soon match the behaviour of his/her peers. Manifestly, management will have demonstrated that they say one thing and accept another. If there is a discrepancy between the two, employees deduce that what is *accepted* is really what is expected, and these become the standards to which they conform. Companies in fact get no more than the behaviour they have come to accept. And what they accept becomes, in large part, their culture.

INFORMATION AND CONTROL SYSTEMS

Computerized information and control systems have undoubtedly had the biggest influence over the last decades in reshaping the structure and processes of companies in every kind of business. Many jobs have been completely transformed, while the ubiquitous microcomputer now appears on virtually every office desk. But not all the changes have been for the better. Some years ago, if you received a reminder about your gas bill, you could go down to the local office, the clerk would open a great ledger and in a few minutes confirm that your payment had indeed been received, and all was well. Nowadays, the clerk may say: 'It's in the computer somewhere but, I'm sorry, we don't get a print-out until two weeks on Friday'!

And fear and complexity of the computer system can often develop an extensive subculture of systems to manage day-to-day affairs. One British engineering company, which supplied complex machinery specific to customer requirements, installed a comprehensive materials requisition planning system several years ago. It was designed to receive customer orders, organize the relevant engineering drawings and materials for the job, and present these to shop-floor production managers on the appropriate day to meet customer requested delivery dates. The system could have worked well until planners found that manufacturing sometimes slipped up on promised completion dates.

Some planners started to put in false early delivery dates to give themselves some secret leeway in case manufacturing failed to produce. Before long all the planners were doing this until eventually no one could tell from the computer list what really had priority. The computer continued to issue production lists but these were ignored in favour of handwritten lists which showed what was *really* urgent. Progress chasers were also added to help 'walk orders through' when necessary. Despite a sophisticated production control system the subculture ensured that what was actually done was what progress chasers pushed, what senior management thought would help their figures, or what the managing director countermanded to keep irate customers at bay.

Such a vicious circle of hectic and *ad hoc* decision-making can be very difficult to break. There is a feeling that if you once let up on the frantic pace the whole edifice will collapse. That is why introducing any system which fundamentally changes long-established company practices needs detailed and sensitive handling, comprehensive training and extensive trials before it disrupts the whole business and kills morale. Thorough preparation definitely pays off. That is just what a Midlands company found when it developed and introduced a computerized information system which completely transformed their business.

Copystatic of Nottingham rents office equipment (photocopiers, fax, printing machines, etc.) to its customers together with maintenance services guaranteeing repairs within short time-scales. To help them offer a service as short as 'repaired within one hour of your phone call', the company developed a system with which they can contact their repairmen by radio 'on the road' and direct them immediately to any company making a repair request. The time of the call is logged and the clock starts ticking. The repairman knows the speed of service the customer has contracted for and knows exactly within what time-scale the repair must be completed. When he has completed the repair he informs the office direct. The repairman knows that back at the company the MD has on his desk a computer screen which will warn him when any contracted repair falls behind its precise schedule. None of them likes to hear from the MD.

Back at base in the evening the repairman leaves his hand-held terminal which has recorded a list of the parts used during the day on his customer visits. When he returns in the morning his van has been completely restocked. The stock carried is determined by the accumulated computer data showing which parts are most used, and giving the repairman a stock of parts which will allow him to deal with the vast majority of repairs without returning to base. The computer data is also used in another interesting way. If a customer who has some outstanding unpaid bills calls about a breakdown, the computer automatically switches the call instead to the credit control department. They immediately say: 'We would be happy to come out, Mr Customer, but could you settle your bill of last April, please.' It works like magic.

Computer information and control systems can radically change the operating culture of any company, for good or ill. Disruption, morale problems and contorting complexity are the penalties of rushed introduction. The antidotes to these dangers are taking the time and trouble to make detailed preparation, to train operating staff thoroughly and to bring them with you every step of the way.

LEGISLATION AND COMPANY ENVIRONMENT

Multinational companies who have developed corporate mission statements or policies to guide the company world-wide are well aware how these have to be interpreted by their operating units round the world to accommodate the legislative and national cultures in which they operate. One large food company prefers to work its assets full out and favours round-the-clock working in all its plants. In France, however, Sunday working has to have special local government permission and they are never very keen to grant special concessions for mere efficiency reasons. It also costs treble time payments for the hours involved and obviously makes it less cost-effective as a result. At their Austrian plant this point is not a problem, but the grape harvest is. Set in a wine-growing area, many of the company's employees grow grapes, and whatever the company says, they have to be gathered when they are ripe. Accepting the obvious, the company plans its operations and shutdown times round the yearly harvest, which of course varies depending on the season.

Another multinational business, which has plants in the USA, Australia, Britain, France, Holland, Germany and Italy, finds Trade Union patterns and legislation differ in each. In the USA the company is largely non-union, while in Australia recognizing unions and negotiating annually on pay and conditions is part of the scene. In France the company must by law hold elections in which employees vote on whom they wish to represent them on the company's consultative system. The first round of voting is restricted to employees who represent recognized Syndicats (trade unions). Only if they fail to gather sufficient votes can the company then hold a second ballot in which employees can elect non-union representatives. In Germany, for companies greater than a threshold size, a Supervisory Board and a Works Council are by law necessary elements in the company's organization. Whenever the parent company plans to introduce changes in policy or operational arrangements, the constant worry of the German managers is how they will 'get it through the Works Council'.

In many cases, corporations have developed core philosophies which apply across continents, but inevitably the legislation and the culture of the environments in which they operate have material effects on how the philosophies are actually carried through in practice.

PROCEDURES AND POLICIES

When Harold Geneen was in charge of ITT, the American telecommunications giant, it had some 350 businesses in 80 different countries, around 350 000 employees, and sales of over $16 billion. His theory about how to manage this huge conglomerate was disarmingly simple. He did not believe in pat or sophisticated management theories, business was just too vital and dynamic to be contained in any formula or theory. He thought the best way of running any business was to 'cook as you would on a wood-burning stove'. You follow a recipe to some extent, but you add something of your own and as things are cooking *you keep your eye on the pot.*

His way of keeping his eye on the pot was in fact quite elaborate, and produced a procedure which strongly shaped the culture and lives of everyone in ITT. He required the managing directors of all ITT subsidiaries round the world to submit to Head Office in New York monthly reports showing specified financial and performance figures, together with their detailed plans for the following four quarters. Between 15 and 20 pages each, Geneen and his five executive vice-presidents at Head Office read every one of them. Each month he and his top 40 executives from headquarters would sit down face to face with all the chief executives from the American subsidiaries and go over each unit's operating report in a week-long general managers' meeting. He and his 40 executive staff would then decamp to Brussels for a further week-long meeting with the bosses of all the other ITT units.

Geneen and his team went through this punishing monthly routine – one week in New York, one week in Brussels – for ten months of each year. Meetings would last from 10 in the morning to 10 at night and often beyond. Tough questions were asked: Why are sales down this month? Are you sure you know the real reasons? Have you checked this yourself? How? What are you doing about it? What can we expect next month? Do you need help from headquarters? How are you going to stay ahead of the competition? etc. Geneen wanted no surprises. He had previously issued memos condemning vague and indefinite reports and demanding clear unambiguous statements of actions proposed and supportive reasoning. Another historic memo issued in exasperation insisted on nothing but 'unshakable facts', and not apparent facts, assumed facts, reported facts or hoped-for facts. So you can just imagine the charged atmosphere in these meetings when you were challenged every month in front of tens of other executives about your company, its figures and its performance. There was no hiding place.

Most business procedures do not have such profound and widespread effect, but many company policies can be the source of much employee frustration. In the 1960s Frederick Herzberg conducted some revealing research into those factors in organizations from which employees derive the greatest satisfaction or dissatisfaction in their work. With evidence from a wide variety of businesses in different countries, 'company policy and administration' consistently topped the list as the factor causing most of the negative feelings about work. Company procedures and policies are necessary as guidelines to help employees do a consistently good job for their company, but when they are implemented rigidly they deprive employees of the authority to act promptly in difficult situations and imply a lack of confidence that the employees can be trusted to do a good job. Employees then effectively pay the company back for their lack of trust by exercising no initiative when they otherwise could, and letting the company suffer for its inflexibility. On the one hand, the procedures and policies of any company have a prime role in shaping its culture, while on the other, they can also be the major source of employee frustration and alienation.

REWARDS SYSTEMS AND MEASUREMENT

Companies generally measure what is important to them, for example, sales, costs, profit, market share, return on capital, output, quality. Many companies produce figures monthly with actual achievement set against forecast figures for the month and year-to-date. As a result, managers get regular feedback on their performance, and paying attention to the numbers becomes a habit, part of the culture. If bonuses and promotions are also awarded to those who do well on the numbers, then that behaviour is reinforced and repeated throughout the company. If, in addition, you have to suffer a Geneen-like examination every month, then you pay even more attention to the numbers and take action to avoid any possible post-mortems and public embarrassments.

It is also true that *what gets measured becomes important*. Those who wish to transform their company culture have to start measuring what they want employees now to treat as important. The Rank Xerox company is a good case in point. Rank dominated their market for decades, and suffered from that near-fatal disease of arrogant complacency. Their copying system, well protected by patents, meant they could produce copies which put others in the shade. They also had armies of maintenance technicians who would get faulty machines back in production in a few hours. However, when their patent protection ran out, competitors like the Japanese introduced machines which could not only produce good copies but did not break down as often. Xerox's share of the market started to plummet, and financial performance suffered too.

The UK company believed some fundamental structural change was necessary to make sure everyone got the message that the world had changed out there. They began regularly surveying their customers on their level of satisfaction, and taking notice of what they said. Nothing radical in that, you might say. Then they made senior management bonuses dependent on the satisfaction scores achieved. That helped to get more attention. At first the bonus amounted to just 4 per cent of pay and covered only the top managers in the UK company. Now, the amount of bonus these top managers can earn goes up to 18 per cent of salary, and everyone in the company is involved in the bonus arrangements. As you might

expect, there have been significant improvements in the customer satisfaction scores, and more and more the company is
coming out top of the heap on the competitor comparison
surveys. The fact is, when you measure it and reward it, the
whole company takes a different attitude.

ORGANIZATION AND RESOURCES

It has been the fashion to put together huge conglomerate
companies on the basis that diversity brought protection against
vagaries in any one market, and that size brought purchasing and
marketing muscle. That may be true but conglomerates are hard
to manage. Often, nothing is common but the fact that they all
look at financial numbers and employ people. What works in one
industry just does not apply in the next. Products are different,
markets are different, countries are different, processes are different, customers are different, technologies are different, and so on.
As a result a common culture becomes well-nigh impossible.

Moreover, the performance of conglomerates overall is not
spectacular. Their ordinary financial results lead to raids by
predator investors, until now 'unbundling' has become the
fashionable trend. Far from giant corporations being able to
turn their wide experience into strong results in a variety of
industries, it seems that diversity generally means mediocrity in
productivity. A recent study carried out by Columbia University
concluded that 'the greater the number of industries in which a
plant's parent firm operates, the lower the productivity of the
plant'. Increasingly, conglomerates are realizing that having a
holding company acting as banker, and using different goals
and cultural norms for the different industries or countries in
which they operate, makes more business sense.

At the same time, the availability of resources to get the job
done can make a crucial difference to management attitudes.
With adequate resources managers can gain the self-confidence
to deliver excellent performance, but starved of resources,
managers may resign themselves to cutting corners and just

doing as best they can. Employee morale stays low as they struggle with inadequate and hand-me-down equipment, and mediocre performance becomes the norm, just part of the culture.

The point became clear to me while on a tour of the Bordeaux vineyards. The high price obtained by Château Haut Brion (a Premier Cru vineyard) for its wines enables it to employ modern stainless steel fermenting vats, to use 100 per cent new oak barrels each year in which to mature the wine, to send grape-pickers out several times at harvest time to pick only the ripest grapes, and to reject large percentages of the grapes that are considered not good enough to make the best wine. As a result, the quality of their wine is always outstanding and commands top prices. The money they get gives them the resources to continue to use the best equipment and techniques, and to stay among the very best. At the lesser known 'Petits Châteaux' they cannot always afford the best and latest equipment, they might only be able to use 25 per cent of new oak barrels each year, and they cannot afford to pay pickers to visit the vineyards several times. Similarly, they cannot be so selective about their grapes: since their wine commands lower prices per bottle in the market they can only increase their revenue by producing greater quantities. That inevitably means lower quality, which in turn means lower prices, and so the cycle is perpetuated.

The people who live within a business adapt their behaviour to cope with the structures and constraints they have to live within until it becomes part of the normal way of doing things, part of the culture. Not all constraints are changeable, for example, wine-growers may have to live with the soil and climate they are given, but most organization structures are, and that undoubtedly makes a difference to how people behave.

GOALS, VALUES AND BELIEFS

In his book about IBM, the son of the founder, Thomas J. Watson Jnr, attributes the long-lived and astounding success of the business very firmly to its strong set of beliefs, first articulated by his father and still guiding the company today. They are:

- Respect for the individual.
- To give the best customer service of any company in the world.
- To pursue all tasks with the idea that they can be achieved in a superior fashion.

These were no 'motherhood' statements just to hang on the boardroom wall. As Buck Rodgers, Vice-president of Marketing for 10 years, said in his 1986 book: 'The Watsons didn't simply comunicate a set of principles to hear themselves saying something nice. They lived by their beliefs in their everyday work.'

Beliefs sincerely held, of course, translate into action, and it is by their actions that employees judge their companies. Did they really mean 'the best customer service *in the world*?' Yes, they really did. Watson Jnr tells how in 1942 an official of the then War Board called his father late in the afternoon of Good Friday, gave him an order for 150 machines and challenged him to have them installed by the following Monday! By contacting IBM offices all over the country, Watson and his staff located the machines, arranged round-the-clock transport and sent cables to the War Board or the official at his home every time a truck was sent on its way. They even set up a miniature factory in Washington to handle the reception and installation of all the equipment. There were plenty of sleepless IBM and War Board people in Washington that Easter weekend . . . but they got the machines there on time.

Such is the stuff of legend. And such are the stories that show employees what the company really values. When they start to believe you are really serious, soon they start doing the same until there are so many stories from everywhere in the business you can't believe people will go to such lengths to fulfil the company's goals. That's when the beliefs have penetrated deep and become part of the company's culture, part of 'how we do things round here'. They affect how people act, talk and think.

Employees begin to identify with their business: they take pride in it. They don't say 'I'm a systems analyst' any more, they say 'I work for IBM'.

The goals a company sets and the values it truly believes in have more influence in *transforming company culture* than any other factor. The goals are the true engine of change and excellence. But, as we shall see later, if they are to stand the test of time, they are not arrived at lightly. IBM's have lasted more than seven decades. It is to their outstanding customer service rather than their products that they attribute most of their long and outstanding success. They are not always first in the market-place, they do not always have the best products, and they are often expensive. But they still sell more than anybody else. That is the prize of simple, solid goals and beliefs.

KEY POINTS SUMMARY

Many influences have shaped your company's culture, but the overwhelming majority of these will be contained in the following 12 key causal factors:

- Influence of a dominant leader
- Company history and tradition
- Technology, products and services
- The industry and its competition
- Customers
- Company expectations
- Information and control systems
- Legislation and company environment
- Procedures and policies
- Rewards system and measurement
- Organization and resources
- Goals, values and beliefs

3

Where are you now?

KNOWING WHERE YOU ARE STARTING FROM

Most managers are particularly vague and even inarticulate when asked how they would describe their company's culture. Basically there is no generally accepted 'language' or terminology to describe it. With the 12 factors you can be much more specific and incisive about the formative influences which have produced your own organization's culture. That knowledge is in fact an essential prerequisite to making the moves and changes which will take you successfully in the direction you want to go. You need to know exactly where you are starting from.

The practical approach to compiling such information is to conduct a company audit. This information will become the foundation data for future action. The advantages of using internal staff to conduct the audit are that they know their company from the inside, and it is cheaper. However, employees may get treated like 'prophets in their own country', i.e. not listened to when they come to present their report, and they may well be blind to important factors which they have simply come to live with. Consultants have the advantage of being able to tell it as they see it with no worry about damaging their promotion prospects, their experience and expertise in the subject can be useful, and they tend to be listened to more readily by senior management. However, they can be expensive. The choice is yours.

CONDUCTING AN INTERNAL AUDIT

First it is useful to examine how you can conduct an audit of your own, using the 12-factor analysis, and assuming that there is a real desire among the leaders of the business to move the company in a different direction, to *transform company culture.* Conducting a comprehensive audit needs to be a team job, and the audit team should be carefully chosen. Normally it should consist of a diagonal slice of members drawn from the company who know the business from various levels and areas. In addition, a balance of skills and personalities in the team is important. Preferably you should have a mix of practicality and intellect, long-service people and newcomers, an 'ideas' person, a 'worker/organizer', and at least one member with enough organizational clout and authority to carry weight with top management. If members of top management are in fact part of the team, so much the better.

Audit teams can vary in size but companies have worked quite effectively with groups of anything from 6 to 12 people during this phase. Using a systematic process can help enormously, of course, and the following is a procedure which has proven its worth in practice.

1 Team members first become acquainted with the 12 factors and discuss these together until they have *common understanding*. This is an essential first step as it is important that, whatever the dictionary definition of the factors, team members know what they mean when talking about their company.

2 A simple *pre-think document* is distributed. This lays out the 12 factors in tabular form, and enables team members to note the particular influences under each head which they believe are, or have been, important in shaping the company's culture. A suggested format is shown at the end of this chapter (Table 3.2).

3 During an *interval* of 10 to 14 days, team members are asked to give the matter considered thought and to note their

personal views under each factor. What they are particularly trying to identify are those influences which:

(a) affect most, or large numbers of, people in the business;

(b) shape how they behave and do their everyday work;

(c) have over time formed the habits of 'how we do things around here'.

4 Having made their notes they are also asked to give their view of the *weight* they would attach to each factor. They do this by spreading a total of 100 points across the factors.

5 The team then meets together to compare opinions, and in discussion to arrive at a *consensus* view.

The normal sequence of events is for each member in turn to display his weighting scores under each factor and to explain to the rest of the team why he (or she) comes to these conclusions. Team members may ask questions, but at this stage questions are confined to matters of clarification rather than argument. The discussion is then open, during which the team agrees on which are the key elements under each factor and the appropriate weighting score. This discussion can be deep and wide-ranging and may well take several sessions to complete. But when five or more people, who know a business well, come to a fair consensus, then they will be pretty close to the truth about the major influences shaping the company's culture.

6 The next stage is for the team to identify among the factors what they *value*, what in their culture they particularly want to preserve.

When companies have decided they want to make fundamental changes in how they operate, they inevitably swoop on what they think is *wrong*. They can then too readily start uprooting trees, getting rid of whole procedures or making major organization changes to the business. That is a mistake, at least until they have identified what is *right* with the business, what they specifically want to preserve for the future. In making rushed or drastic changes they may well send out the wrong signals – that nothing from the past is of any value – and inadvertently find themselves throwing out precious babies with the bathwater.

7 The team then identifies the habits which are positive *hindrances* to the company improving its performance: in financial terms, with the customers, against the competition, or in its key standards of performance.

8 Finally the team prepares and *presents its findings to top management*, generally in the form of a presentation and report. Remember, the team is not necessarily making proposals for the future: they are merely saying how it is now. But the data can be used as the base from which the top management team can prepare clear and actionable company goals (see Chapter 4).

ASKING THE RIGHT QUESTIONS

People inside a company are often too close to it both operationally and emotionally to take the detached 'helicopter' view that is required in this situation. Even with the 12-factor process they may not always know the appropriate questions to ask. Table 3.1 shows some of the questions, under each of the factor headings, which you should find helpful in isolating the key factors and influences that go to make up your company's culture. These should be used in conjunction with the factor analysis forms you will find on pages 43–44.

Questions you will see in the next few pages are not the only ones which could be asked, of course, but they have helped to get some deep and far-reaching discussions going. The important outcome is to identify the major behaviour- and culture-shaping influences on the business and to get a large measure of agreement on what these are. Some purists might feel the use of open-ended questions (rather than questions which can be answered simply by a 'yes' or a 'no') would be preferable in such initial audit discussions. In practice, when team members give their opinions and on the weight they attach to the factors, their colleagues tend to ask for examples and justification, and

Table 3.1 Isolating the key factors and influences

Factors	Questions
Dominant leader influence	Do we currently have a leader, or leaders, in the business whose ideas, energy, personality or management style dominates how things are done across the business.
	What are the positive and negative aspects of this?
	Are there positive factors of the influence of a previous leader, now gone, which we wish to preserve?
Company history and tradition	Are there traditional elements in how we work or make the product which customers value?
	Do we own brand names with a long history which are positive assets?
	Do we have traditional ways of operating which are actual preventions to improvement or to beating our competition?
	What disruption might be caused by changing our traditional ways of doing things? (Trade unions may have vested interests, for example.)
Technology, products and services	Does the nature of our business have a major influence on our culture?
	Does the nature of our business make us adaptable to change, or get us stuck in old ways?
	Is service all that really counts in our business, and are we all aware of it?
	Are we a business with such diverse products and services that our people find difficulty identifying with us?

Table 3.1 (*cont.*)

Factors	Questions
The industry and the competition	Are we unduly influenced in our style of operations by what the rest of 'the industry' does, or is our image and culture unique and distinctive?
	Does our dominant market share give us an arrogant culture?
	Does our minority position in the market make us act 'second class' or like also-rans?
	Does our monopoly position, or the irrelevance of competition, make us lethargic and slow to innovate?
Customers	Does our dependence on one major customer largely shape our actions and our culture? What are the positives and the negatives?
	Do the wants of our customers dominate our actions? Should they?
	What do our customers say our culture or mode of operating is as they see it? Should we find out?
	Do we have two levels of customers and what do they each think? (For example, the motor industry, where vehicles are sold first to dealers and then to users, is in this category.)
Company expectations	Are we clear enough about the behaviour we expect of our employees, and do we follow through on what we say? (For example, on matters of safety, co-operation, absence, performance.)
	Have we a 'commitment culture', or do we say one thing and accept another?
	Do we make our expectations clear at induction? And do our managers follow through?

Table 3.1 (*cont.*)

Factors	Questions
Information and control systems	Has the installation of new information and control systems radically changed the jobs of many employees? What have been the positive and negative effects on our way of doing things? Are our present information systems a help or a hindrance? Have we altogether too much information and paper?
Legislation and company environment	What effects does the national culture have on how we implement company policy? (For example, are we peculiarly British? Or American? Japanese?) How does national legislation affect how we do things? What local and environmental issues shape how we operate in the business?
Procedures and policies	Does the planning and reporting process in the business shape much of how things are done in the business? Should it? Do we have procedures which make the handling of recurrent work problems easy, or are we a company which '*ad hocs*' much of the time? Do our people feel empowered to do what they think is right at work, or do they feel restricted by company policy? What company policies and procedures cause employees most frustration?

Table 3.1 *(cont.)*

Factors	Questions
Rewards system and measurement	What are the principal reward systems here (pay, bonuses, promotions, awards, etc.) which shape behaviour in the company?
	Are we a company which 'chases the numbers'?
	Which numbers, and how does it affect how we operate in the company?
	Do we have different reward and measurement systems round the business which cause differing priorities and lack of co-operation?
Organization and resources	Are organization reporting relationships clear throughout the company?
	Are there confusions in decision-making authority?
	Does the diverse nature of the business produce a complex organization and mediocre performance?
	Does lack of resources make us act in struggling 'second-class' mode?
Goals, values and beliefs	If employees across the business were asked to write down the prime goals and beliefs of the company, would we get anything like the same answers?
	Do our leaders and managers demonstrate genuine and daily commitment to our published company goals?
	Are our business goals clear and consistent, or do we keep 'moving the goalposts'? Are we subject to the 'flavour of the month' syndrome?

it is in these clarification debates (and arguments) that the culture picture becomes clear.

Audit teams may also decide to conduct formal surveys with employees, customers and suppliers to provide additional qualified evidence to supplement their own discussions. The combination can then provide a fairly robust picture of 'where the business is now'.

USING OUTSIDE HELP

The dangers may still exist, however, that insiders may not acually recognize the significance of certain debilitating factors that they have simply come to live with, or may be afraid to raise certain issues at senior level because it is not politic to do so. For these reasons, many companies prefer to use consultant help. Outsiders have the further advantage that employees, customers and suppliers are all likely to be more frank in their answers, especially if their opinions are to be treated confidentially and they will not thereby risk damaging their standing in the business. Thus the real truth may be better revealed.

The nature and scope of such a study will naturally vary depending on how important the matter is to the company, how big or complex the business is, how much management is willing to spend on it, and so on. However, broadly there will be both quantitative and qualitative findings. The quantitative evidence is likely to be of the type: 37 per cent of staff believe so-and-so, while 82 per cent of your customers think such-and-such, and so on. The qualitative evidence is likely to describe, for example, what people said in discussion, the stories they told, the quotes they made. This tends to flesh out the audit, to paint a fuller picture, to add substance and background to the bare statistics. Both kinds of evidence are important.

Consultants also vary in their approach to conducting audits, but generally they will first want to know from top management why they want to conduct an audit at all, and how they plan to use the results. Motivations can be multifarious, from discontent with prevailing attitudes or performance to losing market share to competition, so some probing and mind-clarifying discussion can be invaluable at this stage. It makes simple common sense that when the objectives are clear the audit format can be better designed.

GOOD AUDITS WILL POINT THE WAY

A large UK insurance company decided in the late 1980s that if they were going to increase their business versus the competition and protect their margins they would have to achieve clear *'differentiation in the eyes of our target customers'*. They concluded they would have to: provide their staff with better systems to provide better service; motivate them better; gain a much clearer understanding of their customers' needs; and to deliver consistently on their commitments. Easy to say, of course, but harder to do.

With their consultants they started asking questions: of their staff, their managers, their agents and their customers. Staff were asked to complete a specially devised questionnaire, and this was followed up by conducting discussions with small groups of staff drawn from different areas. What they found was:

- Staff were motivated more to please the boss than the customer.
- There was an emphasis on 'following the rules'.
- Decisions were constantly referred up the organization.
- Decisions were based on what the company wanted, not what the customer wanted.
- There was strong control from head office, i.e. remote from the customer.
- There was rivalry between departments.
- The reward system reinforced the *status quo*.

The agents, who sold the policies to customers, said the company was no better and no worse than most of the other insurance companies. That meant they were not very flexible to customer requirements, telephone respondents often did not know enough to give authoritative answers on the phone, and getting prompt quotes was difficult. Customers themselves said they tended to get shunted from one person to another when enquiring about their claims, answers were deferred, and who-ever you talked to seemed to have to get someone else's say-so before they could make a decision.

Much of this came as quite a shock to senior management. It can be quite embarrassing when customers and employees hold up the great mirror of truth, especially as you may (blushingly) just recognize yourself. But it certainly acts as a stimulus to change. In fact the great value of a good audit is: it shakes out any residual complacency among senior management; it gives a kick start to the change process; it provides the justification of the need to improve; and employees and customers show you exactly where you need to target your actions.

DISCOVERING THE PATTERN OF YOUR CULTURE

So what sort of question do consultants ask? Normally, they begin by asking some simple, open-ended questions of key interest groups, or stakeholders as they are sometimes called. Stakeholders are all those who, one way or another, are affected by the fortunes of the company. These can include: customers, employees, suppliers, local communities, shareholders and the financial community. The approach is likely to differ in each case.

For example, the starter questions with customers might be:

'What do you value about doing business with XYZ?'
'What problems do you have in dealing with XYZ?'
'How do XYZ compare with their competition?'

Their answers to these initial questions allow them to ferret out further interesting or important information. Once they have visited a few customers, similar points will begin to emerge and patterns begin to form of how the company actually appears in the customers' eyes. And it is the *pattern* that is important; that is what the company will have to work on if it wants to change its company culture. Some investigations may be more complex than others, of course. For example, if the company is a car manufacturer, it will have to talk to its first customers (the dealers) and the final customers (those who buy and use the cars). Garage mechanics and storemen will also be worth consulting to see what problems there are in keeping customers happy after the sale, the part which helps make customers into repeat buyers.

Suppliers may have quite a different picture of the company, however. For example, have the suppliers been taught to see themselves as part of a chain in satisfying the eventual customer, or do they just keep the company's buyer happy? Do they have a 'partnership' relationship with the company, or are they just treated as 'a supplier'? Are they made to jump through hoops by the company, and are they paid on time, etc? If the supplier is largely dependent on the company, he may be less forthcoming in his responses, of course.

For example, one large car company declared in its mission statement that 'suppliers are our partners. We must work together to meet our common objectives.' It went on to say that 'good working relationships are founded on trust, respect and fairness'. Suppliers said in practice, however, that they were pressed severely on price, that they could not get definitive schedules from the customer to plan their work sensibly, given schedules would change arbitrarily at very short notice, they were given little sympathy for the problems that were created, and buyers threatened them with the loss of business if they did not keep quiet and respond as directed. The message is really quite clear. It is not what the company says in its mission statement that counts, it is how it *behaves* in practice that actually determines its culture.

DIFFERING PERCEPTIONS

Employees will also have different perceptions. Normally, an internal audit will start by talking to 'focus groups', i.e. small groups of staff in various areas and at various levels in the company, focusing on different aspects of company life. Starter questions used here might be:

'What is your view about XYZ as a company to work for?'
'What do you like, and not like, about working at XYZ?'
'If you were the managing director, what one thing would you change which you think would make the biggest difference to the success of the business?'

The use of small groups of employees generally gives staff more courage to say what they really think, and often comments by one employee will raise useful thoughts in the minds of others and produce richer information. However, employees are often worried about confidentiality. If the consultants or questioners can give assurances that no comments will be traceable to any individual then generally this produces more open discussions.

The various stakeholders will all have different interests in the business, and naturally different views about it. Employees, managers and customers are generally those whose views are most taken into account, but others, such as members of the local community or shareholders, may also have substantial influence in shaping the company's behaviour. Often a push–pull strain can be set up by the different interests. For example, the local community may be pressing for the company to reduce the pollution it causes around its plants, from noise, effluent, smell, chimney emissions, traffic, etc. But the financial community and shareholders may downgrade the company's rating if, for purely environmental reasons, they see them adding substantially to their costs relative to the competition. Hard as it may be, the company has no alternative in shaping its behaviour but to take the varying stakeholder interests into account and to strike a sensible balance while, of course, achieving the economic results that ensure its survival.

UNDERSTANDING THE FACTS AND THE FEELINGS

Changing the culture of any company is a matter of changing both the *facts* and stakeholders' *perceptions*, and it is as well to know what these facts and perceptions are before you begin. That is the function of a well-conducted audit. Managers should be aware, however, that the act of conducting an audit raises expectations around the business that 'something is going to happen', so unless there is visible action soon afterwards, many interest groups may show their disappointment. No one person – inside or outside – can know everything about the business. A good audit invariably opens management eyes with things they did not know before and virtually always produces gems of ideas which can set minds thinking and excitement rising. Knowing the important facts and perceptions about the organization gives you a much clearer vision both about the culture and habits you have now and where you want to be.

KEY POINTS SUMMARY

- Before you launch into a revolution in your company's culture find out exactly where you are now. Conduct an audit.
- If you choose to do this internally, use a team of people with a balance of skills, experience and personality. They have the advantage of knowing the company from the inside, and costs are minimized.
- Use a step-by-step process such as the one explained in this chapter. The 12-factor framework and sample questions given earlier will provide a solid basis for the study. (See Table 3.2)
- The study needs to identify the major culture-shaping

Table 3.2 Factor analysis form

Factors	Notes	Weighting
Dominant leader influence		
Company history and tradition		
Technology, products and services		
The industry and the competition		
Customers		
Company expectations		

Table 3.2 (*cont.*)

Factors	Notes	Weighting
Information and control systems		
Legislation and company environment		
Procedures and policies		
Rewards system and measurement		
Organization and resources		
Goals, values and beliefs		
	Total Points	100

influences affecting the company, in particular those elements which are most valued and those which may be acting as hindrances to the company's moving in its favoured new direction.

- Using consultants to conduct your audit has several advantages: they may have experience in the field; they are more independent; people may be more frank in their answers to them; they may be less afraid to tell it to you like it is. However, they can be expensive.
- Do not confine your audit investigation to employees of the company. The views of outside interest groups such as customers, suppliers, the local community, shareholders and the financial community can all cast revealing light on the culture and habits of your organization.

4

Being clear on goals

If there is one influence that shapes a company's culture more than any other it is the goals the senior management of the business set and consistently pursue. A favourite starting-point of mine with groups of directors is to ask them each to write down the top three goals of the company as they see them. Invariably there is some degree of overlap, but lists in the range of 20 to 40 goals are common and I have never yet had a list in single figures. It is only too obvious that if top management are not clear where they are going then there is no chance at all of junior managers or employees knowing any better. In such situations directors have differing views, department heads have differing views, supervisors also have their own views, and with no unifying direction they are each likely to pursue their own sectional interests first and to think about the company only second.

MISSION STATEMENTS

If the job of directors is anything, it is giving that clarity of direction to the business which will unify efforts across the organization, be straight and simple enough for employees at every level to understand and to which they can all make a personal contribution. It has become popular in recent years to draw up mission statements as a means of achieving this objective. This could be an encouraging trend but in practice many turn out to be nothing more than 'motherhood' statements which do little to alter the direction or habits of the business. Drawn from actual company statements here are just two examples to illustrate:

> To ensure the company is able to maintain a high position in the competitive market by reason of its standards of price, quality and service to customers. This involves research, development and achievement of high technical and organizational efficiency.

> To provide good jobs, wages and working conditions, work satisfaction and opportunities for advancement conducive to the most productive performance and also the stablest possible employment.

Such expressions could be taken on by virtually any company yet create no distinctive difference in its performance or daily operations. They may be the kind of statements that make senior management feel better, or which they can show to visitors, but they do little to inspire employees or customers.

There can also be a strong tendency to overelaborate. Companies may start with a business definition, a statement of purpose, or a vision, then follow up with statements of business ethos, values, beliefs, principles, strategy, objectives, targets, or whatever. Eventually the statement may cover all the bases, but it becomes just too long and complicated to remember. If a director in your business has got to rummage around in a drawer to find the company's mission statement because he cannot remember it, then it is just too long. If he cannot carry it around in his head then it is not achieving its fundamental purpose, which is to affect and shape his everyday behaviour. It is written on the paper and not on his heart.

THE LAUGH FACTOR

When a company first issues its carefully honed mission statement, there is one factor which can kill it before it ever gets off the ground: the laugh factor. On one occasion, when working with the directors of an automotive parts supplier, I noted the mission statement of their biggest customer on their boardroom wall. My reference to it was greeted with cynical smiles and laughter. That was for the birds, they implied, and for the next half an hour they regaled me with stories to show what things were really like in practice. When employees, customers and suppliers believe reality is actually miles away from the mission, then they simply do not treat it seriously. Far from changing their behaviour they conclude that senior management is just out of touch.

This laugh element can be a serious problem for many companies who may accept that their performance is presently not all it should be, but who nevertheless want to make a start along the long tough road. British Rail is a case in point. Some years ago they embarked on an advertising campaign, using well-known personalities and based on the slogan 'This is the age of the train'. Those who experienced late trains, cancellations, dirty or cold compartments and indifferent service treated the whole thing with undisguised contempt, and comedians added to the agony by regularly making it the butt of their jokes. Later BR changed the slogan to 'We're getting there' but the scorn and the jokes continued unabated. In the face of such derision it is hard for employees (or directors) not to give up and resign themselves to a never-can-win situation.

THE VALUE OF GOALS

BR may despair of ever producing goals which will not immediately result in a derisory laugh. But with care it can be done. For example, rather than go public with a slogan, BR could start with a simple *internal* goal like:

> 'Every month we aim to make improvements in every area which are *visible to the customer*'.

Now that appears modest, but employees at every level would feel they could 'get their arms round it', and every department in the company could become involved in the process right from day one. Because the improvements sought would apply both to fare-paying customers and to internal customers, each department could be asked to plan and show what it was doing each month to make their contribution. Their progress could readily be checked by asking their customers what they had noticed! No doubt the doers would find better ways just to make their customers *aware* of the improvements they were making, but then customers only start to change their opinion when they actually *perceive* the improvements, so that would be a benefit in itself.

On their visits, the chairman and senior managers could ask to see what each team had done this month, and what they were planning next. Employees could then begin to show some pride in the job right from the outset, especially if they were regularly getting pats on the head from the most senior people even for their modest (but visible) achievements. Everyone in the business, managers and staff, would realize they were all engaged in exactly the same process and begin to feel they were in it together, to feel more like a team. After several months of activity the whole business would be intent on doing things to please their customers. It would simply become part of the ethos of the business, part of how we do things around here. And that, as we know, is what culture is.

GOAL CREDIBILITY

The prime reason that mission statements suffer from the laugh factor is that employees, customers and suppliers perceive a great yawning gap between what is preached and what is practised. Management say one thing but actually do another. You see, the culture of the business is not about what is written on paper, but about how the company *acts* in its everyday dealings.

One of the problems with statements is that they can imply you are there already. Statements like: 'We respect the contribution of every employee' will be treated with disdain by employees if they do not see evidence of it from the managers they deal with every day. Assertions like: 'Suppliers are our partners. We work together to achieve our common objectives' may be hotly denied by suppliers if the company's buyers apply undue muscle or coercion to force compliance. On the other hand *goals* recognize you are not there already, but they make clear what you are genuinely striving towards. That is something employers, customers and employees can respect.

I encourage you to steer clear of the elegant but anodyne mission statements which sound good, cover all the political bases or look good on the boardroom wall. Clear goals are needed, which will galvanize the whole business into action and affect how everyone in the company behaves every day; goals which will touch the minds and imaginations of the employees doing the front-line work of the company. What customers think of your business will not be based on any well-meaning mission statements emanating from the board, but on their actual experience of how they are treated by the employees they meet. These are the people facing customers and clients daily and, for good or ill, creating the true image and reputation of the company. These are the people who make the products or deliver the services which customers buy and which pay every salary in the business.

GETTING THE GOALS RIGHT

No leader can make it all happen on his or her own. He or she has to engage the support of the employees making the products and giving the services. That is why the goals need to be few enough for everyone to carry around in their head. They need to be so understandable that the words do not need further explanation. They need to be sufficiently actionable that everyone knows exactly what they can do to make them happen.

Employees need to believe that their senior management are truly committed to the goals for them to feel it is worth committing themselves. They will hesitate till they see telling evidence. They will want to see management spending time on, and paying attention to, the measures that indicate how well the company is doing on its chosen goals. They will be even more convinced when the company starts recognizing and rewarding the successes that are achieved.

All this is not easy. Producing goals that will eventually transform the culture of your business is a tough task. It will probably take several attempts and a lot of thought, discussion and deliberation to get it even near right. However, if the job of the leaders is anything, it is distilling the essence of what the business is and what it wants to be. No other job is more important. That is why it takes time, effort and attention. Here are some clear rules you can follow which will help keep your thinking on track.

Make sure your goals are clear and simple

This seems such an obvious point but it is the rule most frequently violated. Directors can wax lyrical when it comes to encapsulating the ethos and goals of their company, and often get so carried away by their own soaring inspiration that they forget the most important factor, namely that it must all be clear and unambiguous even to the most lowly member of staff.

One well-known British company was painfully reminded of how damaging it can be not to be disarmingly clear and simple in getting important messages across to employees. During 1990 they were targeted as a company for selective strike action by the Engineering Union in support of their campaign for a shorter working week. Senior management decided to conduct a series of meetings with all employees on site to make clear the company's position and indicate the undesirability of work interruption given their full order books and the pressure on production capacity. Such was the commitment of management that the general manager and his directors conducted 28 such meetings to get their points across. The general manager felt the points they made were crystal clear. But were they?

While discussing the situation some two weeks later, the directors were asked to write down the two most important points that the meetings were trying to communicate. When the answers were revealed no two directors had the same messages. If the directors (who had heard the message 28 times) did not know, what were the chances that the workforce had picked up the right message? The employees hadn't. Following the 'talk-ins' the company experienced the longest strike in its history. The workforce, previously piqued by pay increases below the inflation rate, had interpreted the unprecedented meetings as evidence that on the subject of working hours they now had management 'on the run'.

MIND-BLOWING SIMPLICITY

The point about simplicity was also driven home very clearly to Sweden's airline Linjeflyg in 1978 when they decided they had to get their planes in the air for more hours per day to generate greater growth and profitability. They had been offering a Y50 deal: basically this was a 50 per cent discount to all young people under 27 to anywhere in Sweden as long as they travelled on off-peak flights. This had been successful but they felt they now had to go one better. They came up with something even simpler: travel anywhere in Sweden for just 100 kroner. Parent company SAS decided not to join the scheme as they estimated the new deal would only produce 5000 or so more customers. Linjeflyg went ahead anyway. But its new 'hundred note' offer did not just attract 5000 more customers, it pulled in 125 000 in the first summer alone!

Why did they think it had worked so well? 'The answer was simple,' said the company, 'no one could figure out what a Y50 discount was but everybody knew what a 100 kroner note was.' That sort of simplicity is not only understood by all the employees, it gets right through to customers as well. The company galvanized its whole workforce into generating more profitable business with this and other projects. And what made them all join in so wholeheartedly? The company believed it was 'because they all understood our goals and long-range plan. We communicated a vision of what the company could be, and they were willing to take responsibility for making it work'. That sort of simplicity is worth working for.

SIMPLE CLEAR STANDARDS

In some businesses repetition is an inherent feature of the work, as in making the same product hour after hour, or delivering the same service day after day. In such situations clear and unambiguous standards are critically important for the front-line staff doing the work. That is a feature of Japan's bullet train service. The rules are simple. The train arrives precisely on time. It spends exactly one minute in the station to allow passengers to get on and off. Painted on the platforms are lines and numbers which indicate where the doors of each carriage will stop, and they do. Passengers know exactly where to stand to get on to the right carriage and find their seat. On the train itself, as it approaches each station an announcement is made automatically at intervals of two minutes and one minute before arrival saying what is the name of the next station. And the trains are clean.

Compare that with good old British Rail. BR currently have an unofficial target of 82 per cent of trains arriving within five minutes of their schedule, but passengers never know when they are going to be among the unfortunate 18 per cent. Carriages on longer-distance trains differ: sometimes the first class carriages are at the front, sometimes at the back, sometimes there are two carriages, sometimes one or less. The buffet car you see listed in the train schedule may be there but may not be open if the member of staff concerned has not actually reported for work. Some trains listed in the timetable may not run at all because other difficulties have appeared. All this can be confusing and irritating to passengers. But it seems there is no clear and consistent standard for employees.

In the Japanese train service all the employees know precisely what they have to do: the train *will* arrive on time, it *will* stop in the station for exactly one minute, it *will* stop at exactly the right spot, there *will* be exactly eight carriages so that passengers find their carriage easily, etc. They do not have to wait to hear what their supervisor tells them to do every day, they know what is required and do it. When employees find themselves having to compromise on standards every day because equipment is not there or whatever, they have to keep checking with their supervisor: 'Is it all right if . . .?' Then their supervisors find themselves having to agree to compromises because it is 'the best they can do', i.e. approving work which is actually below standard. Not only that, it takes so much more time for supervisors to get any kind of job done if they have to spend their time assessing and making decisions on non-standard situations every hour of the day. So they spend more time rushing around feeling busy but ending up doing an inferior job. Worst of all, it all soon becomes 'how we do things around here', just part of the culture.

SIMPLICITY TILL IT HURTS

The antidote to overcomplexing your goals and standards is 'simplicity till it hurts'. Keep refining and simplifying till they are clear and unambiguous to everyone in the business. If you go too far it will begin to get crude: that is when it begins to hurt. There is no mathematical formula; you have to exercise management judgment. Your customers will be your acid test of whether you have got it right or not. Take Marks and Spencer as an example. Years ago they decided to stock only high quality goods – goods they would be happy to have in their own homes – and to take anything back if it was unsuitable in any way. That is the image they project to their public. The standard is so clear and simple, not only do the employees know it, but the customers know it too.

Federal Express, the parcels delivery company, have a simple three-word ethos in their business: People, Service, Profit. On the 'People' side they believe that if they treat their employees well they in turn will want to do the best job they can for their company and treat their customers well. Federal Express employees are among the highest paid in America for their type of work. Their 'Service' standard is simple: it means 'absolutely, positively overnight'. Federal fly their packages into Memphis, Tennessee from all over America every night and deliver from there to everywhere in America during the following morning. When you ask employees in any department what the 'Service' part of their slogan means they inevitably say: 'by 10.30 next morning'. Customers do not have to pay if they fail to deliver. 'Profit' means they want to do enough profitable business to enable them to pay above average benefits, fund their future growth and keep their shareholders happy. Customers understand Federal's standards so clearly they have made them into the biggest parcels carrier in the USA.

If two of the best companies in the world can make it simple, so can you.

Make your goals actionable by every employee in the business

If companies are going to have any chance of getting all their people working like a team they need to have goals which can translate into practical action at every level in the business. Otherwise the goals get firmly stuck in the boardroom and do not penetrate down through the company. One of the big four UK clearing banks has for some time pursued the goal of maximizing 'return on equity', but most of their employees – front-line people who face customers every day – do not actually know what 'equity' is, and would not know what a good 'return' was if they saw it. Even if they did, what could they do about it in their everyday work? When return on equity figures appear in the company annual report the employees who do not understand what it all means presume it must have some financial benefit for directors and senior managers, and that makes for feelings of alienation rather than teamwork.

To get strong team feeling in an enterprise employees need to feel that:

- the boss of the company knows what he or she is aiming at
- they understand and buy into his goals
- they know the practical things they can do to help
- they will get recognition and support for their efforts from the top
- they get co-operation from other departments who also understand and support the goals.

TRYING TO UNITE THE TEAM

This is much easier to say than to do, as the London Metropolitan Police found out. Worried about their image with the public, in 1989 they called in a company of consultants to help. Following an audit the consultants reported that 'there is no overall consistency of view on the mission of the Met. nor on how each individual contributes to the whole. . . .That is why different standards of behaviour and action co-exist and why they have been noticed by both police and public'. The Police Commissioner decided to draw up a statement of common purpose. This took the form of a set of 10 values designed to help the police in their work. This was the list:

- To uphold the law firmly and fairly.
- To maintain public peace.
- To act with honesty and integrity.
- To adopt the highest standards.
- To be compassionate and courteous to others.
- To uphold individual rights.
- To behave in a manner which is neither sexist nor racist.

- To serve the public.
- To be a cost-effective service.
- To co-operate with and consult the community and other agencies in pursuing police purposes.

Despite the best of intentions the list looks very much like a collection of 'motherhood' statements, i.e. things that no one could really disagree with. But does it actually help the constable doing his everyday job on the beat? For example, what does 'to adopt the highest standards' actually mean in practice? If a constable is called to sort out a family feud, which 'individual rights' should he choose to uphold? Many members of the police felt the list was more political than practical. Some policemen expressed the view that whatever two values they upheld at any time their boss would no doubt get them for their failure on the other eight! If you cannot write goals which unite the whole team and make clear what everyone can do to contribute positively, then it is better not to publish anything at all.

TURNING VALUES INTO ACTIONABLE GOALS

Consider the difference, however, if the police (or the Met.) were to choose instead of a blanket list of values just three simple actionable goals:

- To reduce crime.
- To make it safe for anyone to walk anywhere at any time in the UK.
- To treat everyone fairly.

No list is perfect or fully comprehensive, of course, but simple goals like these would have several crucial advantages:

1 Every member of the force at every level would be able to understand them.
2 Everyone in the police could carry the goals around in their head and *do something about them every day*. And everyone would

realize that their personal contribution was important to the success of the whole organization.

3 Targets based on the goals could be agreed at every level throughout the force – country, region, district, section, individual – and performance measured against them. Working on exactly the same goals, the whole organization would be seen to be pulling in the same direction.

4 Most importantly, instead of worrying about criticism and fault-finding from above, constables on the front-line would be able to count on willing support at every level for what they knew they were all trying to achieve.

When you first see simple, actionable goals like those above, it all looks quite easy. It is not. It takes contemplation, effort, discussion and struggle. But it is fundamentally important.

Only choose goals which management will live in practice

When company goals are first announced employees look on keenly to see whether management actually means what it says. One manufacturing company produced the slogan 'Quality Is No. 1' and launched a strong campaign to improve its quality performance using employee presentations, videos and posters in support. Quality inspectors withdrew all previous 'concessions' and insisted that products 'conform to specification' without exception. This was supported by top management despite pressure from production managers who wanted to hit their output targets and from operators who found their production bonus affected. The company said it really wanted a change of era.

However, the crunch came within two months. A large export order which by itself amounted to more than half the monthly sales value was due for shipment. The company had experienced endless lingering problems with 'part shipped' orders in the past, so the strict rule was: export orders must be shipped complete. Late in the month one vital casting was found to be porous while in work, and a new casting had to be rushed through from an outside supplier. In addition, several key parts were being specifically nursed through the plant. In the event, work on the vital new casting in-house did not clear inspection, and metal housings from an outside supplier were scratched on arrival and in one case did not fit. But the managing director decided the order would have to be despatched 'as is'. Its absence would make too big a hole in his invoice figures for the month and would be embarrassing to have to explain at head office. Of course employees got the message loud and clear. 'The Quality is No. 1 campaign is only the latest flavour of the month. What really counts is getting stuff out of the door and the boss meeting his budget figures. Add quality if you have the time.'

BE PREPARED TO ACT LIKE YOU TALK

Naturally, production managers again started to use month-end pressure to press for quality concessions, quality control found themselves cornered into agreement, and top management wondered why they were still making no progress on the quality front. The lesson of course is obvious. Don't declare a goal unless you are fully determined to carry it through, even when the pressure is on. It's not only embarrassing, it kills your credibility. The cynics have a field day: it is just another demonstration of the fact that you cannot believe anything management says. Subsequently, it is very hard to get employee support for any other move you may introduce. If employees are in any doubt they will revert to the behaviour that kept them safe before, i.e. old era behaviour.

Lenin once said that 'the peasants will vote with their feet'. Similarly, employees observe less what management say, they watch what they do with their feet. Make sure anything you announce publicly is something you are all going to be able to live every day, against all the odds. And if the goals are designed to transform your company's culture then you are entering into a long-term commitment; it is not something you can just switch off when the going gets tough.

During the oil crisis years of the 1970s Ford of America had been losing out to Japanese competition whose smaller cars used less fuel and were very reliable. The company realized it had to change and Chairman Philip Caldwell announced in 1978 that from there on quality was to be the company's first priority, 'Job One' as they called it. In 1981, they took on quality guru W. Edwards Deming as a consultant to help make their goal a reality. The company struggled for three years to fully embrace their new philosophy, and in 1984 Henry Ford II announced a new 'Mission and Guiding Principles' to senior management. Prominent among the principles were:

> 'Quality comes first. To achieve satisfaction the quality of our products and services must be our number one priority. Customers are the focus of everything we do. Our work must be done with our customers in mind, providing better products and services than our competition.'

Employees, however, were much less convinced by the fine statements than by what they saw management do with its feet. After several years developing a new Thunderbird model, which was confidently tipped to win 'Car of the Year' title in 1983, Ford decided not to release the car because 'it was not up to production standard'. Quality really was coming in front of marketing, advertising and meeting schedules. Their decision to give up on the title, and all that it meant in terms of publicity and prestige, sent 'a shot heard round the world', as one senior executive called it.

Some time after companies go public on their goals or mission statements there comes a 'crunch event', an event which puts their seriousness to the test, where employees are looking on to see whether management's feet will follow their mouth. Do not go public on any goal if you are not willing to stand up and be counted when the crunch comes, as it surely will. Ford bit the bullet and sent out a strong message: it really was a new era. Employees contributed ideas from all round the company and customers came back to boost the company's market share. From a loss of $1.6 billion in 1980, Ford produced a profit of $4.3 billion in 1984, and in 1986 profits exceeded those of General Motors for the first time in their history. In the recession of 1990/91, Ford suffered just like other car manufacturers, but their new quality ethos will not disappear from their culture.

Keep your goals constant

It is a perennial complaint from managers that the goalposts seem to keep moving. 'One year we are concentrating on market share, next year it is product quality, the year after that it is cost-saving. No sooner do we start to get our act together on one subject than we switch our attention to something else'. That sort of switching may convince senior management that their company is fast-moving and 'with it', but it can leave managers and employees confused and frustrated. They then give lip service to the latest drive but continue to pursue their own personal objectives to give some constancy and structure to their lives.

What is needed are some over arching goals which will mean something in every department of the business and keep everyone heading in the same positive direction over a period of years. The goals need to keep everyone stretching to improve so that the stumbling efforts they make in year one become the learning experiences that help them to do much better in years two and three. That is exactly what happened in Pedigree Petfoods, the biggest operation of the Mars Group in the UK.

SIMPLE BUT STRETCHING GOALS

Late in the 1970s, Pedigree commanded between 60 and 70 per cent of the prepared petfood market in the UK and had a productivity performance some three times better than their competitors. The directors felt they could easily become complacent if they did not set themselves some stretching goals to maintain their considerable edge over the competition. Accordingly, they decided to set themselves the goal of achieving an annual 9 per cent improvement in productivity; for a company in a mature market this represented a doubling of output per head every eight years or so. Every division of the company, even the administrative departments, was required to make their contribution to the achievement of the productivity goal. In year one they actually achieved an increase of only 8.4 per cent, followed by 8.7 per cent the next year. However, in each of the next five years they were always in double figures, with a high of 17 per cent. Why? Because, with practice, everyone learned how to do it better.

Production people started to investigate what new methods, new plant, new layouts and new technology they could use to hit their target not only that year but the year after that. Their time horizon immediately lengthened. Engineers started looking around for the manufacturing concepts which would simplify operations, save labour and produce leaps in productivity performance without compromising on quality. Personnel came up with a written guarantee of 'no redundancy as a result of new technology introduced by the company'. Employees may not have the same job but they would always have a job. That gave solid feelings of security, made change and redeployment much easier, and sent the strong message that change and learning was now the norm for everyone in the business.

GOALS WHICH DEMAND CONSTANT INNOVATION

A second goal produced more strategic thinking around the company. It was to keep the prices of the company's products to its customers to no more than 80 per cent of the annual rate of inflation. This would not only expand the market by giving customers ever better value for money, but keep tough pressure on the competition. Immediately marketing managers conferred with research colleagues about how they could maintain product palatability but use alternative cheaper materials. One of the costly materials was carob which was used to produce the clear aspic-like gel for the company's canned meat products. R&D people discovered that a yam-like plant grown in the Far East could produce a similar gel but much more cheaply. However, there was just not enough in the world to serve the company's large requirements. Aware of their long-term goal the company embarked on a large-scale growing programme in Indonesia (grown under the trees of banana plantations) which at the end of several years development produced enough volume to satisfy the company's large requirements. That is the sort of strategic advantage the competition find it impossible to keep up with.

The company was also a huge buyer of cans, the biggest in the UK, and knew that miniscule savings on each can would produce handsome dividends. Up till then they had used three-piece cans (a body, a bottom and a lid) but two-piece cans (a drawn-out body and a lid) promised a better, cheaper future. They put their ideas to their existing suppliers, but they generally dragged their feet and refused to make the required plant investment. The company then approached a UK conglomerate with a proposition: set up a two-line can manufacturing plant with our help and we will take your entire production for the first two years. They did it. Pedigree was the first company anywhere to put food in two-piece cans. But they would never have done it without that demanding strategic goal.

For seven successive years, with retail price inflation in the UK then at low levels, the company kept price rises on their products to less than half of the rate of inflation. When managers and technicians in a business realize that this year's stretching target will still be there again next year, pretty soon everyone begins to think more strategically. They embark on the thinking and the planning that produces the quantum leap solutions that keep the competition scrambling and shaking their heads.

Companies who know where they are going do not keep moving the goalposts.

Make your goals measurable

Some writers on goal-setting say that company goals should not be too specific as they can quickly get out of date. They should simply define the *direction* in which the company wants to go. That allows room for manoeuvre, and the development of specific activities in support of the goals as time goes on. In my view, no measurement simply means avoiding the truth. The personnel director of a large container manufacturer found just this picture when he suggested to his board that the company should undertake an employee attitude survey. 'That could be like opening Pandora's box', said one director, meaning 'we might not like what we see' or 'if we don't know about it, we don't have to worry about it'.

If you are really serious about your goals (and that seriousness is a large determinant of how successful you will be in reaching them) then you will want to know exactly where you are now and just what progress you are making. And when you start measuring for the first time, even when you thought you knew your business well, you can often get some eye-opening surprises. In 1990, one large UK engineering company conducted an employee attitude survey for the first time. Because directors when they see the results have a habit of saying 'Oh well, I could have told you *that*', each director was asked to forecast the results of 10 key questions for the company as a whole and for their department in particular. As generally happens, no one predicted correctly, but on some questions some directors were as much as 70 points adrift in their forecasts versus the actual scores. Don't kid yourself that you know. Find out the truth. Measure it.

MEASURING IS REVEALING

Measuring was what one of the leading paint manufacturers in the UK decided to do and they got quite a surprise. Pressed by ever-improving competition, they reasoned that they could develop a further edge by working on their service quality to customers. They recruited a senior executive from another large organization which had gained a public reputation for measuring and improving their service to customers. With him they initiated a programme of customer visits to assess how well they were doing. During one visit to a large and important retailer they asked: 'How do you rate the service we give you now?' 'Oh, very good,' came the reply, 'If all our suppliers were as good as you, then we would be doing well'. Later they asked: 'Overall, what score would you give us out of ten?' 'That is difficult to say', said the manager, 'there are quite a lot of factors to take into account'. So they then asked the key question, which happened to be their prime measure within the company: 'Out of the last ten deliveries, how many times did we deliver your order *complete and on time?*' 'Oh, that is easy,' said the manager, 'none – you never deliver everything we order.' The company knew exactly where to start.

Using goals which you subsequently find difficult to measure, or failing to dig out the information which will tell the truth about where you are, means you are simply not serious about your goals. If top management in a company is not genuine and serious about its stated objectives then the rest of the company will not be either. They can mouth them as often as they like, but if they do not follow up employees will treat it as so much window dressing.

NOT NUMBERS, JUST MEASURES

Does this mean that every goal must have numbers attached? Not at all. But it does mean choosing goals which are *measurable*. When goals are measurable it clarifies to everyone in the

business what the company really means (including top management): it is a test of whether the goal-setters are sincere and
prepared to face the truth, and it is a measure of your real
performance and progress. Otherwise they simply become
'sound-good' statements, which will have precious little effect
on changing the culture of the company.

When goals are first mooted there are some 'acid test'
questions which you should ask immediately and which will
clarify your thinking. As you formulate each goal, ask:

- *How will we measure that?* If you cannot measure it, start
  worrying. Inevitably people round the business will interpret the message in quite different ways, or just ignore it
  altogether. If lip service is all that is required you will get
  that a-plenty. When you have to face up to some hard facts,
  people start paying attention.

- *How will we collect the data?* Be specific and detailed. Clarify
  who will produce the data, in what form, how often it will
  be fed back and to whom. If there is already too much data
  around check what measures can be dropped. The ones you
  are not willing to drop may well be your true goals.

- *Are we prepared to face the consequences when we see the facts?*
  Companies who have set goals of delivering 'superior customer service' have sometimes been shocked when they have
  done some 'benchmarking', i.e. gone out to see what their
  competitors or the best companies do, or collecting hard
  data from their customers. Only choose goals which you are
  publicly willing to stand by, come what may.

Those who choose goals that are not too measurable often wax
poetic about them but you never get the impression of real
substance behind the talk. Those whose goals are supported by
real and measured facts talk with a conviction and attention to
reality which shows through in bottom-line business performance. That is the difference.

KEY POINTS SUMMARY

- The one influence that shapes a company's culture more than any other is the goals set and consistently pursued by senior management.

- Clarity of goals starts with the directors. Employees cannot help the company achieve its aims if they are not clear about its goals.

- Beware of fine-sounding mission statements which mean little in practice.

- Beware of mission statements which fall prey to the 'laugh factor'.

- Rather than statements which presume achievement, choose credible, practical *goals* which imply striving and long-term commitment.

The cardinal rules for setting company goals:

- Make sure your goals are clear and simple.
  - Do not risk misunderstanding either by your employees or your customers.
  - Use clear standards which can be easily remembered and implemented every day. Banish complexity. Pursue simplicity till it hurts.
- Make your goals *actionable* by everybody in the business.
  - Common actionable goals produce a strong team feeling throughout the company.
  - Avoid long lists of perfectionist standards which promise failure and discourage striving.
- Choose only goals which management will live in practice.
  - Management credibility is not proven by what they say but by what they do.
  - When the crunch comes – as it surely will – prove equal to the test by sticking with your goals.
- Keep your goals constant.
  - Make your goals stable and for the long-term. Employees learn better every year how to make the goals a reality.

- With practice and further innovation by the company on the same theme every year, it gets more and more difficult for the competition to catch up.
- Make your goals measurable.
  - Do not be afraid to measure: it is the only way to know whether you are really improving. It is all just talk unless you measure.
  - Confidence comes from knowing the truth, and the truth showing you really are excellent.

5

Visible management commitment

ACTION IS ALL THAT COUNTS

Transforming the culture of any organization requires a clear vision of the future, with actionable goals that everyone can identify with. But that is just the first step. Making the goals a reality takes real management commitment. That commitment has to be consistent and it has to be visible. Top management may well be genuinely committed to their goals, but if employees don't see visible evidence in their own areas of work they simply don't join in. Talk, however loud and strident, is not enough. Action is all that counts. If they don't see management making step changes in their own work habits to fit the 'new era', they don't change their habits either.

It is important not to minimize the degree to which old work habits can pressure you into the old ways, despite your best intentions. The managing director of a large UK engineering company – part of a large conglomerate – was convinced of the need to change his operation from an era of work by management edict and control to one of work teams using strong two-way communication to contribute ideas and improve performance. He and his senior management in a series of retreats hammered out the key messages which were to represent the company's goals over the following decade and shape its future. In a series of meetings covering every manager in the operation, the MD announced the goals that the whole top management team were committed to, and that he himself believed were critical to the company's future success. He realized their success in implementation depended hugely on their own dedication and commitment, and, with real sincerity, he asked them all to 'devote themselves not only in practice but with their hearts, their minds, and their very souls to making them a reality' throughout the company. They were impressed, to say the least.

Over the following months, managers across the business all met, in their work teams, to work out exactly what they were each going to do to make the new company goals come true in their areas. The MD undertook to attend the end of each session over several months to hear a presentation from each of the management teams in turn. These sessions created a lot of enthusiasm and a lot of positive and practical actions to help the whole process move forward. However, many of the old pressures which had produced the old habits were still there. Senior corporate executives still demanded the MD's presence, often at short notice, at meetings away from site, on subjects unexplained to those at the company. As a result, despite his own enthusiasm, he could not turn up at a number of team presentations, and several were deferred more than once. Immediately top management commitment began to be questioned.

COMMITMENT UNDER PRESSURE

The company also had a strongly rising workload, and the pressure to meet production schedules was enormous. The big expansion in output was accompanied by serious shortages in materials and in sub-assembly equipment from outside manufacturers. As a result, the company's executive meetings spent much of their time talking materials and schedules with discussion on the new goals falling on the priority list. Outside pressures from customers and head office grew on the MD and his diary arrangements became subject to short-term change.

Managers throughout the company were working everywhere in 'rush mode', and the pressure became the excuse for delaying work on the company goals. Follow-up review sessions, planned for the executive to monitor that the actions agreed by each management team were being implemented, were deferred or forgotten.

The reality is that, however sincere you are about your goals, the pressures of work will force you into the old undesirable habits unless you are prepared to grit your teeth in the eyes of the storm and follow through. Employees are not understanding about the pressures. They only know you told them to embrace the goals 'with their heart, mind and soul' and already management are doing what they have always done. If even the boss is not dedicating himself to the goals, why should we? It is not the talk that counts, it is the *example*. It is what you do that convinces employees of your real sincerity. If employees have to interpret between your words and your actions, they believe what you do is your true motivation. And, regretful as it might be, they are absolutely right.

Employees actually send you a silent message: 'when you become truly committed, so will we' and that commitment becomes visible to them in how you are seen to spend your *time, attention, effort and money*. These are the signals that show what you really believe is important.

DEVOTING TIME TO YOUR GOALS

Managers basically spend their time on three categories of item: what they think is important in the job, what is presented to them and demands their attention (visits by others, phone calls, letters, reports, meetings), and what they find comfortable or enjoyable. Many managers allow their whole lives to be dominated by category two, and there is a great seduction in believing that being incredibly busy is being effective. You may be responding to pressures, but that may in fact be *preventing* you from devoting time to the goals you profess to be important.

Conduct a little exercise with yourself (or better still, get your secretary or someone independent to do it for you). Have a look at your diary over the last three months and see what time you have actually devoted to the pursuit of your transforming goals. If it does not amount to 40 per cent or more of your work time then you are not really serious about your goals. And that is the message you are sending out to everyone who is looking on: 'just do it when you have got time'. You may protest that there are so many pressures, or life is not that easy, etc., but if you allow the circumstances to manage you then you really have not much hope of transforming the culture of your company. It is tough, but it takes determination and consistency to win through.

Take Sam Walton of Wal-Mart, now with more than 1500 retail stores in the USA. Sam has this touching conviction that it is only the experience and service that customers receive in his stores that ensures the company's growth and success, and it was some years ago that he decided he would visit each one at least once a year. He believed it was 'terribly important to get out into the stores and listen to what the associates have to say. Our best ideas come from clerks and stockboys.' When he had 18 stores visiting was relatively easy, now it dominates his life. But he did not give up. When asked about the enormous amount of time he spent on visits, travelling with truck drivers, turning up on loading docks at 2 a.m., etc., he said: 'I spend about four days a week in the stores and one day a week in the office. I am trying to cut down on the time I spend in the office'.

Do Sam's people know what he sees as important in the business? They certainly do. And it is all out there in the stores where the action is and where the customers are. He has been visiting stores constantly since 1962, literally decades of time commitment to his goals. You may think that is going over the top. But Sam must be doing something right. Wal-Mart's sales have grown from around $45 million in the 1970s to some $30 billion in 1991, to knock Sears Roebuck off No. 1 retailer spot in the USA. In 1990, the UK *Sunday Times* nominated Sam as one of the richest men in America.

GIVING YOUR GOALS CONSTANT ATTENTION

Now, what about the matter of attention? Here is a little exercise you can conduct to test what attention you are actually giving to the goals you have chosen. Many executives become slaves to their in-tray or to their telephone. So take your whole in-tray and classify it into piles either on your desk or on the floor: piles for the goals that are going to transform your operation and a pile for 'other'. These piles will tell you a story. What you read is your management diet, and you are either working towards your goals and a corporate body beautiful or you are in danger of staying a slob on a diet of junk food.

Be ruthless. Take action. Stop the reports which are not about the key goals and performance of the business, or have the reports reshaped to give you the facts and feedback you really want. That will immediately send signals to your people about what is important around here now. Then start asking questions about the reports you read, searching questions, awkward questions. Give plaudits where they are deserved and make sure others know what is valued. Do not put up with bluff answers; send a few people scrambling, cause a few public embarrassments where necessary. If you do that bit well, you will not have to make sure others hear about it. The message will flash round in no time at all.

The basic rule is very simple: your people pay attention to what you pay attention to. If you are consistent, persistent and insistent they will be too. That is how it was with 'old man Marriott' of Marriott Hotels. He hated carelessness or inattention to customer service at any of his hotels and for more than 50 years he read every customer complaint card sent to the company. Did that get his hotel managers to pay attention? It certainly did. Nobody wanted to hear the old man's voice on the phone saying he had just received a complaint from a visitor to their hotel . . .. Said one executive: 'Mr Marriott's habit meant that you had 140 property managers working 28-hour days, 15-month years, to make sure the old man had a very, very light reading load!' That is the power of attention.

THE HAWTHORNE EFFECT

The classic example of the power of attention was the series of experiments conducted by psychologist Elton Mayo way back in the late 1920s in the Hawthorne works of the Western Electric Company in Chicago. Most people remember that Mayo introduced a number of environmental changes to a group of girls making telephone relays, and that productivity seemed to go up no matter what he did. Output improved, for example, when Mayo increased the lighting, but it also increased when he went back to the old lighting. Productivity seemed to rise almost every time he introduced a change or benefit, yet it hit an all-time record when at the end all the benefits had been removed.

All that was surprising enough. What most people are not aware of is that the Hawthorne experiments lasted for over five years. During all that time Mayo paid lots of attention. An observer was permanently stationed with the girls, keeping them informed about productivity and other aspects of the experiments, asking for advice and information, and listening to their complaints. The observer also regularly measured temperature and humidity in the work area and other environmental conditions, and conducted interviews with the girls individually about their views and feelings as the test proceeded. Mayo was not only interested in productivity but about everything that could possibly affect the girls and their environment. The lesson of Hawthorne is still very relevant today: consistent management attention to key goals, combined with adult, genuinely concerned treatment of those involved in the work, can produce not only record-breaking performance but a breaking of the limits that old cultural habits have imposed.

MAKING VISIBLE EXTRA EFFORT

Employees are much more likely to be persuaded that 'the new way' is the way to go when they see their own managers making special efforts in that direction. Naturally, the more senior the manager, the more convincing it is.

The biggest plant of Baxter Healthcare in the UK is at Thetford, in Norfolk. They make medical products like plastic containers for holding blood and systems for intravenous feeding. They have always been highly quality conscious given the products they make, but since 1986 they have been running a Quality Leadership Programme, and with notable success. Process control charts are around everywhere, and at least one department has been operating at a level of zero defects for more than two years. That only comes from commitment, application and effort. The effort shows right up to the general manager. The company recently decided to enter for a prestigious quality award. Seven teams, each made up of managers, staff and shop floor employees, began concentrating on different aspects of their quality performance. The general manager himself became trainer/leader of one of the groups. Employees saw him taking four hours per session and obviously spending more time in preparation and follow-up. To them the message is quite clear. The GM would not be making all this effort if the company were not fully committed to its quality initiatives. And it is just that sort of effort and commitment that convinces employees to buy in and help.

Another UK company intent on changing their culture and their outlook on quality is Grace Dearborn, in Cheshire. Part of the international company W. R. Grace, they make water treatment products, like corrosion inhibitors, scale dispersants, etc. They have been pursuing a quality drive for several years now, but the commitment of their managing director does much to convince employees how serious the company is about it all. Four times a year or so they hold Quality Action Days which the MD runs personally. About 60 employees from across the site come together in groups of 15 to talk quality. After the MD's initial talk they split into working groups of five or so, each with a facilitator, to work on determining specific quality improvement actions the company can take. Later the facilitators collate the suggestions and present them in a feedback session to the MD who clarifies, modifies and approves the action lists employees have drawn up. The final action list is then communicated to the full 60-person group. Six months later they meet again with the MD to review implementation and progress. Did we do what we said we were going to do? Are we seeing genuine improvements? People tend to get things done when they know the managing director himself will be reviewing their earlier commitments and will be doing his review in public. It concentrates the mind . . ..

The MDs who make these sort of efforts are actually sending strong signals round their companies. 'If I can take the time out of my busy schedule to do these things, I expect you to do the same'. Those who follow up religiously send more signals: 'Lip service is not enough − I want to see results'. The plain and obvious fact is the efforts and commitment you get from your employees is simply a reflection of the efforts and commitment you demonstrate yourself. Nothing more and nothing less.

PUTTING YOUR MONEY WHERE YOUR MOUTH IS

What impresses employees most of all, however, is what managment is prepared to put real money behind. If management expend time, effort *and* money on something, they reckon, then they really *must* be serious.

That was the message that came across from Jan Carlzon when he took over at Scandinavian Airlines in 1980. The company was heading for a loss of around $10 million, and everyone realized radical moves were necessary away from the old habits and the old culture. Instead of simply cutting costs Carlzon and his team decided they needed to become a much more service-oriented business, in particular for their regular business travellers, the only passengers who paid full fare. They decided in fact on the goal of becoming 'the best airline in the world for the frequent business traveller'. That goal led to the examining of every activity, procedure, policy and cost for what it was actually contributing to their goal of serving the business traveller. The review resulted in the closing of some departments and redeploying the people, tossing out all the old thick reports, and cutting the costs which were not directly contributing to their new purpose. But achieving their aim was also going to mean *spending* money, especially if they were going to achieve what their business customers told them was one of the things most important to them: flying on time.

A study conducted by the company estimated that flying every plane punctually to schedule would cost around $1.8 million a year. Was the company going to spend that much? Yes, was the answer. Was the company going to stop the practice of 'consolidation', where they saved money by cancelling those flights that were less than half full and putting passengers on the next available plane? Yes. Were the planes to take off on time even if they were waiting for passengers from their own connecting flights? Yes. Were they to take off on time if they were some meals short or one of the crew had not turned up? Providing it was safe to travel, the answer was yes. They were going to do whatever it took, spend whatever was necessary, to be the best businessman's airline. Now, that's commitment.

In fact, the company authorized 147 different projects costing some $45 million in capital expenditure and resulting in an increase in operating expenses of $12 million a year. This was bold stuff for a company looking at potentially large losses in a stagnant market at the time. However, at the same time a huge project named Trim helped them save some $40 million by cutting out all those activities not helping the company towards its prime goal. And what was the result? In 1982, to even their own amazement, they turned in a profit of $70 million. In 1983, *Fortune* magazine voted them the best airline for business travellers in the world, and *Air Transport World* named them Airline of the Year.

Many companies can articulate a good mission statement. But it is not the words, it is what management do with their feet that counts. When management invest significant lumps of what is really important to them – their time, their attention, their effort and their money – then employees begin to take them seriously.

IT TAKES PASSION AND DEDICATION

The boss of the business cannot change the culture of his organization all by himself, of course. He needs a 'critical mass' of managers and staff who are just as convinced as he is if the change is going to be deep, widespread and permanent. However, once the momentum has really started and more and more people join in, then the bandwagon begins to roll along. Up till then it is nothing but hard work. As Ian McInnes of Baxter Healthcare says: 'It's a bit like pregnancy: there's nine months you've got to go through before you can start enjoying the fruits of your labour!' In some cases, it can take even longer than that.

So are you willing to endure the blood, sweat, toil and tears? Can you be a missionary for your company's mission? Because that's what it takes. That's one of the key factors that distinguish the best leaders, according to Warren Bennis. In publishing his book, *Leaders*, in 1985, Bennis and his colleague Nanus interviewed and studied 90 leaders ranging from chief executives of big business to football coaches, university presidents and orchestra conductors. They found that leaders are very clear where they are going, their people 'know where they are coming from', they stay with it persistently. To quote: 'Leaders are reliable and tirelessly persistent . . .. Ultimately, it is this relentless dedication that engages trust . . .. The truth is that we trust people who are predictable, whose positions are known and who keep at it.'

One man who is convinced about the value of persistence is

Ray Kroc, founder of the McDonald's hamburger chain. Prominently displayed in his office, as in virtually every other McDonald's office, is a framed statement by Calvin Coolidge, 30th President of the United States. It says:

'Nothing in the world can take the place of persistence.
Talent will not: nothing is more common than unsuccessful
   men with great talent.
Genius will not: unrewarded genius is almost a proverb.
Education will not: the world is full of educated derelicts.
Persistence, determination alone are omnipotent.'

Do not pursue a goal or a culture change for your organization to which you cannot feel yourself wholly dedicated. It will show through in a thousand ways and the result will be frustration and disappointment. Your employees' dedication and attention will be no greater than yours. But when you can pursue your goal with a passion, your zeal and sincerity will be contagious, and your people will follow on with enthusiasm.

GRABBING ATTENTION

Sometimes, to get people out of their old habits, the way we have always done things, it takes some spectacular action on the part of the boss to get the message home. That is how it was with Marcus Sieff of Marks and Spencer when he undertook Operation Simplification. Sieff believed that the company was awash with duplicated paperwork, and that much of it could be eliminated by trusting employees to do a good job and to use common sense in solving day-to-day problems. He started with a team to examine the company's paperwork to see what could be cut out. They had some early successes, for example, the first experiment cut out six million pieces of paper a year. He still felt they had to do something dramatic to get the message across.

At the time, stock-rooms in each store were protected by

walls, and floor sales staff had religiously to complete stock-order forms to get stock-room staff eventually to bring down the goods they wanted to their counters. Sieff decided at a stroke that sales staff should be able to go and fetch their own stock direct from the stock-rooms. The chief accountant protested that there would be a huge increase in stealing, but Sieff went ahead anyway: he believed most people could be trusted. In the end, the level of stock loss was no greater than before, but in the process they eliminated some 26 million forms and documents, sold off 1000 filing cabinets they did not need any more, and 1000 stock-room assistants were able to be transferred to the sales floor. At the same time, Sieff reinforced his trust in his people by getting rid of several hundred time clocks and punctuality actually improved.

Do you think the message got round the company? Without doubt it did. People may hear you spouting about simplification and trusting employees, but they are never quite sure whether you mean it, especially if they have a boss like the chief accountant. It often takes something sweeping and dramatic to convert the doubters and sweep away the prophets of doom. When Sieff later took over as Managing Director he had another go. He spent nearly a year eliminating another 27 million pages of company paperwork (it creeps back so quickly), piled tons of it together and had a great celebratory company bonfire. These are the images that make employees sit up, these are the stories they remember and repeat over and over, and these are the stories that characterize and transform the culture of the company.

THE 'PARABLES' OF THE COMPANY

The stories Christ related to his followers each had a message within them. Parables are not only easy to remember, they are designed to shape the listeners' behaviour. So it must be with the parables of the company. The stories they tell in your company are integral parts of its culture. What are the 'parables' they tell in your company? Perhaps you need to create a few, with some memorable actions that send a clear message about what the company values and what it wants to be.

That is what Rene McPherson did at Dana Corporation in the USA. 'Almost every executive agrees that people are their most important asset,' he said, 'yet almost none really lives it'. When he took over as Chairman he felt the company was far too bureaucratic and centrally controlled, effectively stifling people's initiative and ideas. When he piled the corporate policy manuals on top of one another they measured over 22 inches! He threw them all out and replaced them with a one-page policy statement. Said a vice-president: 'We have no corporate procedures at Dana. We threw the books away. We eliminated reports and sign-offs. We installed trust.' That trust showed in reducing corporate staff from 600 to 100, leaving factory managers alone to mind their own 'store' and do their own buying without interference, and, as McPherson said, 'turning the company back over to the people who do the work'. But the parable was the throwing out of the manuals, that was the story that stuck.

Peter Edwards, Managing Director of Granada Computer Services in the UK, is obsessive about customer service and measures it continuously. In his last company, when he was Customer Services Director, he found that managers spent time each week in meetings at several levels identifying complaints that were most likely to result in an irate customer phone call to him the following week. It was complaint handling by escalation. He insisted that managers went out and talked directly to the customers and solved their problems. Despite his efforts they still continued to spend too much time in-house. Then he hit on an idea. He locked them out of their offices! At first they were disorientated. He would not give them the keys; they were holding clandestine meetings in corridors, and generally feeling sorry for themselves. The story echoed all round the business, and the message was crystal clear: desk-work comes second, satisfying customers is the first priority. The customer satisfaction surveys that Edwards also installed showed that the percentage of customers who rated the company 'good' or 'very good' for service doubled within two years. People still tell the story about the managers with no offices!

USING SYMBOLS

In 1989, Frank Burns took over as Director and General Manager of Coventry Components, part of the Unipart Group. His factories supply exhaust systems to the UK car industry and in 1989 they won the contract to supply high specification exhausts to Honda. He was anxious right at the beginning to make the point that he wanted the whole business to pull together as one team, and that he valued the contribution of every employee. Soon after he arrived he got the whole company together to tell them how he intended to run the business. He explained his philosophy of management and that he intended there should be a few changes around the place. 'In fact, I am making the first change today. Just look out of the window over there.' A handyman was unscrewing the names of the directors from their privileged parking spots. There was a huge and resounding cheer. 'I'll never forget it, as long as I live', said Frank. Of course, it was only a symbol, but symbols can be very powerful. This one sent a clear signal: privilege and division have no place here any more; we're all in this together and from now on we work as a team.

TAKING RISKS

Taking risks can also emphasize the degree of management commitment to the new goals and create an atmosphere where everyone realizes there is no going back. You will remember the risk Ford took when they decided not to release their new Thunderbird model when it was tipped to win the 'Car of the Year' title, to prove they really meant 'Quality is Job One'.

Carrying through that commitment, the managing director of Ford Belgium a few years ago authorized his dealers to resolve all warranty claims directly with the customer irrespective of settlement cost. Everyone, including the finance director, had nightmares that the dealers 'would give away the shop'. But that is not what happened. In fact warranty costs per car went down. Previously claims would shunt back and forth to head office and up and down the hierarchy with the customer and the garage getting more and more mad at each other. Now the dealer had the authority to act there and then and make the client into a lifetime customer. Management showed its commitment by putting its neck publicly on the block. That kind of risk-taking not only convinces dealers that you are serious, more importantly, it impresses customers as well.

PRISM, a Florida-based company specializing in pest control in hotels, restaurants and other premises, must offer one of the best examples of head-on-the-block commitment. This is their guarantee to customers:

> You do not pay our initial charges until we totally eliminate every roach, rat or mouse nesting on your premises. If you are ever dissatisfied with our results and want to cancel our services we will refund up to one year's service charge and pay the cost of another exterminator of your choice for one year. Should a roach or rodent be seen by one of your guests, WE WILL PAY THEIR BILL, send them a letter of apology and invite them back as our guest. We will PAY ALL FINES that may be levied against your hotel or restaurant by the health authorities for the presence of roaches or rodents, and further . . . Should your hotel or restaurant ever be closed by the health authorities, PRISM will PAY PROFITS LOST while you are closed, plus $5,000.

If you were a potential customer and PRISM's representative presented you with a card showing that competition-blasting guarantee, what could you say? Providing the price was not ridiculous you'd have to say 'I'll buy it!' But think what it says to employees: 'We do a thorough job *every time*. Zero defects is the only standard.' It sets expectations well and truly, for customer and employee alike. That is no-escape commitment.

ALL-THE-WAY-THROUGH MANAGEMENT COMMITMENT

One has to remember that however wedded top management may be to their company goals, employees seldom meet top management. Mostly they see front-line managers, or if they are lucky, middle managers. To them the managers they actually meet *are* the company, and if their commitment is intermittent or lukewarm, employees simply assume that is how it is with the company as a whole. That is why support and conviction down through junior and middle management is critical to the success of any business intent on changing its culture.

The normal role of middle managers is to carry out the expressed wishes of the company. But if in the culture change process their role is to change substantially from the one they have known, their fears and anxieties may in fact result in resistance. After all, the performance and behaviour they demonstrated until now have fitted the company's needs outstandingly: that is why they were promoted. So a change of role, especially in middle age, is not something that is welcomed with open arms. That is the kind of role change that happened in SAS, the Scandinavian airline, when they decided to become the best businessman's airline, extensively trained their front-line staff in customer service skills, and gave them authority to act to solve customers' problems. The middle managers suddenly found their role had changed from one of giving instructions to one of enabling and supporting. But could they all adapt? Here's how Jan Lapidoth, Vice-president put it:

'There's one group of people in our organization that concerns me deeply, and that's middle management. In a traditional corporation decisions were made at the top of the pyramid and executed at the bottom. Top management handed down the orders, middle management interpreted them according to the rules, and then passed them on to be implemented. Basically, they were the messengers for top management. Now, when you create a freer structure and encourage front-line people to make their own decisions, then you undermine middle management in a terrible way. You may not say so, but you question their *raison d'être*.

First you promote a middle manager, then you say to him [or her]: "It is no longer your mission to give orders to the people who work for you. Now you should be their coach and *serve* them so they get the help they need to do the best job". That won't go over too well with the neighbours when you're asked to explain what your new job is. The problem is that you need much less middle management when you have delegated responsibility far down the line. The problem will only go away when people get to feel comfortable in their new roles.'

GETTING MIDDLE MANAGERS ON BOARD

Middle managers can either be a strength or a problem when effecting a major culture change. When they are neglected or forgotten about, and treated as 'assumed supporters', they may secretly pooh-pooh the changes to their people, drag their feet and create resistance as a way of protecting their own positions. When they are clear about their new roles and understand they have got a future and a key part to play, they can be part of the company's engine of change. Their authority and experience give them great influence around the organization. That is why you need to take the trouble to get them on board.

Firstly, if the changes mean there are to be fewer middle managers, the organization needs to be thought through and redrawn precisely. This may be difficult as top management may not be clear themselves how the organization needs to shape up, but they have to make the best decisions they can. Nothing gets managers more disorientated than uncertainty about their future. (Even those who have got a job may think: 'It could be me next'.) Those who are to be displaced need to be given other useful roles which will help the company make the desired transition. For example, systems and administration processes will need to be changed in a new regime, and experienced people given the opportunity to adapt and simplify processes to suit the new culture will undertake the work with gusto. Those who will be departing need to have separation packages prepared in detail which will ensure that they leave the company 'with a sweet taste in their mouth'.

Secondly, those who are staying need to be specifically helped to 'discover' their new role. Even though it may not be clear what the new roles should be, you need to be as specific as you can. A project team, composed of specially selected senior managers and some personnel specialists, can be a great help here. Ask them to describe the new middle management job in terms of the outputs required, and under each heading the measures by which they can judge their success (the latter will concentrate the mind!). Get them to do the same for the front-line jobs, to show how they are changing and how they fit with those of the middle managers. A direct comparison of the new job outputs with those of the jobs as formerly done will help make the differences clear.

Most companies put this kind of task in the 'too hard' basket, and hope it will go away. It does not go away. If you do not pay the price of taking the time and trouble to get it all clarified at the front, you pay the price over the following two or three years in terms of disruption, disaffection and deteriorating attitudes. One of the key factors supporting the success of many Japanese companies is the thoroughness of their preparation before embarking on major changes. Changing a whole culture deserves just that sort of detailed, painstaking attention.

KEY POINTS SUMMARY

- Clear goals are essential, but what succeeds in transforming the culture of any business is real, consistent, visible management commitment. Without that commitment, it simply does not happen.
- Beware of the old habits and pressures. Without determination and resolve, they will drive you back to the ways of the old culture.

Top management's visible commitment to their goals shows in:

- How they use their time.
  - If at least 40 per cent of your time is not spent doing things to further the goals, then you are just not serious about them.
- What they pay attention to.
  - What top management constantly review and check on is what the rest of the employees treat as important.
- What they make special efforts about.
  - If management make special efforts, it sends a signal to everyone else.
- What they spend money on.
  - The most convincing signal of all. If the company is spending money on it, then it must be important!
- Transforming company culture is not achieved at a stroke, it is a journey. Do not start on it unless you are willing to stick at it through thick and thin.
- Grab employee attention by doing something dramatic to show the company's commitment.
- Retell the dramatic stories which show what the company values. These will become the 'parables' of the company and part of its culture.

- Use symbols which crystallize the new character of the company.
- Take a few risks (like unusual customer guarantees) to demonstrate the company's commitment.
- Take the trouble to get middle and junior managers with you all the way. Their support will be critical to your success.

6

Blackpool rock: the role of communications

GETTING THE MESSAGE ALL THROUGH THE BUSINESS

Many companies treat employee communications as if it were an 'add-on' to the business, something done 'because it is a good thing', or 'to keep employees informed'. But communications is not something that is confined simply to what is said in monthly meetings or team briefings: it is going on continuously in every business, every day of the week, every hour of the day. And communications are not simply the words that are spoken. There are endless other *signals* that are all conveying messages: what front-line managers do and say every day, what top management shows concern about and follows up, what different departments treat as important, how they deal with each other, etc. Communication is a continuous two-way process that influences both the culture and the health of the business. If you are intent on transforming company culture then all these communication signals need to be pointing in the same direction, and your messages need to be consistent and repeated all across the business.

The analogy which stays most in my mind is Blackpool Rock. As a youth I once spent a holiday in Blackpool and watched them making the rock through a big plate-glass window in one of the main street shops. British people will know that rock is a stick of hard candy made in a tube shape about 10 inches long, which is generally pink on the outside and white on the inside and sold in many seaside resorts. Through the window you could see the confectioners lay out the pink outer cover, about 4 feet by 3 feet, on a large table, and place a second white layer of the same size on top. Then they took 4 foot strips of red and white candy and laying them carefully along the length of the cover they fashioned them till at one end you could clearly see the letter 'B'. The process was then repeated for 'l', 'a' and all the other letters, spelling Blackpool. At the end the whole thing was rolled up like a great fat carpet, and then through an inch-wide die they pulled the roll into thin pieces and cut them into 10-inch lengths.

It was endlessly fascinating to watch. The reason they took so much trouble in making the rock was to give it one unique feature. When you break a piece of Blackpool rock at the top you can see the word 'Blackpool' spelled out round the edge. When you break it half-way down or at the bottom, the message is still the same: it says 'Blackpool'. And that is exactly how it needs to be in companies who know what they want their culture to be: the message has to be the same all the way through, from top to bottom.

CLEAR MESSAGES, OFT REPEATED

The advertising business has much to teach us about how to use messages. They inevitably make them simple and easily remembered. They know that if they do not they will not get through to their public, and, most important of all, they will not influence their behaviour, i.e. their buying behaviour. That is the purpose of it all. So they boil all the many wonderful attributes of their client's product down to one key message. Then they repeat it and repeat it and repeat it until we all know it by heart. These are the techniques advertisers have used for years to work their way into our consciousness and influence our behaviour. And if it works with people outside the company, it will work with people inside the company too.

Whether they are about the mission, the values, the principles or beliefs of the company, the messages that are communicated round the business must not just be 'understood', they have to be specifically chosen, worded and repeated often. It follows that if they are to be repeated they need to be easily remembered and trip easily off the tongue, even of the lowliest of employees. You need to be able to hear first-line managers saying the same words daily to their people. That way the messages will start to affect behaviour, i.e. to start moving the habits of the company at every level.

For example, one large engineering company had a long record of always meeting its production programme, although on many occasions they had to scramble through to meet their schedule. However, only production felt the constraint of that record, so the message was changed to: 'We meet our *targets*'. That led to teams of managers from all *other* departments in the business meeting to set their own targets in support, and targets which they were all committed to meet. One manager reported:

'I was keen to set ourselves some ambitious targets but several of my team said "It's all very well getting brownie points by writing these marvellous objectives, but *we meet our targets* means we've actually got to meet these targets now." That made us start writing objectives which were more practical and realistic. And two months down the road, when we had trouble making a date on one job, the whole team worked evenings and the weekend to deliver on time. Before, they would not have been so committed. Funnily enough, I don't think I would have asked as much of them either . . .'

That is the value of consistently repeated messages: people begin to live them.

THE BENEFITS OF A COMMON NEW LANGUAGE

Another great benefit that communications can add to the process of changing a company's way of life is the use of a common new language. The fact that the phrases are new emphasizes that things are indeed changing, and the fact that everyone understands them and is using them helps to make the changes simply 'part of how we do things around here now'.

That is how they found it at Baxter Healthcare, the company we mentioned earlier. It was in 1986 that they started in the UK with their Total Quality programme and have been continuing ever since. Using the Phil Crosby approach and terminology they first conducted a Quality Leadership training programme with all their managers to introduce the concepts, and gain understanding and acceptance. There they discussed their COQ (costs of quality): how much it was costing in manufacturing to have separate people inspect the products after others had made them, to carry out rework and repair on products not made right first time, to deal with complaints about products in the field, etc. They started talking about 'zero defects', about whether it was actually possible and how you could get there. They talked about 'error cause analysis', about 'prevention not detection', and about quality being simply 'conformance to requirements'.

That is indeed the first stage in using a common language: understanding what the new words and concepts actually mean, and just as important sometimes, what they *do not* mean. After training, those who understand the new terminology feel an immediate affinity with others back at work who are 'in the know', because communication seems so much easier with people 'who understand each other'. Also, when someone first starts conducting an 'error cause analysis' to tackle some perennial problem which may (as it often does) spread over several departments, they find interdepartmental co-operation is so much readier with people who understand why it is all being done.

TWO POINTS OF CAUTION

This leads us on to two other important points. If training in the new language and concepts is spread over too long a period, those initially trained and anxious to exercise their new skills and knowledge may find themselves stymied back at work by those who are not 'in the know', and do not want enthusiasts upsetting their established routine. That kind of discouragement can seriously damage the company's efforts to change. People give up early if they run up against too many blockages, and the successes recorded can become both patchy and disappointing. Everyone needs to be brought on board as soon as possible.

Secondly, there is a tendency with companies starting down new cultural paths for the trainers to be seduced by the charm of all the new language and smart phrases, and to give participants too much to digest at once. That can lead to confusion, lack of focus, and widely different initiatives being undertaken. Companies need to be jealous of the number of ideas and initiatives they introduce at any one time if they want to see coherence and concerted action in the changes they are introducing to the organization.

Over the four years since Baxter introduced their programme of change at Thetford, Ron Feakes, Technical Director, believes they have learned that 'in the end, communication is what it is all about, and the commonly understood concepts and language certainly helped us break down barriers between departments'. Baxters do not depend on quality control checkers to get their quality right any more. Production operators have now taken over full ownership of their own processes and realize that the only standard is to get it right first time. And the operators certainly understand the language of quality: they have process control charts everywhere and talk knowledgeably about them to anyone who cares to ask. Even directors have changed their conversations. Said Bob Clarke, their Quality Assurance Manager: 'I heard two directors say the other day "Yes, but have we got a process which is capable of meeting these limits?" That kind of detail and precision would not have come into director discussions three years ago'. Gradually the common language is shaping the focus of the whole business.

It takes time for everyone to get used to a new common

language, of course. At the beginning, using the new words and concepts can feel a bit awkward, rather like wearing new, elegant clothes, one feels slightly self-conscious at first. As one gets accustomed to them, so the whole thing becomes more natural. That is how the new vocabulary becomes just part of the company's culture.

SELLING THE CHANGES

When companies first embark on a process of change, they often have to sell the need for the changes to their people, in other words, to do some intensive internal marketing. In this respect we could do well to take a few lessons from those who successfully market branded consumer goods. When a company like Heinz decides to launch a new canned food product, for example, they know the product has to have something different or new about it, or be clearly better than what was available before. They do not start unless they have that kind of distinction.

They then work out the *exactly worded* messages that they will use in their advertising, and repeat on the can, in poster hoardings, in magazines, on TV, and in the shops. They plan their calendar of launch events meticulously. When housewives, who have seen the adverts the previous evening on TV, arrive at their supermarket, they find posters about the product outside the front door, special displays inside, promotional offers, balloons for the children, etc. There is no escape. And the weight of the communications and selling effort just carries everyone along. That is how it needs to be planned when first communicating and persuading employees of the worth of your company's new goals and the need for constructive change in the business.

COMMUNICATIONS BROCHURES

That is where special communications brochures have a useful role to play. They can clearly set out the company's goals or explain the reasons behind the company's change of direction. Putting a copy in the hands of every employee ensures at least that everyone gets the same message. They can even add a bit of spice and excitement to the process.

When Jan Carlzon started on the process of turning around SAS in the early 1980s, the company issued a little red book to every one of their 20 000 employees entitled *Let's Get in There and Fight*. With pictures and cartoons the book gave concisely information about the company's goal and vision which had already been approved by the board. However, Carlzon felt they simply could not risk the message becoming translated and distorted as it worked its way through the company. So he spent lots of his own time conveying the message personally all over the business. During his first year in the company he spent exactly half of his working hours out in the field talking to SAS employees. It was his way of demonstrating in a very visible way that his enthusiasm and involvement were genuine. 'From my first day at SAS,' says Carlzon, 'I've made communicating with our employees a top priority.'

In the case of Kodak, the situation was a little different. The company had been losing market share to other competitors, but in 1984 the decision to award the Olympics contract to Fuji Photo sent a message which shocked the company into action. Company leaders Colby Chandler and Ray Whitmore embarked on a fundamental restructuring of the business which included laying employees off for the first time in Kodak's history and abandoning the traditional functional organization for one in which a number of independent business units were created. They also published an eight-page brochure in which they both praised the company's past achievements and explained the reasons for the changes. Not only did every employee get a copy of the document, but meetings were held all round the business to make sure everyone got the message both as an individual and in a group where they could ask questions and discuss the implications of the changes. In addition, videos featuring Whitmore and Chandler were shown to employees during the next year to reinforce the messages and keep minds focused on doing what was necessary to guarantee a better future. The messages must have got through. Three years later *Business* magazine carried a feature article titled 'Kodak Makes An Olympic Comeback'.

USING ALL YOUR MEDIA TO CARRY THE MESSAGE

There are many media which can carry the company's message, of course, but if you are going to communicate effectively with employees, then you have to use effectively all the media at your disposal. In fact, it is not until you actually make a list that you realize how many means really are available. The list below is not exhaustive, but they are all 'media' with the potential to influence employees and help gain their involvement and support.

Notice-boards
Information briefs
Monthly team briefings
Pay packet inserts
Special launch brochures
Training sessions
Trade Union representatives
Cassette tapes
Campaigns
Static displays
Special competitions
Congratulation boards
Big boss visits
Award ceremonies
Company magazines
Magazines sent home
Manager/employee team talks
Senior management
    presentations
Mass meetings
Problem-solving groups
Specialist consultants
Videos
Posters
Information on personal
    computers
Attitude surveys
Local newspaper articles

The more the same messages and signals reach employees the more they become convinced that that is how the company is, and wants to be. Indeed, the companies which communicate best make sure the messages carried by their various media are all pointing in the same direction. They do not want to risk any diffusion or confusion of message.

COMMUNICATIONS MANAGER OR NOT?

This is where some overall orchestration of communications can be helpful, but I am not an advocate of appointing a Communications Manager if that gives line managers the impression that they are thus relieved of ongoing communications responsibility. Effective two-way communications need to remain firmly with line managers. However, a Communications Support Manager or Facilitator can play an important role in providing useful material for managers, and in planning and co-ordinating the material presented in the various media round the business.

This is particularly so when companies first decide to launch out on major changes to the company's style of operation or focus on new long-term goals. That is the time when it makes sense to list all the media that can be used, and to plan carefully month by month the calendar of the events and communications that is to take place over the following period. Using a simple matrix of this kind both prevents clogging the calendar with too many events or communications at one time (especially in the first flush of enthusiasm), and reveals the gaps in maintaining the communications flow after the early months of special effort. To be effective, communications have to be planned, ordered and sustained.

GETTING MANAGERS TO LIVE THE MESSAGES

Let us assume then that the company has launched out in a chosen new direction and has put together a coherent communications programme to get its messages across. So far so good. However, to make the changes stick the whole management team needs to be conveying the same messages, speaking the same language, actually living the talk. One good way to encourage this is to transfer ownership for the actions that need to be taken over to the managers themselves, by asking:

'What actions can you take now, and over the next few months, which will signal to all your people that this is indeed the start of a *new era*?'

'What in our current actions are signals of the *old era* that you think we should now take steps to remove?'

When managers meet in working groups to discuss the actions they can take to advance the company's development moves, they generally come up with lists of realistic, down-to-earth objectives and decisions. When they begin to discuss the old era signals, almost invariably they home-in on attitudinal factors which act as real hindrances to change. As they list items like 'not doing what we say we will do', or 'not co-operating well with other departments', participants each realize they all bear some guilt in these areas, and that can strongly reinforce everyone's commitment to change.

NEW ERA/OLD ERA SIGNALS

That was the experience of managers at the Peterborough plant of Molins, manufacturer of high-speed cigarette-making and packaging machinery. They chose as two long-term annual goals: 'record-breaking company performance', and 'record-breaking service to the customer'. All round the business managers in their working teams met to decide what actions thy could put in place to make the goals a reality right from year one. Every team came up with objectives and actions which they then presented to their respective bosses for their approval and support. When they discussed new era/old era signals the kind of point that appeared in their old era lists included items like: failure to produce on time, missed target dates, poor communications with production, too much moaning and not enough positive action, lack of co-operation and understanding with customer service department, criticizing our department to outsiders, delays in attention, talking down the company, and so on.

The managers soon get their own message: it takes effort on *everyone's* part to make changes happen and become the company's way of life. Of course, as a result of these revelations there was no sudden revolution where everyone magically changed their attitudes overnight, but their combination of actions was enough to see customer lead times immediately reduced, and for productivity in the first year to beat their previous best by some 36 per cent and to keep improving ever since. When managers own the objectives and actions they are planning their commitment becomes all the more intense, their communications have the ring of sincerity. They become not only communicators but advocates as well.

THE KEY ROLE OF FRONT-LINE MANAGERS

However, in most companies 85 per cent or more of employees are non-managers, and to get the change of attitude and culture you seek, the message has to get through and be taken on board right down at the lowest level of the organization. The stark fact is that they are the people who make the products your customers buy and by which your company is judged in the market-place. They are the people who actually deal with clients face-to-face every day and make or break the reputation of your company. And the person who communicates with them most and influences their behaviour every day is their immediate boss. That is why the front-line manager has a key role in the communications process.

Fortunately this has two inherent advantages. Firstly, there are by definition more front-line managers than any other kind! Any company which gets its front-line managers in departments all across the business speaking and acting in support of the company's drive to change has a veritable army which becomes difficult to resist. But equally, if they are forgotten, their cynical remarks can quickly kill the credibility of the company's efforts, and lead employees to make no serious efforts to change. That is why you need to get them on your side if you want to see visible and positive changes across the organization.

THE PREFERRED COMMUNICATOR

The second advantage is that employees actually *prefer* the information they get to come via their immediate boss. When MORI, the polling organization, conduct attitude surveys, they ask employees questions about the sources from which they *actually* get their information, and which sources they actually *prefer*. Respondents are usually asked to nominate their top five choices from a list of sources. Combining employees' top three choices, Table 6.1 shows what they typically find.

Table 6.1　Preferred communication sources
(from a 2000 person survey)

	%
My immediate manager	85
Monthly team briefings	59
Notice-boards	35
Printed material sent to me	29
My manager's manager	29
Direct from senior management	15
Personnel	15
Trade union sources	12
Audio-visual presentations	6
House magazine	4
The 'grapevine'	4

With a little thought it becomes quite obvious why the immediate boss is the communicator employees consistently prefer. He is the face of the company they see every day, the one who helps interpret company goals and policies into working practicalities. He understands their everyday problems, he talks their language. When he communicates with his people, they can ask him questions in their own words, i.e. he makes the communication two-way and at the employees' own level. That makes the communication much more personal than a notice-board, a video or a magazine. He probably talks to them more than anybody else in the business. Quite simply, he is their natural choice.

And think about this. Your formal company-to-employees communications process may only take up two or three hours a month, but the first-line manager is actually communicating with his or her people every hour of the day, that is, around 160 hours a month. What he or she says and does in all these hours will overwhelm anything the company says through its formal communications by a factor of around 80 to 1. Employees take their example from their boss, and if they do not see him or her actively supporting the company's goals, they won't either. They are a powerful force either for you or against you.

In the end, there is no viable alternative but to develop your first-line managers into the company's best two-way communi-cators. That means giving them the appropriate communi-cations material, pitched at the level of their employees' understanding, to help them get the message across. It means giving them whatever training and retraining is necessary until they can perform their communications role with confidence and conviction. When they run up against practical problems, they need to know where to turn for help. You need to do whatever is possible to help them do it well. That is the kind of training and support that pays off in the process of shifting attitudes and changing culture.

ENCOURAGING UPWARD COMMUNICATION

A common problem with most company communications sys-tems is that they focus almost exclusively on the downward flow of messages and information. But employees begin to mobilize

most strongly behind the company's goals when the communications flow *upward* through the business is as easy and as
respected as the downward. Companies may have communicated their principles and goals to their employees clearly, but
they never really know whether the graft has taken to the root
stock unless they examine the plant closely and cultivate it with
care. That is where feedback is so important to the culture
change process. You need to ask your employees if you are
being true to your own principles, if at every level in the
company you are doing what you said you would do.

Mars Inc. runs just this sort of health check on itself every
two years or so. Some years ago the company published a
booklet, with a copy for every employee, laying out the Five
Principles of Mars. These were Quality, Responsibility, Mutuality, Efficiency and Freedom. A copy of the principles appears
on the wall of every Mars unit across the world. In the booklet
John and Forrest Mars said:

> 'We have tried to state in a simple, direct way the guiding
> principles of Mars. But principles don't live in words on a
> page. They only come to life in the hearts and minds of
> people, and people have always been the core and driving
> force of our company.
>
> So this is simply the first step. The second and far more
> important one is up to you. We ask you to make these
> principles your own. When you do . . . when we all do . . .
> our future will bring success in every sense of the word.
>
> The principles are demanding. They are often difficult to
> get right, and we realize we don't always get them right.
> However, we do see them as being fundamental to our way
> of doing business.'

Every few years Mars conducts a company-wide survey to check
whether round the world they are still being true to their own
stated principles. The confidential and anonymous survey tells
them what their associates really think, and that kind of upward

information flow allows the company to put attention where it is most needed.

ACTIVE LISTENING

Active listening is a key part of the upward communications process. That is where the company learns to listen to its own employees about what does not fit with the new culture, about what is wrong, and to their ideas for change and improvement. It can be tough going at first with seemingly endless nit-picking and faultfinding. But if the company reacts patiently and constructively, soon the positive ideas start to come through, and that is when active listening comes into its own. Listening to the legitimate points employees raise, but doing little about them, means employees perceive you as only *hearing* what they say. They do not reckon you are actively *listening* until you do something positive about what they say.

It is at that point they begin to think that what they say is actually worth listening to. In fact, it does not need to be something major, just something visible. Here is a very simple example, from a large engineering company in the UK Midlands, which will illustrate the point. Pieces of heavy machinery were assembled in stages on large jigs, and moved by heavy crane to other areas of the factory for further work as they progressed. When the crane arrived to lift a piece on to the next stage the driver would generally have to manoeuvre around to get in the right position each time. One operator suggested putting a paint mark on the crane beam exactly at the spot where the crane was directly over the work, so that he did not have to shunt back and forward every time: a simple idea, but very effective. Of course, it is not just a paint mark, it is a public mark of recognition, to the operator and to everyone else looking on. Mentally the operator says: 'That's me up there, I did that. My input actually makes a difference in this place.' When your people genuinely believe that, then they really start contributing.

FOSTERING CROSS-COMPANY COMMUNICATION

Lack of communication *between departments* can often be one of the biggest blockages to implementing effective change. So introducing specific mechanisms to stimulate cross-company interaction becomes an important element in the process. One of the effective ways of doing this is to *structure* situations where this kind of communication becomes virtually unavoidable.

For example, as part of the company's focus on new goals, each department head can be given the task of establishing who exactly are the department's 'internal customers', that is, those departments to whom they supply information, materials or finished work. They are then required to meet with these department heads within a specific timescale to determine (just as they would with a customer) their specific requirements, particularly in the context of the company's new goals. Their discussion needs to establish clearly:

- The customer department's top three priority requirements.
- What they 'contract' to do on each of these.
- How the supplier department will measure their success on each.
- Regular dates when they will meet together to review progress.

This kind of exercise takes time to complete, of course, but when department heads all over the business become engaged in the process, it certainly gets more cross-company communication going than ever before. Getting the new culture and attitudes to grow throughout the organization can be a long and sometimes slow job, but this exercise, in a 'what can I do better for you' context, certainly accelerates the process.

USING CROSS-FUNCTIONAL TEAMS

Another technique for developing stronger cross-company communications is to use multi-disciplinary teams to undertake important projects designed to advance the company on the path of its chosen goals. For example, the company might be a manufacturing business which has chosen to become much stronger in the area of 'customer service'. But they realize that there are many departments which affect the company's ability to deliver what the customer would see as good service, namely sales, order recording, planning, production control, manufacturing, quality assurance, transport, invoicing, service engineering, etc. To get the whole bundle right, they have to select key people from each of the departments involved to get together as a team to discuss the whole in-company sequence and how it can be improved.

In the process, team members begin to understand how things happen in other parts of the business, they learn about their colleagues' problems, and feel united by what has become the common goal of improving the company's service to the customer. They also begin to talk the same language the more they meet with each other, and develop useful relationships with people in other departments which they can then use later to get things done. Most important of all, they begin to talk like *businessmen* instead of just production people, planners or accountants. As time goes on, departmental isolationism and the 'not invented here' syndrome become less and less appropriate: it just does not fit with the new culture.

LOOKING TO THE OUTSIDE

A fundamental reason why any company embarks on a process of culture change is for the positive effects it will have on its image and relationships with its many audiences *outside* the business. Part of the communications support manager's role will be to examine what signals the company is sending to its customers, its suppliers, its local community, its shareholders and its industry. Are they noticing the difference and do they realize the company is changing for the better? For example, are the invoices and paperwork sent to customers showing positive signals? Do they get better treatment when they telephone with queries? What about the company brochures: do they carry the new messages? Does the talk of the salespeople reflect the changes? Do visitors to the company get a positive impression right from the reception desk? Is the difference noticeable when you phone in? Do people in the neighbourhood notice any difference? These are all legitimate areas for the communications manager to examine. And getting departments all round the business to respond to his or her inputs means the company can not only build up an image of itself which all hangs together, but which gets across to its publics with positive impact.

EMPLOYEES AS THE COMPANY'S BEST AMBASSADORS FOR THE COMPANY

A fact which may not have occurred to many is that just as people talk to each other across the business, so they also talk about what is going on in the business to their families, their friends and acquaintances. After all, if work occupies half of their waking day, it is frequently bound to be a subject of their conversation outside the company. And if their comments are largely favourable it can materially affect the company's image with its various publics.

Comparative market research surveys are often conducted to assess the reputation of companies with the public. One of the key findings of these studies is the virtual direct correlation that exists between how well companies are known by the public and how favourably they are regarded; in other words, the data regularly confirm that 'familiarity breeds favourability'. When asked how they know the various companies, people cite different reasons such as 'I use their products', 'I have seen their advertising', 'I have often seen their name on buildings or vehicles', or 'I know someone who works there'. By analysing the various ways people say they know the company, the degree

Table 6.2   Companies favourability scores: impact of factors

Factor mentioned	Uplift in 'favourability' score (%)
I have seen their advertising	+2
I have heard or read news about them	+5
I have often seen their name on buildings / vehicles	+7
I use their products / services	+12
I know someone who works / worked there	+30

of uplift each factor gives to favourability can be worked out. Taking a mid-1980s survey as a typical example, Table 6.2 records what the data showed.

The figures vary from year to year, of course, but each year the company's employees are shown to have the greatest impact on companies' favourability scores. The fact is *the company's best ambassadors are its own employees.*

When one stops to think, it all becomes quite obvious. Employees will talk about work to their friends and acquaintances anyway. If they are involved in making positive changes within the company's culture change programme, if their comments and ideas are being actively listened to, then they are going to say favourable things. No one wants to admit they are working for an awful company since it tends to reflect on their own mistakes or show themselves incapable of getting a job with a good company! So the tendency is to want to say something good about your company, if nothing else but for the reflected credit it implies. Several companies in fact produce little booklets of positive facts about their companies for distribution to employees. They know that not only will employees be able to take some pride in their achievements, but they are bound to use the information in conversation, and that will have positive impact on many of the company's key publics. In the business of communications companies regularly neglect one of the most powerful forces for their own good: their own employees.

KEY POINTS SUMMARY

- In companies who know what they want their culture to be, the message has to be the same all the way through, from top to bottom, just like Blackpool rock.
- Whether they are about the mission, values or beliefs of the company, the messages have to be specifically chosen, worded and repeated . . . often.
- Whichever discipline or approach you adopt, use of a common language brings people together, and makes change easier to implement.
- Two cautions. Teach everyone the new language early. Do not let trainers or enthusiasts cause indigestion by introducing too much new jargon at once: keep it simple.
- Generally, you have to sell the changes to your employees. Brochures which explain the changes and have visible support from top management can create good initial impact.
- Use all your media to carry the messages. Show signals of your beliefs and culture everywhere.
- Use a simple matrix calendar to plan and orchestrate your communications both inside and outside the business. By all means use a communications support manager, but keep the responsibility for communications firmly with line managers.
- Enlist managers' help in speaking, and living, the messages. Get them to undertake actions across the company which will signal everywhere that this is indeed the start of a *new era*.
- Front-line managers have the greatest influence on the attitudes and behaviour of most of your employees, i.e. the non-managers. They set the daily example which employees follow. It pays to have them on your side.

- Front-line managers are actually your employees' preferred communicator. Use, train and support them as your best communications asset.
- Encourage *upward* communication by getting feedback from employees on how your practices fit your goals, and by active listening, i.e. taking action on the constructive suggestions they give you.
- Structure events and encourage procedures which get departments communicating productively with each other.
- Remember: in creating your image and reputation, employees are your company's best ambassadors.

7

Train employees to help you

SIGNING ON TO THE CHANGES

It is only when everyone is involved in doing things differently in a business that truly the culture has moved, both in depth and for the long-term. In starting the process it is not enough just to mouth slogans like 'Total customer satisfaction is our goal', or 'Now quality is everyone's responsibility', and expect things to change. Most employees actually want to help their company to change and improve, *but they need to know exactly how*. Every employee needs a specific answer to the question: 'What should I now do differently to what I was doing before?' That is where training comes in.

Firstly, the training needs to explain to every person why the company *wants* to change. In this context, it is not a good idea to 'rubbish' all that has gone before as a way of emphasizing the need to change. Most listeners will have been there at the time, and unless things have obviously been mismanaged, may feel emotional attachments with the past or with former bosses. They may feel they were doing the best they could under the circumstances, and do not appreciate their efforts being denigrated, even by sidelong comments. Generally it is better to give due credit to past work and successes, and to allow proper mourning at the passing of old times as a way of helping employees to make the transition.

Thereafter, initial explanations need to concentrate on the

present, on customers' ever-increasing expectations, on rising product reliability and quality standards, on the pressures being brought to bear by competitors, and on the necessity to keep moving ahead to guarantee a successful and secure future. If the company can also point to the resources it is devoting to its effort, affirm that they are committed to long-term change, that they have confidence in their management and employees to reach the goals they aspire to, then all of that helps convince employees that the company is really serious. And in painting the future scenario, there is no substitute for enthusiasm. When employees see real fire in the eyes of the boss and their senior managers, there is a great inclination to sign on and be part of it all. That is the kind of excitement that needs to come across to get employees inspired and enthusiastic about the future.

MAKING THE TRAINING RELEVANT

Secondly, the training needs to focus on what every person in the organization specifically needs to do to make their own individual contribution to the change. Everyone should not only have a *stake* in making it work, but a *role* in making it work. That means the training needs to be adapted for specific groups, to giving the knowledge, skills and tools which employees can put to use as soon as they get back to the workplace and begin to see positive differences. It also means that everyone should realize that the whole company is involved; that employees are all attending different training sessions, but with everything 'hanging on' the same company purpose, namely making the chosen new company goals come true in practice. That way the training begins to have coherence and *meaning*.

In this initial phase of development, drop all training which does not directly support the company's new goals or culture. Demonstrate that management knows what it wants. Do not carry on with, for example, 'Finance for Non-Financial Managers' or 'Interviewing Skills' while running the programmes that are planned to change the whole culture of the company. It dissipates resources, energy and attention. Employees may also conclude that the new training sessions are merely another training course, just the latest flavour of the month, and that is not the message that needs to come across. It needs to be made clear that this is all part of a lasting 'sea change' which is vitally important to the company's future, and that everyone needs to give it their full and undivided attention.

START AT THE TOP

This may seem all too obvious, but if top management do not get involved early in the training they imply that they feel no need to change, and that it is only the more dim-witted junior managers and employees who need to have their minds rewired for everything to come right. By taking part themselves they also send other signals round the organization, like: 'Changing our culture means changes in the habits and behaviour of everyone in the organization, and we recognize that this must start at the top', and 'We are giving this the highest priority at our level, and we expect everyone else to do the same'.

In the early days training for the most senior executives may be of quite a different nature to that planned elsewhere in the company. Initially, for example, they may invite outside experts to come and give presentations on subjects such as introducing Total Quality Management, flattening the organizational pyramid, developing exceptional customer service, and so on. Comparing and discussing the varying approaches can be educational by itself. They might also read recommended books or view a variety of videos and discuss the implications for the company together. They might visit other companies regarded as benchmarks of excellence on specific subjects and learn directly about the practical things that can be done, and about the dangers and the problems. All this opens windows in minds and gets senior management to consider new possibilities.

Experience shows that senior managers often have likes and

dislikes which can influence how well they take to the training. For example:

- They are receptive to outsiders who have recognized authority or experience in the subject, but experts within their own company are generally treated as 'prophets without honour in their own country'.
- They welcome the opportunity to learn from the experiences of senior executives from other respected companies.
- They are very willing to visit other companies who have established reputations in the subject, e.g. organized visits to a series of companies with records of excellence.
- They prefer to attend training sessions with managers of the same level.
- They prefer their training sessions to be off-site, in pleasant locations where they can concentrate.
- They are not keen on being trained by their subordinates.
- They hate to be treated like schoolboys.

HOW TWO COMPANIES STARTED

Companies often use a workshop format with their top team as a start to the training process, but the pressure to change varies widely from company to company. In the case of Legal and General Insurance in the UK the stimulus for a culture shift came as a result of a strategy meeting held by the senior executives of the company. They sell most of their business through agents and 'intermediaries'. Realistically they concluded that they were not going to increase their total sales volume, and at the same time sell more via larger intermediaries, unless they started to differentiate themselves clearly from the competition. This they decided to do on the basis of service rather than price, but they realized that meant they would need to initiate changes throughout the whole organization.

Consultants conducted an audit for the company and gave them independent feedback on 'how things are now'. Over several months the directors read some key books on customer service, submitted themselves to intensive discussion sessions on the subject with their consultants, and firmed up on exactly where they wanted to go. They concluded they needed to develop a set of values and practices which would pervade the company and actively support their new service objectives. Using further survey research, both internal and external, and following on several Directors' Workshops, they decided on four key goals for the company. They were:

1 Customer orientation at all levels and at all times.
2 Partnership between departments.
3 Empowerment of front-line staff, so that decisions can be taken as near to the customer as possible.
4 Continuous staff training and development.

These then became the focus of their efforts over the next two years. During that time they ran a whole series of training 'events' involving every member of staff in the organization. They used a Front-Line Road Show to present the vision, held intensive week-long residential training sessions for managers, organized training sessions for staff dealing directly with external customers, and more for those dealing with internal customers, produced and distributed an internal video, conducted audits to see how far the changes had penetrated, and ran 'focus groups' to home-in on specific problems and issues of internal communication. Two years down the road, Director Rod Young emphasizes they still have a long way to go, but he is in no doubt that the change in their culture is irreversible . . . and it started at the top with the Directors. That is where the discussing, the mind-opening, the training and the clarity of vision have to begin.

At Honeywell Information Services in the mid-1980s the situation was somewhat different. President Jim Renier had announced to the company's top executives and to the press that the company intended to remain a force in the computer industry and planned a closer association with the Japanese manufacturer NEC. Many executives had open reservations about the strategy, however. Renier realized that their commitment and co-operation were critical to its success, and as a consequence he organized a five-day workshop for his top 25 executives to address their concerns and try to engage their active support both in succeeding in the market and in changing the culture of the business. Not the easiest task, but some of the more unusual items on the agenda helped mould common views within the team.

For example, one element in the workshop was for each executive to tell a story which represented values they thought the company should work to preserve and another to show the kind of things they wanted to change. That by itself was revealing. Another item involved teams analysing the company's current practice on things like strategic planning, financial reviews and management potential assessment, and indicating how they would have to be changed to suit the company's intended new style. This they had to present in the form of two sketches, the first highlighting the negative aspects of how they then did things, and the second showing how it could work in the future. This made the process both learning and fun. Held in a farm location, the group also took part in a number of outward-bound team-work exercises, but at the end of the workshop they each had developed a written plan of what they were variously undertaking to do, to gain commitment to the company vision and to make things happen in their respective areas. The distinct progress the company made thereafter was attributed by many of the executives to that initial formative experience together.

The situation, problems and opportunities will be different in every business, but the education and learning process has to start at the top. That is where the change in mind-set begins, where minds need to become clear about the company's goals and the kind of culture they would all like to see. That is where company-wide commitments are made, and they are the only team with the authority to put in place the resources, communications, training and actions needed to make the goals a reality.

TOUCHING EVERYONE IN THE BUSINESS

Early in the training process it often helps to launch a major training 'event' which involves every person in the business. That kind of experience can give a kick-start to the whole process of change and grab employees' early attention. That is precisely what British Airways did in the mid-1980s in their bid to become one of the world's best airlines in the eyes of their customers. Two-day training events, under the title 'Putting People First', were held for BA staff all over the world, and brought together people who might normally never meet each other. Baggage handlers joined in syndicate sessions with pilots, cabin crews, freight people, office staff, cleaners, maintenance men and managers to talk about how they might serve customers better and get more of their business.

In the UK, participants were welcomed to the training sessions in a large, specially prepared auditorium at Heathrow airport. With name tags for everyone, they were seated in mixed groups of eight to ten people where they introduced themselves to each other and told each other what they did. Sir Colin Marshall, the Chief Executive, and his team of directors opened each event in person by explaining where the company wanted to go and why, and emphasized the importance of their individual contributions to the company's success. It was quite clear to employees that Sir Colin would not be turning up himself, and the company would not be expending all this effort and money, if they were not serious about it all. When he appeared again at the end of the two days, the point was doubly reinforced.

During the two days, participants were both entertained and educated. For example, they enjoyed seeing the lady trainer show, with a handsome steward picked from the audience, how body language could convey clear messages all by itself, and the importance of the 'first four minutes' in creating a good impression with customers. They also learned about:

- The difference between winners and losers. In particular, winners do not blame everyone else, they take on ownership of the problems and solve them
- Developing better relationships with others
- The importance of attention
- Making eye contact with customers
- Giving and receiving strokes
- Being assertive and not aggressive
- Dealing with difficult people
- Handling stress
- Positive versus negative thinking
- Maintaining adult to adult communication

Nearly 40 000 people attended the training sessions between November 1983 and June 1985, with the company spending several million pounds on the programme. But it did have impact. In 1985 BA was named 'Airline of the Year'. In the same year (from losses exceeding £1 billion in 1981), the company turned in a profit of £176 million. Of course, the service training was not the only thing the company undertook to improve its performance. Under the strong leadership of the Chairman, Lord King, a great list of other projects were put in place to increase its market share and expand its activities. And, although no one pretends that things are perfect, the company keeps performing well. It carries far more international scheduled passengers than any other airline, it is among the most profitable companies in the industry, and in 1991, for the fourth year in a row, *Business Traveller* magazine voted BA 'Best Airline Overall'.

TRAINING MIDDLE MANAGEMENT

Middle managers often feel threatened by major changes in their company's style or structure. They get worried about whether they can adapt to the new demands, about whether old dogs can learn new tricks, and about whether their position will suffer. These anxieties have to be confronted early in the training. With middle managers there is one particular advantage, however. They positively see themselves as part of 'management', and generally see it as their job to carry through in practical terms company plans and instructions. When they have had the 'why' of the changes explained – preferably by the chief executive himself – mostly they will want to help.

However, they also need an answer to the question: 'What do you now want me to do differently to what I was doing before?' That is where part of the training has to be practical and in-depth discussions about precisely how their role will change, with the differences highlighted by a direct comparison with what it was in the past with what it will be in the future. When Scandinavian Airlines gave authority to their front-line employees to make decisions to solve customers' problems, they found managers continuing to override their decisions. It was only when they made it clear that the managers' new role had to be one of support, of supplying their people with the information, systems, equipment and resources necessary to do a good job, that they became part of a fully integrated team.

With clarity about their new role, managers immediately begin to feel more comfortable with the changes. What also helps reinforce their commitment is to ask them to develop a set of positive actions during the training that they are prepared to take to help *make* the company goals a reality. One effective approach is to have managers agree what actions they can take *now*, within the following 48 hours, to show the process of change has started in their area. This is supplemented by more substantial actions that they undertake to put in place over the following three months, to drive the initiatives forward and indicate that the changes are here to stay. Seeing and discussing what fellow managers are prepared to do helps make managers feel they are all part of a team, and gives them more confidence to take action in their own areas. A strong feeling of ownership is also created if each manager has to write his chosen actions on a flipchart and explain them to the assembled group. And, as we know, ownership generates commitment.

A POTENT FORM OF FEEDBACK

Sometimes managers can be reluctant to change, even when the 'why' of the change has been explained in detail. To help the process of 'unfreezing', both Honeywell and Legal and General used a form of feedback to managers to show them how they were actually perceived. In the Legal and General case managers were each given a dozen questionnaires which they were asked to pass on to five or six colleagues (at the same level) and to five or six subordinates. The questionnaires asked the respondents confidentially to score the manager on a number of topics, such as customer orientation, interdepartmental co-operation, people management, attitude to the company-proposed changes, etc. Managers were also asked to rate themselves on the same factors. Respondents sent their questionnaires anonymously to a central point where the scores were collated, and later this was fed back to the managers at their training sessions.

The impact on the managers was considerable. Some were quite pleased with the results, some were shocked. However much they thought they were supporting the company's goals, there was no escaping the 'facts' of their fellow employees' perceptions. Part of the training procedure was for each manager to explain to his or her group what they had learned from the information, and to seek their input, advice and help in handling it. Since everyone was pretty well in the same boat, they all felt sympathetic. During the sessions managers were also asked to declare what specific actions they would be taking 'back at the ranch' as a result of what they had discovered.

All these building blocks – clarifying managers' changed roles, getting commitment to specific action steps, giving feedback on attitudes, getting managers to share problems and ideas

– are ways in which middle management training can help get a 'critical mass' of managers behind the company's aim of creating real cultural change. Some old-style managers may continue to resist, of course, but the tendency simply to dismiss them should be resisted. Often, when they are finally persuaded, they can be the new style's strongest converts. However, it is not acceptable to resist for ever, and, for the sake of the company, those who will not adapt should be asked to leave.

TRAINING FIRST-LINE MANAGERS

The task in training first-line managers is both to explain why the business wants to move in a chosen new direction and to put in their hands practical concepts, tools and techniques they can use to help the process. It is important that these tools engage the managers in doing something *structurally* different, that the managers get involved early in a procedure that represents the new era. Attitudes may only change slowly, but the act of regularly carrying out a new procedure quickly develops new habits and soon makes the new approach just part of 'how we do things around here'.

For example, if the company decides to make the concepts of total quality part of its culture, it may wish to educate its first-line production managers in the use of the 'Seven Quality Control Tools'. These tools can immediately be put to use in tackling everyday problems, gathering hard factual data, showing up the most important quality faults, and generally making the production job easier. Providing the concepts are explained clearly, and the learning process taken step by step, supervisors can often get quickly switched on to the potential of such tools to help them do the job better. What is even more convincing is for the training group to take a real work problem and see it resolved before their eyes by the efforts of the group using one of the new tools. That tends to generate impatience to get out there and put the tools to work and that is the kind of energy that is needed to start off the new habits.

On the other hand, the company may be in a service business and want to develop a much stronger customer orientation among employees. Because in service 'people is all there is', first-line managers need to have put in their hands concepts and ideas which will help them deliver distinctive service. Classifying good and bad customer experiences as 'warm fuzzies' or 'cold pricklies' is a concept which can often grab employees' imagination. It may sound gimmicky, but trainees definitely remember the concept, and retention of the key points is half the battle. Another useful concept is 'meeting and beating the customer's expectations'. That emphasizes the very personal nature of pleasing individual customers: that it is only when you do something which 'goes the extra mile' or gives the customer a pleasant surprise that you earn an 'A' on their report card. One fast food business in the USA teaches their staff to imagine a big plus sign on the customer's forehead as they leave as their way of encouraging them to beat their expectations. Service supervisors do not need big books of rules of what not to do; most of all they need simple concepts they can put to use with their people in their everyday work.

POINTERS ON TRAINING FIRST-LINE MANAGERS

Here are some other tips which are particularly relevant to first-line manager training:

- Do not try to teach them too much at once. Many managers may not have been in a training or learning situation for years and can be apprehensive about it. Teach them only as much as they are going to use immediately.
- Have the managers work in small groups of, say, two, three or four people. That way they feel less exposed, and they learn from each other.
- Modularize the training, for example, into day-long chunks. That is enough for them to absorb at once.
- Ensure that they leave each training day committed to an

action assignment which will make use of the lessons they have learned.

- Follow up on their progress. Start the next day's training module by checking up how everyone got on, discussing and resolving their problems.
- Appoint a mentor for every trainee. This can be the trainee's boss or another senior manager, and has two distinct functions. First, the mentor's role is to encourage and support the trainee in carrying out his action assignment back at the workplace. Also, it presses the boss into a support mode for the training and the company's new goals.
- Use workbooks for the training sessions in which key points are listed and in which managers can make their own pertinent notes. If they are succinct and practical enough, managers will use the material back on the job.
- Conduct 'passport' tests as you go along. Experiments in work situations show that the attention, performance and retention of trainees is clearly raised when they know they will be examined on their learning.

It is a good idea to get the chief executive or a member of senior management to open or close the training sessions. This has a two-fold purpose. Firstly, first-line managers hear about the seriousness of the company 'straight from the horse's mouth'. Secondly, they can put to him directly any resource or blockage problems which may be preventing them from delivering even better on the company's goals. Remember, front-line managers are the most numerous group of managers in the business; they are the army which can do most to influence employees and get them to back the company changes. As such, their training is crucially important.

TRAINING FRONT-LINE EMPLOYEES

You may work very hard on changing the company's culture, but it only begins to mean something when customers start noticing the difference. Front-line employees are the people who get their hands directly on the products customers buy and who deliver the company's services face to face. It is the results of their efforts which customers see most and which are a reflection of the culture inside the business. That is why their training has to be directed to 'doing it better for our customers', and 'doing it better than our competition'. They can help provide that all-important distinction in the eyes of the customer.

Like everyone else they need to understand why the company wants to make changes. If that is communicated first in a specially convened session attended by employees of all levels and addressed by the chief executive, then they begin to appreciate that the decisions have been taken at top level and that everyone is involved. That gives their subsequent training so much more purpose and meaning. It also raises expectations: expectations of different behaviour at all levels throughout the business and more attention to customer-pleasing detail. The training will then simply be a process of showing them exactly how.

That 'exactly how' is techniques, practical ways of doing it better. For example, in a manufacturing company seeking better and more consistent quality, there may be an organizational decision that instead of using independent inspectors to check products, production operators will take over control of their own quality. They will need to be made aware of the specific product quality standards, why these are set where they are, and exactly how to use the measuring instruments involved. They may be taught about control charts, how to compose graphs, plot values from real product data and so on.

It is critically important that the training at this initial stage is taken slowly, step by painful step. Operators are generally a bit scared about 'going back to school' (most did not win prizes there), and it is vital that they experience *early success*, e.g. by trainers using short, simple tests every step of the way where the trainees actually see themselves succeeding 90 per cent of the time. If they feel they can do it, their expectations will be exceeded, they will feel good about themselves and act as your publicists by telling their mates that the training is OK. If they find it all a bit complex and difficult, they will complain to their mates, get them worried and 'kill you off' before you start. This is an enthusing as well as a training exercise.

POINTERS ON TRAINING EMPLOYEES IN MANUFACTURING COMPANIES

Here are some useful points and ideas on training front-line employees, especially when an objective of the training is to change mind-sets as well as teach new skills.

- Take the training in bite-size pieces. As a rule, no more than 20 minutes teaching talk without activity or participation.
- The training must be 'hands-on' practical stuff.
- Only train when the employees concerned are actually going to put the knowledge to use.
- Do not assume knowledge. For example, most shop-floor employees will get percentages wrong, and as soon as you lose them, they switch off.
- They must experience *early success* with the learning. If they do, they will plague you to learn more. If they do not, they will give up on you.
- Set little 'hurdle' tests for each half-hour or hour of the learning. Plan the training that way. Like teaching horses to jump, make the hurdles easy to start with, and congratulate them often.
- Review and extend the knowledge at spaced time intervals. Reinforcement of lessons learned and step-by-step build-up is essential at this level.
- Give employees 'credits' when they pass through specific parts of the training. They love to feel they are getting somewhere.
- Get customers to visit your training sessions and talk

directly to the trainees about your products, quality, service, etc., as they see it. Your employees will be more convinced by that than anything you say.

- Take them to visit customers on their premises and talk directly to the front-line people who are using your products. That frequently produces a quantum leap in employees' customer awareness.
- Show trainees competitors' products, literature, advertising, etc., to make them aware of what they are competing against.

TRAINING SERVICE EMPLOYEES

Unlike products which can be checked before they leave the factory, the quality of services is determined at the moment of delivery, by whoever delivers the service. In high contact businesses, like hotels, airlines, banks and shops, the 'moments of truth' experienced by customers with front-line employees in large measure determine the reputation of the company. Your bank may just have launched a super new product with glossy literature, but if when you get to your branch no one has taken the trouble to tell them about it, then as a customer you begin to think the bank does not know what it is doing. That is why educating employees not only in customer skills but in product knowledge is so important in service businesses.

Home Depot, an American do-it-yourself discount warehouse operation, certainly believes in the value of that kind of training. Company employees attend *weekly* classes in product knowledge, and receive up to 20 hours of training every month both from their own inside staff and outside manufacturers. Unlike most discount stores filled with part-timers and weekend assistants, customers think it is great when they ask layman questions about building, plumbing and electrical products that the staff actually know what they are talking about. The training pays off. Home Depot have expanded by more than 80 per cent annually since 1979, with the volume per store increasing by an average of 18 per cent annually, in an industry where 5 per cent is already considered good. And, despite paying above average salaries, the company still clocks up profit margins which are two to three times the industry average. Low prices and excellent service are not incompatible.

Delivering the same service hour after hour, day after day, can be a pretty tedious affair. Sitting at a supermarket checkout for hours, answering telephone call after telephone call all day, or rushing around serving orders for food and drink can be pretty patience-stretching at times, to say the least. That is why service training needs to emphasize with employees the fun and satisfaction in serving the customer well if they look for the signs, to show that customers' reactions are largely a reflection of one's own approach and attitude, and to make clear that customers have different views and attitudes and that, tough as it is, their satisfaction is a very personal business. Using concepts such as 'beating the customer's expectations', 'going the extra mile', or 'warm fuzzies' can help crystallize ideas that staff can carry around in their head every day, but above all the training has to deal with everyday situations and realities, and give employees effective and practical strategies which will help them come out on top most of the time. They need specific answers to their questions of 'What do I do if this happens . . .?', and if the company shows it understands their problems and is putting into their hands practical ways of handling the tougher problems, employees will respond positively.

POINTERS ON SERVICE TRAINING

- Employees need to know exactly, in detail, what excellent service looks like in the most common, standard situations in their job.
- They also need to have some idea what to do, or where to go for help, in non-standard situations.
- They need to be aware of the importance of time in service

businesses in achieving customer satisfaction. Customers want their requests or complaints answered *now*, not later.

- The training must be strongly participative. No more than 20 minutes teaching talk without active involvement.
- Keep training groups small, preferably no more than 20 people. The course leader cannot ensure personal attention and full involvement otherwise.
- Discussing and answering 'What would you do if . . .?' situations can be a good learning format.
- Role-playing helps make situations live and impactful.
- Taking videos of the role-play and playing these back for comment and discussion is one of the most powerful ways to change attitudes.
- Use simple tests to reinforce the learning, to heighten attention and strengthen commitment.
- Give 'credits' for successful course completion. Many service people live repetitive, humdrum lives and appreciate the sense of achievement and feeling more valued by their company.
- Make the learning fun.

GETTING NEW EMPLOYEES TO FIT THE CULTURE FROM DAY ONE

When employees first join a company, they want to please, they are ready more than at any other time to fit in with the company's requirements. It is the crucial time, as we mentioned in Chapter 1, to be clear about the company's expectations. That is something that Disney, for example, are very careful about. Even when they take on temporary staff to take tickets at their theme parks, they put them through three days of intensive training before they allow them ever to take a ticket.

From the start it is made clear that the company is putting on a 'show' for their Guests (capital 'G' please), and that whether they are 'onstage' as Cast Members or 'backstage', they all have an important job to do. As soon as new employees join they are given written instructions on where to report, when to report, what to wear, how long they will be in each training phase and exactly what is expected in terms of appearance, dress, hair-style and length, shoes, make-up, jewellery, etc. Nothing is left to chance. Everyone, temporary or not, must attend Disney University and *pass* Traditions 1 before they get any training at all for the particular job they are going to do. In Traditions 1 they learn how each Division – Operations, Food and Beverage, Casting (Personnel to you), Finance, Merchandising and Entertainment – co-operate to put on the show. They are going to be asked questions by Guests, so they need to know the names of the Seven Dwarfs, and to know about Bambi, Dumbo and Donald Duck's newphews before they ever get out there.

About lunchtime on the first day, a group photo is taken, and before the end of the day it appears with all their names on the front page of the resort magazine. In this way they are already beginning to feel part of the show. Disney know by experience that Guests do not ask all their questions at the information office: they often feel more comfortable asking ticket-takers. They do not risk Guests getting the answer: 'How should I know? I just take tickets here.' So in the following days the new employees find out how to give directions to the restaurants, the toilets, to any attraction on the site, about when the parades start, about when the show closes, what transport is available and a hundred other things. In fact, if a Guest asks a way-out question like 'How many hamburgers do you serve here in a day?' or 'How many bricks are there in the castle?' they know they can pick up a telephone hidden nearby and ask a bank of operators armed with factbooks for the answer to any question. The whole idea is to do whatever it takes to serve the Guest. At the end of their training they are not ticket-takers any more, rather, they have become Walt Disney World *Hosts*. And do you think they play their part when they meet their first Guest? Of course they do. By that time they are already part of the culture.

TRAINING TO A STANDARD

Companies who do not spend time training employees thoroughly when they first join imply that they do not care too much how they do the job as long as they do what they can. That virtually guarantees mediocrity. Inevitably new employees learn from their colleagues and it will be no surprise if they quickly pick up all the short cuts and bad habits they have adopted over the years. So the quality of the existing culture is perpetuated. Merck, Sharp and Dohme, the American pharmaceutical company, are well aware of the syndrome and go to great lengths to train their new employees.

When their new salespeople join the company they first undergo nine to ten weeks of training on basic medical subjects, such as anatomy, physiology and disease, and have to score 90 per cent or better in weekly tests to stay in the program. Phase two of the program consists of three further weeks learning about the company's products and how to present them to clients. They then go on trial for six months, presenting company products to customers accompanied by their district managers. If they get through that, they enter phase three, with three weeks at headquarters in Pennsylvania improving their presentation skills. Even after that salespeople attend regular 'primary didactics' medical classes at Harvard and other Universities. Merck, Sharp and Dohme admit that 'training is our obsession'. That obsession, combined with their care for employees and extensive research effort, seems to pay off with their customers. The company not only earns a hefty 30 per cent return on equity, it ranks consistently high on *Fortune* magazine's 'most admired companies' list, being voted into number one spot in both 1991 and 1992.

The business does not have to be a technical one to justify thorough training. Even when you are selling hamburgers, it pays off. At McDonald's, crew members know how long French fries should be cooked and at what temperature, they know how long the fries should sit before they get thrown out and fresh ones made. Front-of-house staff know to smile and make eye contact with customers, and they know about thanking them for their custom and to say 'come again'. Its staff are all well rehearsed. McDonald's even founded a Hamburger University way back in 1957 to teach their franchisees and managers. The first one was in the basement of one of their stores, but the current one is a $40 million facility which has capacity for 750 students, and is equipped with all sorts of cooking and refrigeration equipment, translation booths, and computer equipment for automated recording and scoring of examination answers. McDonald's food may not be to everyone's taste, but customers flock to their restaurants all over the world, whether in Russia or China, because they know what they are going to get. McDonald's is now the largest restaurant chain, and the largest owner of retail property in the world. And their success owes much to their consistent training and performance standards.

CREATING A LEARNING CULTURE

Business has become like the Olympics: the performances that won gold medals the last time may not be good enough to win the next time. Standards are constantly creeping up, expectations are continuously rising. There is only one way businesses can keep their own performance edging forward, and that is by the knowledge and skills of the people inside the organization being on a continuous upward trend. The continuously learning organization is no longer an option, it is a necessity.

Many companies have already made continuous education part of their culture. Under Thomas J. Watson Jr, IBM took the lesson on board long ago. This is how he put it in his book *A Business and Its Beliefs*:

'There are two things an organization must increase far out of proportion to its growth rate if that organization is to overcome the problems of change. The first of these is communication, upward and downward. The second is education and retraining.'

Buck Rodgers, for over nine years IBM's Vice-president of Marketing, reckons in his 1986 book, *The IBM Way*, that the company makes the largest financial commitment to training of any company in the world. Every year every IBM manager spends 40 hours on off-the-job training, and that extends all the way down the organization. They believe the hours logged in the classroom exceed those spent in any major university. IBM don't stay up there by accident. However good they are now they keep working at getting even better.

YOUR ONLY APPRECIATING ASSET

Virtually every asset a company purchases starts to deteriorate or go out of date as soon as it is bought, whether it is machinery, computer software, communications equipment, buildings, vehicles or whatever. Of course, machines and computer software can be updated or upgraded, but never as effectively as people. With an established 'learning culture' people can actually become the only *appreciating* asset you have got. Yet, in my experience, directors will seriously discuss spending millions on new buildings, capital equipment, or communications software but virtually never on their only appreciating asset. Not only do they grudge the spending but cut the budget mid-term with great regularity. It seems to me an inexplicable management blindness.

Each year Motorola spend 1 per cent of their sales revenue on training their people. That may seem modest but it is way beyond the spending of the average company. Employees get up to 40 hours a year of training on subjects such as product quality, statistical quality control, technical developments, team-working, communication, and problem-solving. Motorola reckons it realizes 30 times its investment in quality training in direct quality savings. At the end of 1989, the company took a full-page advertisement in a national UK Sunday newspaper to tell the world its quality performance had improved a hundred-fold since 1981. It does not measure its defect rate in percentages any more as it has gone way beyond parts per 100, or per 1000, or even per 100 000. It is shooting for a defect rate of only 3.4 parts per *million* by 1992. How do the competitors catch up with that? You can only get that kind of world-class quality with a world-class workforce. You only get a world-class workforce by every one of them being involved in a process of continuous learning.

Another company that fervently believes in the value of continuous education is Quad Graphics, a 4900 person printing company based in Milwaukee in the USA. At Quad they run the printing presses four days a week, but for one day every week everyone gets the opportunity to go to school at the Quad Education Division. One whole day of training every week. We may be admiring of the companies who plan one or even two weeks training a year for every employee, but the equivalent standard at Quad is ten weeks! Managers take weeks off to design and deliver a course. Press workers do the same. They are all training, at every level. The company is a veritable university. Every employee is that much more skilled, that much more knowledgeable, at the end of the year than they were at the beginning. That is how they grow their only appreciating asset to expand their business and leave their competition behind.

KEY POINTS SUMMARY

- Changing the culture of a business means changing the behaviour patterns of people throughout the organization. Training has a key role in showing employees exactly how.
- Firstly, the training should aim to get employees to sign on to the changes by explaining why the company wants to

change and inspiring them with the vision of a more exciting future.

- Secondly, every employee needs specific answers to the question: 'What do you now want me to do differently to what I was doing before?'

- Start the training at the top. Directors are not beyond learning. And the changes need to be seen to have participation and clear support at the top.

- Top executives take best to a workshop format, with carefully planned agendas and input from outside experts. The output of the Workshops should always be clarity of goals and actions which the whole team supports.

- A major launch event, involving every employee, is a good way of grabbing everyone's imagination and giving a kick start to the culture change process.

- Middle managers often feel threatened by changes to the organization which promoted them in the first place. Get their active support by making clear what is their new role, and having them propose positive actions they can take to drive the initiatives forward. Ownership will bring commitment.

- First-line managers need most of all in their training simple tools, concepts and techniques which they can immediately put to use in their everyday work. They need to be engaged in procedures which develop new habits that represent the new era.

- Front-line employees need most of all in their training practical techniques with which they can 'do it better for the customer'. Trainees must experience early success with the training for them to get enthused about using it. Use simple 'hurdle' tests and give credits for achievement.

- Train employees to the standards of your new culture from the moment they join. That is when they are most willing to respond and conform.

- Create a learning culture. Continuous learning can turn your whole workforce into a vast appreciating asset, one which keeps you permanently ahead of your competition.

8

Trust employees to help you

TRUSTING SOME BUT NOT OTHERS

Not so long ago I was consulting in a large plant in the north of England involved in the manufacture of huge pieces of electrical switchgear. I was talking to the superintendent of one large section of the works in his mezzanine office overlooking the shop-floor. Within the space of three-quarters of an hour as we talked, five different people had scurried in and out with pieces of paper looking for the superintendent's signature. On several occasions he scribbled his signature on the paper without taking his eyes off me. Finally, I said: 'What are all these people doing, George?' 'Oh, it's probably just masking tape they're after, or other things to get on with the job.' It turned out that superintendents alone were allowed to sign for *any* materials for use on the job. Supervisors, often in charge of millions of pounds worth of machinery and equipment, looking after large groups of skilled craftsmen, and expertly knowledgeable about the product were having to interrupt their superintendent, irrespective of what he happened to be doing at the time, to plead for masking tape!

Unbelievable? Not really. One sees evidence of this kind of mistrust, of whole groups of employees being treated as second or third class citizens, in just too many businesses. This sort of situation is even more prevalent in many public service and government organizations. A 1991 report by the Audit Commission on the British Police demonstrated only too clearly that far from protecting against mistakes, the process of getting approvals from layers of management can be frustrating, long-winded, inefficient and expensive. To comply with the approval procedure for purchasing new cars, one police force had to wait a year and a half between requesting cars and their delivery, during which time there had been no less than three price rises. The constables of one rural force spent much vuluable time transporting papers between sites until headquarters finally approved the purchase of a simple fax machine. Two police forces drove prisoners and their escorts back and forward from country stations to the city to have their photographs taken until each rural station was allowed to have its own instant camera. These are the sort of frustrations and inefficiences that occur in every organization where top management, remote from the day-to-day work, retain the only authority for action in the company.

SPENDING THE GREY STAMPS OF FRUSTRATION

It was back in the 1960s that, as a result of studies conducted in business and in public utilities with managers, engineers and shop-floor workers, Frederick Herzberg formulated his motivation–hygiene theory. He concluded it was factors such as achievement, recognition, responsibility and the work itself that accounted for most workers' feelings of satisfaction, but by far the greatest sources of dissatisfaction fell under two headings: *company policy and administration*, and *supervision*. In fact, in studies subsequently conducted by Dr Paul Schwartz, these categories accounted for as much as 76 per cent of all the stories of dissatisfaction told by repondents. The stories were to do with items such as 'ill-advised management decisions, hamstringing procedures, red tape, management apathy toward problems, being bypassed in decisions affecting the job, and having requests or recommendations turned down'. Overwhelmingly, employees did not see their companies or supervisors as helpers and enablers, but as obstacles and preventers.

The inability of employees to take commonsense action to help the job, to use their own judgment in handling situations, can be both offensive and frustrating. Staff often give up, adopt a resigned 'why bother?' attitude and may even feel gleeful if disaster strikes as a result of management's failure to listen or consult. Employees may in fact pay their company back with bouts of non-co-operation to get their own back for their feelings of upset and frustration.

In transactional analysis terms, this is much like 'green shield stamps'. Many shoppers save the stamps given them by their local store and later exchange them for gifts of their choice. Similarly, employees perceive episodes of irritation and frustration as being awarded 'grey stamps'. They are not really forgotten. They save them all up in their mental stamp books and when suitable opportunities occur they 'spend' them in the company's shop by making life as difficult as possible. It shows in episodes like: 'So you need some overtime to get this urgent job done for a customer? Sorry, I can't help, I promised my wife I would take our cat to the vet tonight'. It shows in employees leaving as soon as the buzzer goes no matter how important the job, in their finding mysterious difficulties which help to slow up urgent work, in not passing on information to other departments, in making it difficult to introduce changes, and a hundred other ways. Companies actually pay a high daily price for not trusting. They set up a 'tit for tat' conflicts throughout the organization which can be difficult to shift. With employees reluctant to give willing co-operation or to go the extra mile, mediocre performance is virtually guaranteed.

THE TRUST ANTIDOTE

That is not how it is at Nordstrom, the US speciality fashion retailer, which sells shoes and clothes for men and women from their well-appointed stores. They consistently get rave notices about their customer service, and their recent growth has been the envy of the industry. How do they do it? They recruit what they call 'nice people' and then simply trust them completely to do whatever is necessary to deliver outstanding customer service. As soon as they join, every new employee gets a copy of their one-page policy manual. This is what it says:

> Welcome to Nordstrom. We're glad to have you with our company.
>
> Our number one goal is to provide outstanding customer service.
>
> Set both your personal and professional goals high. We have confidence in your ability to achieve them.
>
> Nordstrom Rules:
>
> Rule No. 1: Use your good judgment in all situations.
>
> There will be no additional rules.
>
> Please feel free to ask your department manager, store manager or divisional general manager any question at any time.

That is it. You spend the first day getting to know the various departments, the people you will be working with, and the cash register procedure. Otherwise, it is up to you. From day two you get the whole responsibility of serving the customer well; they assume you will want to do the best job you can, and they trust you to use whatever common sense, effort and ingenuity you think it takes to do it. Wouldn't you respond to that challenge? So will *your* people. Freed from the long-standing bureaucratic rules and restrictions, they will astonish you with their enterprise and commitment. They will actually help you completely transform your company's culture. But you have to do the trusting first.

Of course, Nordstrom does a lot of other things to please its customers. For decades its motto has been *quality, value, selection and service*. To help them live up to that the company carries stocks which are twice the industry norm; for example, they have some 80 000 different pairs of shoes available at each of their branches. The stores are beautifully decorated, many with their own live piano player, and washrooms that are meticulously fitted and a pleasure to use. To give that special service to its customers Nordstrom also use more salespeople than most other stores: about 50 per cent more than normal in the industry. They will also not be undersold on any item, and they will take anything back which the customer returns, no questions asked. In fact, one enthusiastic assistant was said to have taken back a pair of snow tyres, which Nordstrom does not even sell! Of course, one of the penalties for trusting your employees completely is that they make mistakes, but then who doesn't? The liberated salespeople of Nordstrom are simply tops with their customers. So much so they sell twice as much per square foot as their competition. In the ten years to 1990, while some of the best in their industry doubled their business, Nordstrom grew sales and profits by some six-fold. Not bad for a company with only a one-page employee manual.

MANAGERS CANNOT DO IT ALL

The fact is – trust your employees or not – there is no way managers can check every single product or service delivered to a customer. Your company is actually no better than the products your employees make, no better than how they treat your customers when you are not looking. Think about it. Your employees are probably being directly supervised for less than 10 per cent of the time they are at work, but you want them to be doing it right during all the other 90 per cent. There is really no viable alternative to trusting them to do it right, because that is what is happening anyway. Interestingly, though, if you tell them you now *expect* them to handle the job by themselves and that you are going to trust them to do it right without supervision, they immediately feel the weight of the responsibility. They start acting more responsibly, not less so.

Companies in service businesses depend particularly on their employees doing it right every time. What the company sells is no more than the service delivered by the front-line employee at the point of contact with the customer. That is just what Jan Carlzon realized when he began the transformation of Scandinavian Airline Systems in the early 1980s. On average his 10 million customers came in contact with around five SAS employees on each journey, with each contact lasting approximately 15 seconds. These 50 million 'moments of truth' were actually what created the image of SAS in the minds of their customers. Headquarters might provide excellent equipment, marketing might produce interesting or exciting deals, but it was the 50 million moments that ultimately would decide whether the company succeeded or failed. If they were going to transform their company's operation, they could not rely on rule books and instructions from some distant corporate office to do it, it had to be done by the front-line employees taking initiatives and making decisions on the spot to satisfy customers' individual needs.

EMPLOYEES CAN PUT IT RIGHT EARLY

That point is even more crucial in handling customer complaints. Most service employees do not know exactly what they are authorized to do to put a complaint right, so to keep themselves safe they pass it on to their boss. That means doing it twice, with two people involved now. If the boss is uncertain, or feels the customer request does not fit known 'company policy', she may suggest the client 'writes in to head office' to get herself off the hook. Now we are handling the issue three times, with more (and more expensive) people involved. So the complaint goes on, and on.

There are two blatantly clear points here. Firstly, the more times goes by with the complaint still unresolved, the more the customer's initial irritation rises. It takes time and effort to get down to explaining everything in writing for the benefit of head office. So although it may have been a small complaint to start with, now it is becoming a big one. The customer gets more and more determined. 'It's the principle of the thing', they say. The customer now wants to feel compensated for all his extra trouble as well as his original complaint. You may be helping to lose a customer for life, and that can cost a lot of money. There is no profit at all in making it difficult for customers to complain. Secondly, escalating the complaint adds to your costs. You handle the same item two, three, four and more times, with the costs per minute rising at every level. You are actually paying money to irritate the customer more. There's logic for you. You actually save money by *not* escalating, and you keep more customers by trusting your employees to resolve complaints down at the point of contact.

PUSHING RESPONSIBILITY DOWN IN MANUFACTURING

Trust is needed in manufacturing too. Every time an operator manufactures a product, a maintenance man repairs a machine, an inspector examines the quality of the product, you have to trust that they are doing it right. But despite the fact that managers do not put their hands on the products themselves, companies continue to tax managers with responsibilities that assume that they do. Take the following typical list of responsibilities. They describe what is commonly expected of managers and operators in manufacturing companies.

Manager	*Operator*
Output/productivity	Attendance
Quality	Good timekeeping
Operating costs	Meeting performance targets
Administration and records	Flexibility
Good housekeeping	
Scrap/rework	
Safety	
Employee relations	
Training	

As one manager said: 'I would be happy if my operators did just that!' However, ask yourself one crucial question: 'Where do the faults first occur?' Who has the actual power to do it right first time? For example, a little thought will show that the manager is not in charge of output, it is the operator who actually controls that. That goes for product quality, too, and scrap and rework, and good housekeeping. You cannot artificially transfer the responsibility for these things to the manager (where it does not belong) and expect him to police everyone else into it. He simply cannot be there all the time; he is bound to lose that contest. That is where lack of trust gets you: managers scurrying about checking on everything and unable to keep up with the unequal struggle.

There is really no sensible alternative but to put the responsibility where it truly belongs, and to trust and *expect* employees to do it well. It is cheaper, and more effective, too. When employees get the full responsibilities we know they've actually got already, we can then remove the checkers, controllers and supervisors, and the other costly duplications put there to make up for our lack of trust. Of course, operators will need the appropriate training and coaching, but then first-line managers can be released to do *additional* things to support operators doing the job, to *add value* instead of just adding costs.

This is what the new set of responsibilities might look like:

Manager	*Operator*
Section productivity	Output
Operating systems	Product quality
Section operating costs	Scrap/rework
Scheduling	Good housekeeping
Safe working arrangements	Safe working habits
Training	Skills
Innovation	Improvement ideas
Communications	Team contribution
Team development	

In these lists, responsibilities have been pushed down to where they belong. Operators are now clearly in charge of what we know they control anyway, namely output, product quality, scrap, rework and keeping their own workplace clean and tidy. We expect not discipline from above on housekeeping and safety, but *self*-discipline. In addition, we want them not only to 'do the job', but to work well with the team and contribute ideas to improve things. We want them to use their brains as well as their hands.

The manager does not just duplicate, now she adds to and complements. For example, it is the operators' job to work the system, but it is the manager's job to *develop* the operating systems so that productivity and quality can continuously improve. The manager *prepares* the work schedule, and the operators work to the schedule. Many say that you could transfer virtually all of the manager's responsibilities over to the operators, and in time of course you could. But let's take it slowly. Just start with the obvious; that would be enough for most companies to take on at one gulp. That is what trust does for you. You start tapping in to the talents that we all know are out there. And that is real culture-transforming stuff.

EMPOWERING EMPLOYEES TO HELP YOU

Employees do not like doing a bad job or a mediocre job, they actually prefer to do a good job. However, when problems or non-standard situations occur, they do not want to feel powerless to act, unable to do the right thing for the customer there and then or to resolve an obvious production problem without having to run to the supervisor to ask 'please sir, is it all right if . . .'. It makes them feel like children, that nobody in the organization thinks they can be trusted, to the point where they start to lose faith in their own judgment. Judgment is like a muscle: it has to be used if you want it to stay in good condition. Otherwise it atrophies, and people begin to act like children because that is how they are treated.

Won't people abuse our trust if we give it, you may ask? A few may, especially if they feel they have suddenly been released from all kinds of restrictions. But that will fade, and by far the majority will treat it seriously and reward your confidence. Won't they make mistakes? Yes, they will, and we will never be free of that, whether we are employees, managers, directors or presidents. We all learn by our mistakes and employees will, too, given the chance. Won't we be taking a big risk? A calculated risk, yes, but think of it. Transforming the company's culture would not just depend on managers any more. The vast majority of your workforce, the 85 per cent or so who are non-managers, would all be adding their considerable weight to helping the company achieve its goals. The prize simply does not countenance hesitation.

So, what are the practical things to do? You could simply do 'a Nordstrom' and say: use your good judgment in all situations. On the other hand, you may want to move into it step by step. Here are a number of actions of a generic kind which you can take, all of which have been successfully used in other organizations.

Let your people talk to anybody in the organization to resolve problems and get the job done

In many organizations, especially administratively based companies like insurance, banks or local government, managers can be very sensitive about juniors crossing departmental boundaries or meeting privately with managers one, two or even three levels up. It is just not done. Managers, who have worked hard and long to reach their positions of seniority, can get a touch protective about their territory and their positions. Yet these niceties greatly complicate the process of getting decisions taken and resolving customers' problems.

That is the kind of issue Legal and General Insurance were faced with when they first decided to differentiate their business from the competition on the basis of service. Much of their business is conducted by phone, and most of the time the calls require decisions. Previously, if the person taking the call could not give a decision they would have to apologize, and say something like: 'I'll have to check and get back to you'. Often the appropriate person who could give the answer would be at a meeting, on a course, or away on holiday. That generally meant delay, and usually when the item landed on the next person's desk, it was not exactly at the top of their priority list. The person who first took the call could also feel that after they had passed it on, it was now someone else's responsibility. In that respect, Legal and General were no worse than any other insurance business, but their goal was to *differentiate*.

They knew that agents and customers wanted minimum delay and prompt decisions. That meant taking the bold step of 'empowering' front-line staff to give answers rather than make excuses. Staff are now authorized to talk directly to anyone in the company to get rapid decisions or resolve a customer's problem, and senior staff see themselves as very much encouraging and supporting their efforts. Cross-territorial and cross-hierarchical communications are now commonplace. Front-line staff who first hear about a problem do not pass on the responsibility any more, they view it as their job to see the issue through to the end, to resolve it to the customer's satisfaction. It takes time, of course, to change attitudes and habits, and Legal and General are the first to say they are not perfect, but they have already differentiated themselves enough for some agents to have more than doubled their business with the company in the last two years.

A word of warning is important here. Avoid just declaring one day: 'You can now talk to anyone in the business directly to get any problem resolved and the job done'. Unless senior and middle managers are with you the old barriers and departmentalisms will remain. You have to do something *structurally* different to make it *easy* for staff to use the new channels. One sure way to check if you are succeeding is to ask staff by confidential survey if they find cross-boundary communication easy now and 'obstacle-free'. They will tell you. Then you can take further step by step action until the whole process begins to become slick and effective.

Ask employees for their contributions and ideas

Many Japanese companies have developed this approach to a very high level. They take the view that if they are to stay ahead they need to use the brains as well as the hands of all their employees. For example, Pioneer, the electronic audio equipment manufacturer, asks every employee to offer seven suggestions for improvement every month; and they get them. You may feel that is a bit much to ask, but what about just one suggestion a month to start with: would that be too much to ask? Pioneer do not expect them all to be mind-blowing ideas, of course, but they believe it is by making these constant small improvements in every job that they keep getting better quality, better output and lower costs. In addition, because of their monthly commitment, employees are forever *looking for opportunities* to make improvements. A company who leaves the process of making improvements exclusively to management cannot hope to compete with one which has every employee on the job every day.

NV Bekaert SA, the $2 billion Belgian group which manufactures steel wire and reinforcing material for tyres, has taken an interesting approach to getting their employees into a contributing mode. The basic concept in the company is:

> 'Machines are here to work. All the people are here to think.'

Karel Vinck, their Chief Executive, says: 'When management systematically applies that simple principle the result is a revolution in behaviour, information flows, collaboration, motivation and creativity.' Vinck is busy limiting the size of manufacturing units to 300 people, and reducing the number of supervisory levels and staff functions in the process of delegating more and more responsibility to the people doing the front-line jobs. The company's main aim is not just customer satisfaction but 'customer delight', and Vinck is convinced that the critical issue in making that happen is the management of their people. The company's personnel staff are helping by training employees and their managers in the team-work processes that they believe are vital to their success. Vinck says one of their key challenges over the next ten years will be to turn their workforce into a 'strategic competitive advantage'. With the whole workforce in permanent 'think mode', there is no doubt that they will be selling a lot more to their customers than their current $2 billion by the end of the decade.

Give employees full control of their own operations

The basic reason more managers do not give their employees their full trust is that they do not want to take the risk. They think: 'They'll go mad', 'something disastrous will happen', or 'they'll make me look like an idiot'. In fact, the evidence is against them. People do not go mad, they use common sense, *they act like adults when you treat them like adults.*

I will always remember the reaction of people in an electronics factory which came under my management jurisdiction at one point. From setting up the factory, our conviction was that we would get managerial behaviour from everyone if, from the beginning, we treated them like managers. One of the biggest differences in treatment was that managers elsewhere in the company were not paid for overtime. We decided there would be no provision for the payment of overtime to anyone. Interestingly, mechanics recruited from other parts of the company, who had strictly worked bell to bell, started coming in early and staying late to 'get jobs finished'. In its first five years of operation, despite some last minute changes in schedule from customers, the company never missed a delivery date. Staff simply 'flexed' their hours to meet whatever configuration was necessary to respond to customer needs. However, what swelled the chests of operators more than any other action we took was telling them that they did not have to get a signature from a manager any more as formal company acceptance of their reasons for absence. We would simply accept what they said. Surprisingly, that act did more than anything else to convince employees it wasn't any more 'us and them' but we were all 'us'. And attendance improved, too.

Naturally, managers are very loath to give up control, especially in flow-line production situations. Having worked in a car plant as a young manager, I know how paranoid management can get about anything which stops the line. By all means, provide 'floaters' to cover for operators when they need to visit the washroom, or to help out individuals in trouble with the job, but whatever you do, do not stop the line. That is why it obviously took a bit of courage when management at Ford's Edison, New Jersey, plant decided to give every operator a button to stop the line where necessary to put right any quality problem they saw. Did they stop the line? Yes, some 20 to 30 times a day. The average stoppage, however, was only about 10 seconds long. Interestingly, line productivity was not affected. In the first nine months of the experiment defects dropped from

17.1 per car to 0.8 per car, and cars requiring rework at the end
of the line fell by an astonishing 97 per cent! One other useful
side-effect of giving operators more control of their environment
was that the backlog of union grievances fell from some 200 to
an average of less than 12. Even in the toughest situations, when
you trust employees to use their common sense to do a better
job, they will do just that.

Involve employees in selecting all new recruits
Over the years the armed services have developed rigorous
selection procedures, both to help them choose good officer
material and to select candidates for special assignments. It was
way back in the Second World War that studies revealed, for
instance, that trainees were better able to predict who would
make a successful pilot than the instructors themselves! Other
studies conducted in industry have repeated this finding, and
have even shown that subordinates make better judges than
supervisors. So, given practical guidelines and sensible procedures, involving employees in selection procedures may
actually improve the quality of recruits your company takes on.

As when setting job standards, employees tend to set tough
criteria for potential employees. Subconsciously, they all believe
themselves to be good guys, and not any old person off the street
is going to be good enough to do the job they do. So, they are
demanding. Not only that, they do not want to tell potential
employees what a terrible place it is to work otherwise why
would they be working there? Consequently, they find themselves telling candidates the good things about the place,
defending its virtues. In addition, the act of articulating the
positive aspects makes them more appreciative of the company;
it produces more advocates of the company's values, more
perpetuators of the company's culture. Finally, and just as
important, they are likely to choose 'people who fit', both with
the company's values and with their work team. Candidates
also get the chance of talking directly to the people they will be

working with, and that also helps them decide whether the company is the type of organization they would like to join. That is not a bad list of advantages.

It is for just reasons like these that Honda car plant in Ohio involve their shop-floor workers in their careful selection process. First, potential candidates have to complete an application form which asks applicants on the back why they particularly want to work for Honda. Providing their reasons make good sense, they are then invited to take a reading and maths test. Only if they pass do they then get through to the interview stage. Managers and shop-floor operators, in teams of two, then conduct two interviews with each candidate. They are looking for a good work history, a good attendance record and, above all, the ability to be a good team player, i.e. to fit in with the Honda way of doing things. Honda involve the applicant's family as well: when the successful few are hired they are invited to bring along a family member with them to tour the plant where they will be working, and to have a welcome talk from the president of the company. Thus the culture which the company has developed is cherished and perpetuated. Does the tough selection process put potential candidates off? Not at all: in mid-1991, Honda had a waiting list of 30 000 people.

Get employees to train their colleagues

No matter how well you know your job, there is nothing to teach you the essentials better than having to get down to the task of teaching someone else. It helps you to sort out your thoughts, to get your knowledge into coherent order. That is the first advantage of using employees as trainers. In addition, if the job of 'trainer' is given something of additional status ('only the skilled and trusted are chosen to be trainers'), this can visibly increase the employee's self-esteem. Not only do they feel good about it, they treat the task seriously. Also, the initial discipline they teach new employees learning the job affects their own behaviour when they go back on the job themselves.

They feel constrained to be setting an example all the time for everyone else. So good habits are reinforced. Finally, trainers find themselves speaking as advocates of the company's way of doing things: after all, they are now part of it. That means they add their voice to that of managers in helping to defend and support the company's culture.

A word of advice here. Do not choose just anyone to be a trainer. Experiments conducted in America way back in the 1960s in the Metropolitan Insurance Company showed the clear value of training new recruits with your very best performers. Alfred Oberlander, the manager of the Rockaway District Office of the company, had noticed that new insurance agents, regardless of their apparent sales aptitude, did much better when placed with high-performing agencies than with those agencies considered to be only good or poor. To test the point, Oberlander formed three groups of six agents, and placed the top group with his best manager, the second group with his next best manager, and finally the lowest performing group with the least able manager. In the first three months, the performance of the top group surpassed his most optimistic expectations, with the result that in the first year overall performance of the entire agency improved by as much as 40 per cent. Thereafter, he tried always to place new agents with his very best people.

Around the same period, in a study of the careers of 100 insurance salesmen, the US Life Insurance Agency Management Association found that recruits with only average sales aptitude were *five* times as likely to succeed under high-performing managers as under low-performing managers, while those with superior sales aptitude were twice as likely to succeed. High-performing managers taught good habits right from the start, and set high expectations which their recruits clearly responded to. That is a lesson that Honda in Ohio are well aware of. They also place new recruits with trusted workers, who treat their training role very seriously. Instead of two or three days' training as in most other car companies, new employees may spend a full three weeks, training with their shop-floor mentors, or however long it takes to do the job right, error-free. Think how marvellous it would be if all your new recruits performed like your very best workers. The way to achieve that is to give your very best workers the job of training them.

Adopt self-set objectives at every level

In those companies which actually set objectives at a personal level (unfortunately, many do not) there is often a tendency for bosses to 'hand down' to subordinates the objectives they want them to achieve. Another tendency by many is to set objectives which they know to be realistically beyond their subordinates' reach, but are set nevertheless in the hope that they will try harder, and perhaps do even better than they might have done with more realistic objectives. This is a mistake. Firstly, there is no ownership on the part of the subordinates: they do not treat the objectives seriously, knowing that the boss will actually settle for something less. Secondly, the boss is seen to 'talk with forked tongue', i.e. you have to 'interpret' his words, you cannot really believe all he says. That does not make for straight relationships. Thirdly, and most serious, when he congratulates subordinates even when they have fallen short of the objectives, he implies that failure is OK in the business. And that's dangerous.

It is much better to ask the subordinate to draw up the first draft of his objectives. This has several advantages.

1 He has to *think* about the job. Not only must he think about the whole job, about what the priorities should be and about what will fit with his colleagues' needs, but he has to balance this with the company's needs and what he thinks the boss will be pleased with. That is a very good thinking exercise.

2 He has to get *specific*. The task of getting it all down on paper

demands that subordinates crystallize their thoughts, and stand up and be counted.

3 Subordinates tend to set themselves tough objectives. The boss, instead of getting into an 'argue' mode justifying the objectives *he* set, can then adopt a 'help' posture in persuading the subordinate not to attempt too much and helping him to sort out the real priorities.

4 Because they are essentially the subordinate's objectives (he wrote them), he feels he *owns* them, and that ownership brings greater commitment in making them come true.

My advice is to adopt the process at every level, right down to shop-floor employees, even if it takes you time to get there. You will find that trusting the subordinate to set his own practical objectives and agree these with his boss pays both motivational and business dividends.

Adopt self-assessment appraisals

The same applies to performance appraisals. If appraisees are asked to put down in writing how they assess themselves, they are generally pretty realistic about their performance. In fact, more often than not they are modest in their assessment, and tend to underclaim, if anything. That gives the boss the opportunity to be supportive, positive and encouraging. However, if the appraisal consists only of the boss giving *his* assessment of the subordinate's performance as he sees it, the appraisee tends to get defensive to justify himself. That tends to put them in a position of conflict, to put them both into 'argue' mode again. Not a good idea, especially if the appraisal is to meet its prime purpose, namely the further development of the subordinate in a constructive and positive fashion.

There are many forms of appraisal process, but the following format has proved its worth in practice.

1 Privately, the subordinate writes notes on his performance against his agreed objectives, the points he has learned from the successes and failures during the year, his tentative objectives for the coming year and his personal aims for his own further progress.

2 Privately, the boss writes notes of his assessment of his subordinate's performance, the possible learning points, some suggested objectives for next year and his view about his further development.

3 They meet together at a pre-arranged time, quietly, privately, for at least an hour, to conduct the appraisal. The subordinate gets to speak first, on every subject. They then come to agreement about the key points.

4 Following the appraisal, the boss writes up the appraisal assessment, including the specific learning and development objectives agreed for the next year.

5 The subordinate initials the appraisal document to indicate he has seen and understood the assessment and the learning plans.

Give employees responsibility for assets and areas of the company

In discussion in an aero engine factory a couple of years ago, a section manager asked me: 'How can I get my people to work clean? It's important in our kind of work.' He mentioned he had started a Quality Circle a year or so before, and by gentle manoeuvring had persuaded his people to have a 'work clean' campaign. They introduced some simple innovations to help the process, like having white-painted waste bins in prominent places to put the rubbish in. The effects were quite pleasing for the first month or so, but then the old habits gradually crept back and the place was now as bad as ever.

I told him to allocate every operator a defined piece of territory which they would be fully responsible for keeping clean. In other words, the creators of mess would be responsible in every case for cleaning up. That would encourage clean working habits. Unfortunately, he explained, there was a complication. He had a full-time 'sweeper-up' in the section, and because of the recent problems he had actually just applied to have a second one! The silent message he was sending was quite clear: 'I don't expect you skilled men to clean up. That is why we have other lesser mortals to do it'. The point is all too obvious. If you do not deliberately give your people the responsibility, they do not treat it as their responsibility. All other patch-up actions simply will not work.

Exactly the opposite happened at a food processing plant in the UK for which I was indirectly responsible. We decided to treat every employee as a manager, that is, a manager of the company's assets. After all, they were all using equipment, machines, computers, tools, etc., but few felt any real responsibility for them. Having studied the position in some detail, we allocated everyone associated with the manufacturing plant a piece of territory, and the equipment and machines within that territory. Henceforth, they were to be responsible for all of it: its operation, maintenance and cleanliness, and were given clear authority to act on each of these.

What happened was quite a revelation. The housekeeping standards changed overnight, the place had never looked so clean. No one wanted to be seen to have the most dirty area, and with clear accountability fingers could now be very obviously pointed. The copper in the boilerhouse suddenly began to shine, and the boilermen took the initiative to paint the different service equipment and pipes different colours for easy identification. People began to take a pride in their areas. The maintenance men, who were each given prime responsibilities for particular groups of machines, started coming in early to see how 'their machines' were doing, to get there at the double when anything unexpected went wrong, and to instruct operators how to treat their machines better and carry out routine maintenance care.

People want to take pride in something at work. They want

to see the noticeable effects of their being there, to know that the reason something is so good is because *they did it*. Giving employees clear responsibility gives them that opportunity, the opportunity to feel genuine pride and satisfaction in the place where they spend half of their waking hours. It often transforms employees' attitudes to their work; they begin to feel genuinely needed in making their area a success. That's a great feeling: it's a feeling worth coming to work for.

KEY POINTS SUMMARY

- Many companies use procedures that demonstrate every day their unspoken belief that non-managers cannot really be trusted. Employees save up the 'grey stamps' of their grievance at being treated like children and find myriad daily ways of getting back at the company.
- When companies give their employees full responsibility, they start acting more responsibly, not less so, as the simple 'use your good judgment in all situations' policy of Nordstrom amply demonstrates.
- Managers simply cannot do it all. In service situations, for example, your reputation is mostly made in the 'moments of truth' between employee and customer when managers are not there. Front-line employees are likely to be your most cost-effective resource in resolving customer complaints, at an early stage while they are still small.
- Managers cannot do it all in manufacturing either. Press responsibility down for output, quality and good housekeeping where it actually belongs, i.e. with the operators who get their hands on the product. Get managers to stop policing and *add value* by providing systems and support.
- *Empower* employees to help you, in ways like these:
  - Let your people talk to anyone in the organization to resolve problems and get the job done.
  - Ask employees for their contributions and ideas.
  - Give employees full control of their own operations.

- Involve employees in selecting all new recruits.
- Get employees to train their colleagues.
- Adopt self-set objectives at every level.
- Adopt self-assessment appraisals.
- Give employees responsibility for assets and areas of the company.

9

Measuring performance and progress

FEAR OF MEASUREMENT

There is a great temptation not to measure – you might discover things you really do not want to know! So say some managers: it is bad enough trying to cope with the problems one *does* know about without deliberately adding to the burden. You may remember the story from Chapter 3 about the director who advised his colleagues to conduct an employee attitude survey, and use the data to improve on performance and motivation in the business. Several were against the idea. As one said: 'That could be just like opening Pandora's box'. That may avoid looking at the problems, but it is not managing: to even begin to manage you have to know the facts. Deliberately not finding out the facts is the antithesis of good management. I have never seen a company that was better managed on hope than on hard data. Measurement is the test of your good management.

WHAT MEASUREMENT DOES

Measurement tells you whether you are actually making any progress, how well you are doing, how fast, how much or how little. It helps you home-in on the problem areas, identify which approaches produce the best results, and discard the merely 'hopeful' methods in favour of the effective. These are just some of the benefits of measurement.

Measurement deals in facts

It is all hearsay until you start measuring. We would not want to dismiss entirely statements like: 'Well, I *feel* things are definitely getting better', or 'I *think* we are making progress', but we get much greater confidence from statements like: 'there has been a 7 per cent improvement in productivity in the department over the last three months'. That team can be confident it is getting somewhere: it is a fact. You cannot really say you are 'world class' or even 'beating the competition' till you have got the evidence. You are simply kidding yourself by mouthing such platitudes until you have the facts. But when the facts show it to be true, it gives your company and your people the solid confidence to stay on top.

Measurement creates importance

Companies measure what is important to them, generally the facts which will keep the company alive, like sales, costs, profits, cash flow. When senior management check on these figures every month, they demonstrate to everyone in the business the importance of the measures. Measurement and regular follow-up are what create importance. The corollary is also true: what you do not measure loses importance. In changing your company's culture there will be things you want employees to change, to improve, to treat more seriously. That is what to start measuring, and following up. Of course, you will have to show them *how* to measure, how to do it better. Then what you measure will immediately increase in importance, rise up the priority list, focus attention and effort.

Measurement urges correction and improvement

When you start to get data on your performance it is very difficult not to worry whether it goes up or down. Interest is stirred, one is naturally drawn in investigate causes, to try alternatives to improve things, to take actions which will correct deviations and bring operations more under control. The urge is almost irresistible. As employees try things, they find out exactly what works and what does not. They learn more and more in depth about their processes and products, and get ever more refined in their measurements and quality standards. That is probably the key reason why the Japanese, who have been measuring for years, today make such reliable products and keep their competition constantly struggling. Measurement makes a real difference.

Measurement makes you think

When job-holders or managers first decide *what* to measure, they have to ask themselves some critical questions:

- What *are* the critical success factors in this job?
- What do we have to get right in this work?
- What do we most want to improve?
- What really makes a difference?

Just getting these right, or even near right, focuses attention on the critical areas, and may even completely change attitudes to the job. That in itself is valuable. Then the results of the measures, the feedback data, also make you think:

- What can we actually do to improve things?
- What actions can we take to make sure these faults do not occur again?
- How can we make the process fail-safe?

You simply do not get as much of that kind of thinking when you do not measure. That kind of focused thinking going on across your business and at every level will make it a business that never stands still.

Measurement is the acid test

Measurement helps to give you yes/no answers, to avoid unproductive arguments about whether something succeeded or not. It is the kind of thing that happens in personal performance appraisals, where, in the absence of clear and agreed measures, bosses find themselves in conflict with their subordinates arguing about what they might or might not have achieved and, consequently, about how much their contribution might be worth. Much better to have agreed, measurable objectives where the subordinate will know, without anyone having to tell him, whether he has succeeded or not. Life is much simpler when everyone knows where they stand. At the end of the time period the question can be asked: Did he or she succeed, yes or no? There is no argument: measurement is the acid test. Then the discussion will be less about excuses rather than reasons, less about justification and more about lessons learned. If you want to be sure you are succeeding, measure it.

Measurement takes you to the moon
It is a fact that the first moon-shot was on target less than 3 per cent of the time during its trajectory. On-board signals allowed computers constantly to correct the rocket's course to ensure that it eventually landed successfully on the moon. Changing a company's culture is much like that. It is a long journey. Mistakes are made on the way, the project falls off course, but with constant corrections along the way, you will eventually get there. Measurement can actually get you to the moon.

SETTING COMPANY-WIDE MEASURES

Changing the culture of a company means changing how you do things, the standards and the habits of people right across the organization. That is why company-wide measures are so important in this area. They test your commitment, focus widespread attention, and tell you if you are actually moving forward as a company. You may want to become a business dedicated to delivering 'competition-beating customer service,' to creating a 'learning culture', to developing a 'team-working environment', or a company bent on 'continuous improvement' or 'total quality'. Whatever you focus on, you will want to know whether you are making progress on the factors that are due to transform the whole character and excellence of the business.

In addition, in businesses of any size, departments and individuals usually have their own favourite measures, which will vary depending on whether you are in manufacturing, personnel or R&D. What unifies people in a business is to know that they are all, perhaps in their different ways, pursuing the same goals. Having company-wide measures with which they can all identify persuades them they are really all in it together, that they are all playing on the same team. They are also more inclined to help each other achieve their common goals, and all to take pride together when they achieve some success.

Rubbermaid, the US company, has for years used four key company performance measures which concentrate attention and are understood by every employee. They are:

- Annual sales growth of 15 per cent.
- Annual earnings growth of 15 per cent.
- Sufficient new product introductions to ensure that 30 per cent of sales in any year are from products no more than five years old.
- Enter an entirely new market every 12 to 18 months.

These kinds of measures both focus attention and shape behaviour all round the business. The message from the company, despite operating in a market with little growth and strong competition, is that they do not want to hear why growth is not possible – but they want to do whatever is necessary to make 15 per cent plus growth happen. By staying close to their customers and with their new product introductions they have actually seen sales quadruple during CEO Stanley Gault's eleven-year tenure. At the same time, to get earnings growth of 15 per cent plus you need not only to achieve strong sales growth but keep costs down as well. Employees in one division alone helped the company achieve this objective by contributing more than

12 000 cost-saving suggestions. That is the kind of thing that has helped the company more than quadruple earnings during the same 11 years. To a lot of other executives Rubbermaid appear to 'have got their act together', and that perception has made them vote the company second (behind Merck) on *Fortune* magazine's 1991 'Most Admired Companies' list. (Stanley Gault has now become CEO at Goodyear.)

DEPARTMENTAL MEASURES

While company-wide measures take first priority, every department needs to come up with their own self-set measures which will represent their specific contribution to the overall aims of the company. Note that 'self-set' measures are specified here, for all the good reasons listed in the last chapter under Self-set Objectives. The people in the department know the job best, they know what is realistic and demanding and they will be more committed to their achievement.

American Express has become a company strongly committed to delivering excellent (i.e. competition-beating) customer service. There are so many small details to go wrong in a banking and credit card service that the company realized every department would have to maintain and reach its own high standards. As a result there are over 200 service measures used in the company, but all hanging from that overall goal of outstanding customer service. These measures include things like:

- Card application processing time (less than 15 days)
- Lost card replacement (less than one day)
- Error-free statements (presently 98 per cent or more)
- Statements out by due date (100 per cent within two days)
- Telephone response time (less than 10 seconds)
- Correspondence response time (less than seven days)
- Time to replace lost traveller's cheques (within 24 hours)

Every department knows exactly what their contribution needs to be to the company's overall goal. At the same time, Chairman

Jim Robinson knows how important it is that departments do not become isolationist and parochial. As a result, he insists that his senior executives get involved in specific 'One Enterprise' synergy projects every year to encourage interdepartmental and interdivisional co-operation. He even pays special bonuses to reward those who demonstrate the strongest evidence of inter-unit co-operation. American Express Travelers Cheques were 100 years old in 1990, but the company is still very lively. No doubt their customer service and innovation have a lot to do with their ability still to grow revenues by some 20 per cent a year.

SETTING MEASURES AT JOB LEVEL

One of the best ways to get the culture change process right down to individual level is to get the job-holders themselves to develop new measures and standards. That is how it was done in one British manufacturing company. Small teams of job-holders were asked to describe the key elements of their job, and if the company's new standards were going to be achieved, to specify measures of performance for each element, rising through several levels of performance from 'basic' to 'outstanding'. By way of example, here is how it was developed with one group of traditional and strongly unionized tradesmen.

A group of six electricians made up a project team with an electrical manager and eventually agreed on seven elements important to doing the job well. They were:

- Ability to read   (drawings, manuals, diagrams, etc.)
- Knowledge   (of identified pieces of equipment)
- Tradeskills   (measuring, electrical, metalwork, etc.)
- Applications   (specified equipment in the plant)
- Feedback   (of appropriate, timely information)
- Improvements   (introduced as a result of their initiative)
- Departmental contribution

The team produced a matrix document showing each of these elements and identified five rising levels of performance in each. Level one, for example, described basic knowledge, skills and pieces of equipment. Higher levels included more complex skills and equipment. No one was expected to be expert in everything, but at each higher level to be capable of handling two, three or even four additional categories of equipment. Items such as 'improvements' showed interesting descriptions. These rose from 'minor improvements made' at the lowest level, to a top box of 'identifies ways in which equipment and systems can be measurably improved and implements where practical'. The team also devised 'competency' tests, and the whole framework was then used for objective-setting, training and appraisal. Similar projects were undertaken in this company with telephonists, operators, secretaries, invoice clerks, salespeople and other staff all round the business. Employees everywhere became very much engaged in the culture shift.

What was the outcome? Tradespeople were soon attending night-school classes and requesting special training courses. Not only did skills improve, but managers noticed distinct changes in attitudes, too. There was one common and important reaction: once people knew what 'A' class performance looked like, nobody wanted to be 'C' any more. There was a great shift up in performance. Although the standards set were tough, the job-holders in the project team did a much more effective job than managers of convincing their colleagues that the measures and standards were both desirable and achievable.

VISIBLE FEEDBACK MEASURES

Regular, measurable feedback focuses attention, but what grabs employee attention even more is to make the measures both visible and public. It is a communications style adopted by a number of Japanese companies, including the highly successful Nissan car manufacturing plant in County Durham in the north-east of England. There, nothing is kept in the supervisor's desk: all the key information and measures of performance concerning the section are published on the wall for everyone to see. The three examples we show here are not the current Nissan charts, but they indicate the form and value of the information used. Below, for example, in Figure 9.1 is a Section Skills chart.

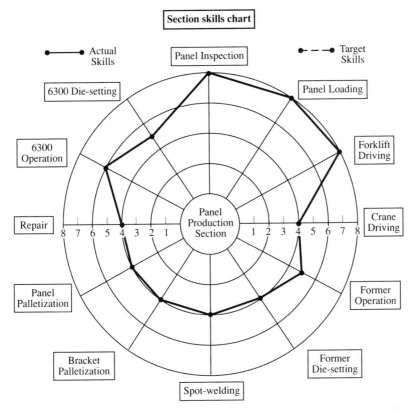

Figure 9.1   Section Skills chart

This chart describes round the edge the specific skills required in the section. Coloured markers then show the *target* skills versus the *actual* skills in the area. Joining the markers then gives the chart an easy-to-read 'spider's web' appearance. For simplicity, only the actuals are shown here.

Housekeeping Responsibility

Section: Front Panels

Area: 4

JIM DAWSON

Title	
SECTION OPERATOR	
In company	4 YEARS
In section	1 YEAR
Other	

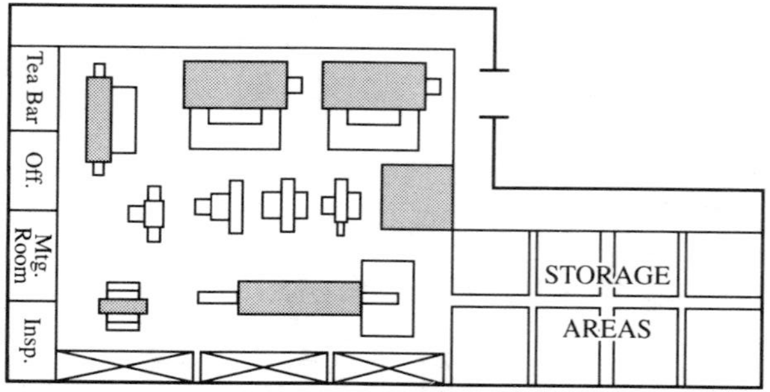

	Items		Items
1	FIRE POINTS – CLEAN, NO OBSTRUCTIONS	11	TROLLEYS MAINTAINED AND CORRECTLY PARKED
2	PEDESTRIAN WALKWAYS – CLEAR, NO PROTRUSIONS	12	JIGS IN PROPER PLACES ON JIG BOARD
3	WALKWAY LINES CLEARLY PAINTED	13	CHARTS BOARD CLEAN AND NEAT
4	ALL FLOOR AREAS CLEANED DAILY	14	MODELS BOARD COMPLETE AND UP-TO-DATE
5	FLOOR FREE OF SCRAP AND LITTER	15	
6	WINDOWS AND SILLS CLEANED WEEKLY	16	
7	CONTROL PANELS FREE OF GRIME AND GREASE	17	
8	ALL LIGHTS AND SHADES IN CLEAN CONDITION	18	
9	PARTS BINS CLEARLY MARKED AND STORED CORRECTLY	19	
10	PALLETS IN CORRECT STORAGE AREA	20	

Tea Bar | Off. | Mtg. Room | Insp. | STORAGE AREAS

Figure 9.2 Housekeeping chart

Nissan believes that the best way to keep the workplace clean and tidy is for every employee to have specific housekeeping responsibilities. In Figure 9.3, a chart similar to the one on the opposite page, individuals' areas are shown as a small section map, with the housekeeping duties described in detail in words.

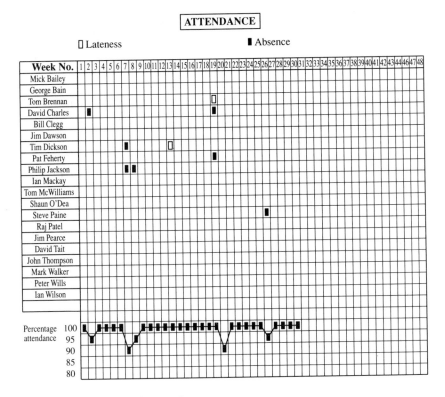

Figure 9.3   Attendance chart

Every supervisor needs to know who is available in his or her team every day. No one clocks in at Nissan, but since the team starts each day with a five-minute communications meeting, they soon know who's there. However, an Attendance chart like the one above helps to show very clearly when the team is up to strength.

QCV (quality, cost, volume) boards are seen in every area of the plant. They display performance data on items such as output, quality, scrap, repair, materials usage, energy cost, attendance, training, safety, etc. On virtually every chart appear control lines or continuously improving target lines, showing the performance levels each team is striving to reach. Not only can supervisors and their people see what is happening in their section, but adjacent departments, senior managers and visitors can all see at a glance exactly how well the section is performing and being managed. It is a powerful incentive to get things right and to demonstrate improving performance.

All employees at Nissan get involved in the business of continuous improvement, whether it's in productivity, quality or their own personal skills. Their photographs and personal details appear on charts in every section showing their responsibilities, skills, etc. And with it all the company has turned in some remarkable results, achieving product quality and productivity figures to rival their Japanese counterparts. In fact, in 1991, the company earned what was for them a cherished accolade – they started exporting cars to Japan! And in January 1992, while other car manufacturers were laying people off, Nissan announced it was to take on another six hundred workers.

RULES ON USING VISIBLE FEEDBACK SYSTEMS

If you decide to use visible feedback systems, here are some guidelines which will help.

The charts should be visible and readable from a distance

If you cannot see the essence of the information from five feet or more, the charts are just too small. They need to have impact.

They should be readily understood by employees or visitors without further explanation

Complex charts, or those with obscure acronyms or too much detail, simply do not communicate well. And that is what charts must do: communicate.

They should be placed prominently at the place of work

Preferably in a place employees pass every day. Even the subliminal effect (i.e. when employees are not looking directly at the information) reinforces the need to maintain standards, to keep performance improving. Don't put them in some obscure corner where nobody goes.

Each chart should show target parameters (acceptability limits) or target lines of improvement over time

Measuring performance and showing information is fine, but target lines focus attention and urge improvement. Using colour is also helpful to make the target lines prominent.

The data should be marked up by team members themselves

If the supervisor alone marks up the data, then the targets are *his* or *her* targets. When the team members enter the data, they become the *team's* targets. That physical act helps to transfer the responsibility.

The information should be constantly referred to by the team leader and team members

Constant reference emphasizes the data's importance. If the information is not looked at or referred to, no one will treat it seriously.

The information should foster good team-work and constant improvement

Information of a competitive kind which sets team members against each other will kill any team-work spirit.

SOME SIMPLE BUT EFFECTIVE SHOP-FLOOR MEASURES

I confess to a long-held conviction of the benefits of simplicity. In the end, it is the simple systems which work best, and stand the test of time. But making things simple isn't easy, it's hard. So that you do not have to 'remake the wheel' here are some simple but effective systems actually being used by other companies which will help you keep operations under control.

SCORE-BOARDS

Keep score-boards simple: just big, visible, on the line, and with boxes for actual and target figures. They do not have to be marvellously beautiful, just a blackboard and chalk will do. In production environments, figures may need to be for achievement every hour on the hour. In other situations, two-hourly or daily intervals may be appropriate: you have to decide. Agree the targets with the team, and get team members themselves to mark up the scores. Generally when the pressure is on, they help each other out to make sure they do not have to chalk up failure scores.

CHARTS

Pictures work much better than words. Statistical process control charts attached to each production machine and filled up by the operator demonstrate very visibly when operations are under control. They have other advantages too. For example, it gives the operator something to think about (namely the key factors affecting his operation), and it urges him to take timely action before faults actually occur. I am amazed at how many manufacturing companies still do not do this very simple thing.

KANBAN

Everyone knows by now that kanban boxes or squares (drawn on the floor) show visibly and exactly how many parts of pieces-in-progress should exist at any point in a manufacturing process. Parts in excess of the specified space are forbidden. Each part or process must be provided 'just in time' for the next process to start. It was Toyota who originally developed the system to reduce costs by cutting inventory and work-in-progress. But the system also reduces lead times (often drastically) by eliminating interim stockholding, and forcing managers to develop reliable right-first-time processes. There is simply no slack to cover for faults and delays. In addition, the kanban system makes immediately and visibly obvious to management any delays or problems in the work sequence, and demands their immediate attention. It may sound tough, but it is basically simple and it works.

KITS

Knowing whether you have enough of just the right materials to get the whole job done is a great problem in many manufacturing operations. In many cases, kitting is the answer. For example, in an aero manufacturing company where I have been recently consulting, kits of parts are prepared by stores people for production operators. Embedded in specially cut spaces in polystyrene foam, you can see at a glance which items are complete or missing. The production operator does not have to go rummaging about in boxes to find the parts, or run out unexpectedly. The same system can be used in both manufacturing and office-based operations.

RED, AMBER, GREEN SYSTEM

Sony Manufacturing in Wales make great and effective use of a system of coloured indicators in their factory. For example, in any operation the manager of a section will display on the information board in his section a list of his people with coloured spots against each name. Green represents 'experienced, fully trained', amber 'improving', and red 'new employee in training'. That alerts everyone to where the vulnerabilities are. Also, employees in training cannot wait to turn green! They also use the colours to indicate performance on quality (good, marginal, not acceptable) and on housekeeping. No one wants publicly to have anything but green on their record.

GREEN TICKETS

Simple systems are effective in administration operations, too. Deluxe Check of Minneapolis produce cheques for use in all sorts of banking and other organizations. Way back in 1936 the founder set as a company standard that all orders should be despatched no later than the day after they were received. Deluxe still use that as their measure of effectiveness today. To help them fulfil that obligation, they use order slips of a different colour every day. Since Tuesday's colour is green, you can hear their plant managers say: 'At four-thirty on Wednesday, we do not want to see any green around here any more!' There are plenty of complexities in today's business life, and having measures as simple as this helps keep everybody's eye on the priorities.

CUSTOMER MEASURES

So often companies assume they know what the customer wants, but even admired companies can sharpen up their performance by actually asking the customer to rate their service. That is what has happened at Avis, the car rental company. It was way back in 1962, when their advertising agency found their only distinguishing feature to be the spirit of the Avis staff, that they came up with the now legendary 'We try harder' slogan. Yet Avis did not actively and systematically measure customer service until 1988. Said Alun Cathcart, their European Chairman and CEO: 'I must admit that measuring and monitoring service, although an ongoing concern of Avis management, was not a burning issue'.

When Avis consulted TARP (Technical Assistance Research Programs) of Washington DC, who have been studying customer service and complaint handling for some 20 years, they found out some sobering truths. Some 45 per cent of the company's transactions could be generating queries or problems for customers, but only 3 per cent resulted in calls or letters of complaint to head office. Some complained at the point of sale, but as many as 30 per cent did not complain at all. TARP evidence showed that unhappy customers recount their stories to three times as many friends as do happy customers, and 1 customer is lost for every 50 who hear negative word-of-mouth advertising about a company. However, the good news is that significantly more customers will use your service again if you search out and handle their complaints satisfactorily than if their complaint is never heard at all. Avis realized that, apart from the natural satisfaction in giving excellent customer service, serving the customer better and dealing with their complaints effectively held real growth and profit potential.

Since 1988, Avis actively seek customer views by sending questionnaires out to customer homes after they have used their service. Figure 9.4 shows their questionnaire. The key questions are numbers 2 and 3: *overall satisfaction* and the *re-purchase intention*.

Data on customer satisfaction are fed back to every Avis station each month. Teams can compare their performance with the scores in their district and in the country in which they operate, and see their 3-month and 12-month average. That helps them focus on the specific areas where customers were less than satisfied with the service. Avis also publishes league tables of the best and worst performing stations and, of course, nobody

HOW WELL DID WE SERVE YOU?

1. Our records show you rented an Avis car in Great Britain on 30/03/92.

Please rate how well we served you. How satisfied were you with:

	Very Satisfied	Somewhat Satisfied	Neither Satisfied Nor Dissatisfied	Somewhat Dissatisfied	Very Dissatisfied
1. Waiting time to get the car	☐	☐	☐	☐	☐
2. Availability of the car group you asked for	☐	☐	☐	☐	☐
3. Type of car you were given	☐	☐	☐	☐	☐
4. Cleanliness of the car	☐	☐	☐	☐	☐
5. Mechanical condition of the car	☐	☐	☐	☐	☐
6. Professionalism of Avis personnel	☐	☐	☐	☐	☐
7. Personalized service by Avis personnel	☐	☐	☐	☐	☐
8. Accuracy of billing	☐	☐	☐	☐	☐

2. All things considered, please rate your overall satisfaction with *this experience* in renting a car from Avis.

Very Satisfied	Somewhat Satisfied	Neither Satisfied Nor Dissatisfied	Somewhat Dissatisfied	Very Dissatisfied
☐	☐	☐	☐	☐

3. The next time you need a rental car, how likely is it that you will rent from Avis?

Definitely	Possibly	Might Or Might Not	Probably NOT	Definitely NOT
☐	☐	☐	☐	☐

4. How often in the PAST TWELVE MONTHS have you rented a car?

Number of rentals: _____

5. How many of those rentals have been with Avis?

Number of Avis rentals: _____

Figure 9.4   Avis customer questionnaire

wants to stay around the bottom for long. In the first year customer satisfaction figures fairly shot up.

The company now composes what it calls a 'Customer Care Balance Sheet', where, by using the customer satisfaction and re-purchase intention figures, they can work out the pound (£) value of customers lost. Comparing figures from month to month gives managers a quantitative handle on how they are doing. And the data has certainly changed behaviour. Said Ian Jarvis, Station Manager at Gatwick airport in London: 'There's a big difference between what customers want and what we think they want. We were working on problems we didn't even have!' Lesley Armitage, Station Manager at Luton Airport said: 'When I first saw the report I was absolutely horrified. It put us near the bottom but we had always had among the fewest customer complaints in the district. Fortunately, the next results showed a dramatic improvement: from a satisfaction level of 60 to 90 in only a month'.

These are the effects of measurement. Avis' experience shows you cannot depend solely on customer complaints to tell you how you are doing. Instead, you have to go out there and ask. By giving employees quantified feedback, the training to do the job even better, and the authority to resolve customer problems on the spot, you can make dramatic improvements in performance. Avis is not Number Two in Europe, by the way. It is Number One. And if their competitors are not taking such good care of *their* customers, then Avis are not going to be knocked off that perch.

SUPPLIER MEASURES

I am often amazed at the energy companies put into changing behaviour inside their businesses, yet they put nothing like the same effort into changing the behaviour and performance of their suppliers. Yet much of your own company's excellence may depend on the materials and service your suppliers give you. That is why you have to get them to work *with* your efforts, to get them to change their habits in line with yours. In the same way that measuring and setting standards can significantly change behaviour inside the business, so it will do the same when applied to suppliers.

Firstly, talk to them and explain what you are trying to achieve, just as you did with your own employees. Because you have the business they want, they will listen. It is important, though, to avoid confrontations such as: 'Unless you people get your act together and meet our tough standards, we are not going to be buying from you any more'. The whole atmosphere should be one of partnership, where you show you intend to work with them to reach your common goals. At the same time, however, make clear that there will no backing away from high standards and continuous improvement: the behaviour change, the culture shift, is here to stay.

Secondly, apply measures. It makes you home in on the specifics (just what *are* you looking for?). It also focuses suppliers' attention and spells out exactly what they have to do to keep your business. British Aerospace at Chester in the UK, for example, classify their suppliers into four categories based on four factors:

- Quality
- Delivery
- Price
- Speed of response

Based on factual evidence and company experience, suppliers are given scores on each of these factors, with a maximum total of 100 points. Suppliers are then graded A, B, C and U (ungraded), the latter category being used when a supplier's total points score fails to meet a minimum threshold, or where they fail to make a minimum hurdle on one of the key factors. Companies graded U know they will be dropped from the company's list if they do not get out of that category. Those graded C are given a specified time period to upgrade their performance. But, as you might expect, there is a great tendency by suppliers to want to graduate to category A as nobody really wants to be second class. In addition, when you can say that British Aerospace classifies you as an A supplier, that gives you a passport to help obtain more business from other customers.

Thirdly, help your suppliers to improve. Instead of shouting at them, get out there and help. Send your best people to help improve their operations, introduce new techniques, install statistical process control, or whatever. It is in your, and their, best interests.

Fourthly, follow up. If operations people are having difficulty with their materials or services, or your quality people are lodging complaints, but your buyers are still placing orders (or even bigger ones!), suppliers just do not try so hard to correct the problems. The messages you send have to be consistent. The new habits, the new culture, has to go all the way through the business.

MEASURING THE SOFT FACTORS

It is relatively easy to measure the things you can count, like production output, sales, profits, return on capital. But what about the 'soft' factors like attitudes, communications, employee relations and team spirit? Shall we just hope? Measures are very relevant there too. Employee opinion surveys can tell you a lot of what you want to know. 'These are just subjective opinions', some say. Yes, but opinions in employee heads strongly affect their behaviour, and in transforming your company's culture that is exactly what you have to change. Having quantified data on the subject is infinitely better than relying simply on 'I think . . .' or 'I feel . . .' opinions. Also, the data will allow you to assess the strength of feeling on any subject, pinpoint the real problem factors and the geographical problem areas.

Probably the biggest influence on employee attitudes is the immediate boss. Any company will have its own peculiar *organization* culture, of course, but attitudes and habits in each area are strongly affected by what the front-line manager does. That is why attitude surveys should be conducted in such a way as to give every manager the scores from his (or her) own team. He is the person who can do most about changing things. In particular, about how he manages his people, how he communicates, and the team spirit he creates. Asking specific questions about these areas, and bunching the scores into *indices*, will give managers a measurement handle on how they are doing, show

Table 9.1   Sample manager feedback

	Your team	Depart-ment score	Rating	Company score	Rating
In our department we are clear about our targets and strive to meet them	66	63	+	53	++
In our department we pay constant attention to our measures of performance	71	67	+	61	++
The people I work with co-operate to get the job done	68	77	−−	74	−
I get credit from my boss when I do a good job	49	51	−	50	

them how they compare with others and what actual progress they have made since the last survey. Measurement like this raises the whole importance in a company of how managers manage their people. In fact, I know of no better way to do that.

Table 9.1 is a sample of scores from one company who uses this approach. Individual managers see the scores they got from their own team, and can compare these both with the average in their department, and the average score in the company as a whole. Scores are also divided into five 'bands' of 20 per cent. If the manager's score falls in the 'above average' 20 per cent band, a + sign appears alongside. If it features in the top 20 per cent, then ++ is the rating. Similarly, a − sign is below average and −− is in the lowest 20 per cent. As the manager looks down his score list, he can see at a glance where he is doing well, and the areas where he has some work to do. Department heads receive their own departmental results and a comparative listing of how each of their subordinate managers have scored. This is used to discuss with each manager individually what has been learned from the scores and what plans he has for future improvement. Continuous improvement is not only necessary in the products and services the company sells, but in how people are managed.

MEASURING THE 'UNMEASURABLE'

Non-profit-making organizations, like churches, charities or local government, tend to feel their work cannot be practically subjected to measurement. I do not accept that. Some may prefer the quiet life where they cannot be called to account for their performance, but if you want to you can produce sensible measures for virtually every organization with a purpose. For example, if you are a pastor, the number of people who turn up to your services will be at least one measure of whether you are serving their spiritual needs *as they see it*. If you are in local government, you can test whether you are serving your citizen customers by *asking* them, by conducting surveys, or having turnround times for completing transactions or documentation. If you are a charity, you will want to be sure you are using your resources well. In his book, *Managing the Non-Profit Organization*, Peter Drucker says 'If a business wastes its resources on non-results, by and large it loses its own money'. It is not enough simply to say you are 'serving a good cause'. Even in a charity, you have to decide how you are going to concentrate the scarce resources you do have so that they will produce the best results. Measuring your competence and comparing your results will help you do just that.

Of course, even in some profit-making organizations some things can be very hard to measure. Take the Joban Hawaiian Centre, for instance, some 200 kilometres north-west of Tokyo. Founded in 1966, it was Japan's first theme park, and by offering exotic Polynesian experiences attracted as many as 1.5 million visitors in a good year. Gradually, however, the novelty faded with both revenues and visitors suffering as a result. But how do you counter that, and the fact that there are now many competing new attractions available? At first, the company began with Quality Circles to help generate ideas and improvements, but their efforts proved unproductive. Then the President, Masao Suzuki, decided they would go all out to improve services using Total Quality measurement methods.

Measures were devised to cover the quality of every activity in the resort. Waitresses noted how much of every dish had been eaten as they cleared plates, dancers scrutinized every aspect of their dances and how they made themselves up, musicians noted how many mistakes they made, stewards videoed reactions of visitors in queues, and on and on. Innumerable changes resulted. Hamburgers were made smaller (children did not finish them all), rice was served with tomato sauce (the children turned their nose up at plain rice). The Hawaiian dancers make-up was entirely revised as it was discovered how pale some dancers looked to large audiences. Musicians were given better lighting and more days off to prevent boredom. Staff found ways to speed up ticket sales so that no visitor would have to queue for more than a few minutes.

The company decided in 1986 to enter for the prestigious Deming Prize, the quality award that can overnight produce a jump in the share price of companies who win it. After an audit by four academics, they told the company that 'you come nowhere near to achieving total quality control', and expressed the view that the executive director was lucky not to have been fired! That put the company on its mettle, and they took to the measurement and improvement tasks with even more vigour. In 1988, they actually won the Deming Prize, the only service business ever to win the award. Not only that, but since their quality measurement efforts had started, visitors to the resort had risen by some 20 per cent and revenues by 40 per cent. If you are keen enough, measurement can help you rise to record levels of performance.

THE DANGERS IN MEASUREMENT

Measurement can be a powerful tool, but there are dangers involved too. Here are some of the worst to beware of.

FIDDLING THE RESULTS

Unfortunately, it does happen. For example, one mortgage lending company had a standard 48-hour turnround time for answering customer letters. However, on investigation it was discovered that the arrival day was actually nominated as day zero by operating staff to help extend the time. Also, the 48-hour measure was used not to despatch a reply, but to get the letter on to the desk of someone who was supposed to reply! In an engineering company, the drawing office had deadlines for the issue of all drawings to production department. They managed to record a 99 per cent hit rate by issuing as many as a third of the engineering sheets blank, and then catching up by issuing so-called 'amendments' at a later date! So you have to make sure the numbers *really* reflect what is happening.

TOO MANY MEASURES

Don't measure yourself out of existence. Internal customers tend to want the earth from their colleague suppliers. First, let them draw up their first 'bid list', then from that decide on their critical top three or four, at the most. Then when the supplier department starts doing well on the most important items, they can think about more in due course.

IMPOSING STANDARDS

Imposing standards does not work – unless you do it by threats or fear. But that is no way to manage. Eventually, employees find ways of fiddling the numbers. It is just not worth it.

NO FOLLOW-UP

Not so long ago, a shop-floor employee complained to me that he had been dutifully filling up his SPC chart but no one was doing anything with the numbers. Do not get employees signed on to a new process and then fail to follow it up. You have to demonstrate interest and importance before they treat the numbers seriously, too.

NOT MEASURING THE SAME THINGS

Often what appears to be the same data from different sections of different plants is actually measured in quite different ways. That kills useful comparison. Also, if you change your method of measurement, that can kill historical comparison of performance too. There is no point in lots of data which you cannot compare: it has to be like with like.

NOT COLLECTING DATA

Failing to collect data is the worst fault of all. You cannot manage on 'gut feel' alone. You have to know the facts.

FINAL WORDS

Some spectacular improvements have been achieved by companies after they started measuring. Motorola, for example, now have quality of such a standard that they measure defects per million rather than defects per hundred. But they simply would not have achieved these gains unless they had started measuring. The lesson is all too clear: start measuring, and keep measuring. Eventually, it can take you to the moon . . . .

KEY POINTS SUMMARY

- Do not avoid measuring because you think you might not like what you see. To even begin to manage well, you have got to know the facts.
- What measurement does for you:
  – Measurement deals in facts. It cuts the argument.

- – Measurement creates importance. People start paying attention.
  - – Measurement urges correction and improvement. People want to do better.
  - – Measurement makes you think. It helps create a 'thinking business'.
  - – Measurement is the acid test. You know exactly when you are succeeding.
- Company-wide measures keep the whole company focusing on the same goals. The sheer weight of attention on a critical few areas will bring about permanent behaviour changes.
- Self-set departmental measures help each area to show their particular contributions to the company's chosen goals.
- Given the opportunity, job-holder teams will develop their own demanding operating standards to help the company's drive for change.
- There is great power in visible feedback systems, i.e. performance charts visibly displayed at the place of work. It creates an open management style and encourages pride in achievement.
- Often the simple operational measures are the most effective, such as charts, scoreboards, kanban squares, kits, colour systems. Develop your own, but keep them simple.
- Ask your customers to measure your performance. There is no need to be afraid. This is the best way to sharpen your attitudes to quality and service.
- Suppliers can greatly affect your ability to perform. Agree some key performance hurdles with them, and watch them jump.
- Measure the soft factors too. Changing attitudes is one of the most important factors in changing your company culture.
- Even in non-profit-making organizations it is necessary to measure how well you are applying your scarce resources to your stated purpose. Continued measurement will bring inevitable improvements.
- Measurement works, despite the dangers.

—

10

Rewarding the behaviour you want to see

THE FUNDAMENTALS

Some years ago I visited Sea World in Florida where they have a magnificent display of all kinds of exotic fish and mammals. The highlight of the visit for most people is to watch the show put on by the dolphins and a killer whale in a huge, green, open-air pool. I sat in one of the front rows, which were empty at the time, and watched the show. After the dolphins had done some spectacular stunts it was announced that the killer whale would also perform some tricks. The finale was to involve the whale hitting a brightly coloured ball placed some 15 feet above the water line. It did not look as if this great whale had a hope of reaching it. But it did: it swam round the pool and jumped clean out of the water to hit the ball with its nose. It came down on the water with a great splat, and drenched everyone in the front four rows, including me!

'How do they get it to do that?' I heard some members of the audience say. The answer is by rewarding the behaviour they want to see. The whale trainers first put a rope line in the water lying close to the bottom, and reward the whale with fish titbits every time it swims over the line. Gradually they raise the level of the line, and keep on rewarding the whale every time it swims over it: but strictly no reward when it does not swim over the rope. Over time, they raise the rope above the water, and with lots of practice, encouragement and food rewards, the whale eventually jumps right out of the water for the reward. It is quite amazing to see.

It was several decades ago that B. F. Skinner, the world-renowned psychologist first described the importance of rewards on learning behaviour. By using food and other rewards to encourage the behaviour he wanted to see, he could teach animals to perform even quite elaborate procedures. Gradually Skinner built up a whole body of theory on learning and education, but none of his conclusions was more important than this basic truth:

The behaviour that gets rewarded gets repeated.

This factor is of crucial importance to companies intent on transforming their company culture. The people in your organization will only change their habits and behaviour *if it proves rewarding to do so.* That is the point that Michael LeBoeuf believes is of such fundamental importance to management that he has written a whole book on the subject and called it *The Greatest Management Principle in the World.* The things that you have previously rewarded in your business are what has helped to produce the culture you have now. If you want to change your culture you have to change the things you value and reward. When you see that new behaviour you have to reward it every time you see it, and keep rewarding it until it becomes a habit . . . just part of the new culture of the business.

Of course, by 'reward' one does not just mean money . . . or even fish. As will be shown later in this chapter, there is actually a huge variety of rewards you can use to help change attitudes throughout your business and produce the behaviour you most want to see. However, it is useful to begin with one of the most powerful ways of changing attitudes: giving employees a financial stake in their business.

OWNERSHIP CHANGES BEHAVIOUR

For a long time National Freight Corporation in the UK was a nationalized company, i.e. government owned. Operating in the road haulage and travel business it was a poor performer by any standards. When Peter Thompson (now Sir Peter) took over, 75 per cent of the business was in general haulage which had never made money. Indeed, several years before, National Carriers, part of the empire, had made a loss of £25 million on a sales turnover of £25 million. Most of their customers, said Sir Peter, actually only used them as a last resort since 'no one believed a nationalized business could be customer-oriented'.

He set about making major changes in how the business operated as soon as he arrived. He and his team reduced the role of headquarters in the decision-making process and created seven autonomous regions. They decided to 'throw away the rule book', while at the same time making every regional managing director fully responsible for meeting their own financial targets. They changed the management structure and made management pay more results-oriented. However, it was when the Conservative government took over in 1979 in the UK and privatization became the norm that major opportunities for even more radical change became possible.

A convinced advocate of the participative style of management, Sir Peter and his team proposed to the government in 1982 the then novel idea of an *employee* buy-out of the company. The government finally agreed a price of £53.5 million, and no less than 82.5 per cent of the shares were bought by the company's own staff, pensioners and their families. That act had a remarkable effect on the attitude of employees. They were now the owners. The company plastered their new slogan 'We are in the driving seat' on every vehicle (thousands of them) and on signs at every depot: the excitement of ownership was really infectious. There were plenty of stories going around, too: like the truck driver at one north of England depot who saw a parcel standing out in the rain getting wet and shouted to staff to get it under cover in blunt and colourful language. 'Of course, I care,' he said, 'I'm a shareholder now'. In touting to take over other companies' transport fleets the company now told prospective customers: 'The driver who delivers your goods will be certain to give good service because now his own money is at stake'; and they believed them. In due course NFC has taken over the transport function for household name companies like Texaco, Sainsbury and Marks and Spencer.

During the following six years sales grew from £493 million to £1255 million, with profits growing during these years by more than 40 per cent compound. The company was so successful it decided to make a public flotation in 1989. It offered its shares at 185p, but at launch the Stock Exchange immediately marked them up to 250p. For the employees who had bought the stock at 2.5p back in 1982, they had seen their investment multiply 100-fold! And the employees keep buying more shares in their own company. Up to 15 per cent of pre-tax profits are distributed to employees every year in the form of free or bonus shares, providing earnings per share keep increasing each year. Naturally, they are more than interested to see their company growing strongly and profitably each year. As the company said in its flotation prospectus: 'The directors attribute a considerable part of NFC's success to the commitment of its employee shareholders'. In fact, ownership has changed the entire culture of the business.

BETTER PERFORMANCE WITH PROFIT-SHARING

However, although every company cannot be in the situation where it is largely owned by its employees, employees can share in the financial success they help to generate. The evidence is strong that not only are employee attitudes in profit-sharing companies considerably better but financial performance, by any measure you might use, is distinctly better too. That is the finding of one of the most comprehensive studies ever under-

Table 10.1   Profit-sharing companies vs non-profit-sharing

Eight-year average performance, 1977–85	Non-profit-sharing companies	Profit-sharing companies	Per cent difference
Return on sales (%)	5.6	8.4	50.0
Return on capital (%)	15.5	20.6	32.9
Earnings per share (p)	12.8	16.3	27.3
Annual sales growth (%)	13.7	15.5	13.1
Annual profit growth (%)	9.7	13.6	40.2
Total investor returns (%)	18.0	24.8	37.8

taken on this subject by D. Wallace Bell and Dr Charles G. Hanson, and detailed in their book *Profit Sharing and Profitability*.

They examined the performance of more than 400 British companies, all quoted on the London Stock Exchange, and taken from business sectors as varied as brewing, building, chemicals, retailing, electrical, engineering and textiles. Their study compared the financial performance of the companies over an eight-year period (from 1977 to 1985) and on nine different ratios covering profitability, growth and investor returns. Their results are summarized in Table 10.1.

The numbers are quite startling. The sample was big (more than 400 companies from very varied business sectors) and taken over a sustained period of time (eight years). Any company wishing to change its culture in a way which materially affects its financial performance must seriously consider having its employees share directly in its financial success. The numbers are just so compelling.

However, don't think that just by installing some profit-sharing scheme employees will all of a sudden change their attitudes and everything will magically come right. Your style has to be 'all of a piece'. You have to be doing other things to convince your people to give of their best all the time, such as having clear, actionable goals to which you are genuinely committed, like treating employees like adults, like training them how to do things better, seeking and using their suggestions for improvement, involving them as partners in every aspect of the business: in other words, all the things we have been recommending in this book. This is how Bell and Hanson put it: 'We do not claim that the results show that profit sharing by itself leads to improved profitability. That would be altogether too simplistic a conclusion. Rather we believe that profit sharing is normally a consequence of the participative style set by the top management in a company; and that it is this management style, with profit sharing as one of the keys to generating commitment to the firm's success, that produces the handsome return for shareholders, managers and employees alike'.

BETTER ATTITUDES WITH PROFIT-SHARING

Bell and Hanson also conducted opinion surveys on the subject, covering more than 2700 employees in 12 different companies with share-based, profit-sharing schemes. Naturally, a large proportion approved of profit-sharing: 91 per cent approved in principle and 88 per cent approved of their own company schemes. Some 96 per cent, however, agreed with the cautionary point that profit-sharing 'is to be welcomed but should not be seen as a substitute for an adequate wage or salary'. Other responses from the survey are shown in Table 10.2.

Profit-sharing gives management an obvious reason for talking to employees about the business, its profitability, its problems and its competition, and employees are much more eager to listen when they know they each have a financial stake in its success. Indeed, one MD in the survey companies said: 'It really is rather silly talking to employees about profit if they don't get any of it'. Of course, employees have the habit at times of asking rather searching questions, but then that may not be

Table 10.2 Employee responses to profit-sharing

	Agree	Disagree	Don't know
Profit-sharing creates a better atmosphere in the firm	65	19	16
It is good for the company and the employees	86	3	11
It makes people take a greater interest in profits and financial results	76	23	7
It strengthens people's loyalty to the firm	47	36	17
It makes people try to work more effectively so as to help the firm be more successful	51	34	15
It can cause disappointment or bitterness, because profits can go down as well as up	42	48	10

a bad thing. The evidence is that some form of profit-sharing not only promises consistently better financial performance but distinctly improved employee attitudes at the same time. In the business of reshaping company culture that has to make the whole idea a very seductive proposition. However, it is not all sweetness and light: there are risks and there are dangers. If you do decide to do it, here is a list of the most important do's and don'ts.

THE DO'S AND DON'TS OF PROFIT-SHARING

Make your scheme as simple as possible so that everyone can understand it

If only the accountant can work out how much it is worth to everyone, it is too complicated. Employees may assume he is fiddling the figures somewhere behind the scenes so the company does not have to pay out what their extra efforts have generated. Then, while you are paying out lumps of money, you may get responses of resentment rather than delight. Don't make the whole thing a mystery: make it clear and simple.

Publish performance figures month by month

Do not wait till the end of the year to tell employees how the company is doing. That is too far away and does little for motivation throughout the year. Show them each month how the company has done, and how much that is worth to them. Put the information clearly and visibly in a location which employees pass regularly, e.g. near the photocopier or the cafeteria. Such action keeps interest high and helps keep everybody's eye on the ball. Show monthly how the profit share amount is accumulating from their efforts. There is as much motivation for employees in seeing themselves 'putting money in the bank' as from getting the money itself.

Pay everyone on the same basis

Pay out the accumulated monies as a percentage of salary or as 'number of days' pay'. That way they can work out what it is worth, and they do! It also makes employees feel they are all in it together, that everyone in the company is playing on the same team. Don't stratify (where senior management are paid out on a much more generous basis). That just reinforces the 'us and them' divisions. Do not sectionalize (where one section is paid on a different basis from another). That can bring horrendous, invidious comparisons ('Why are they getting that and we are only getting this?'), and can simply kill interdepartmental co-operation and team-work.

Make the pay-out 'significant'

By 'significant' I mean large enough to be motivational; worth stretching for, but not so large that it causes serious demotivation when it does not materialize. There is no set formula here. I have seen a week's pay have a big motivational effect (i.e. 2 per cent of salary), and I have seen Japanese companies pay bonuses of five or six months' pay. However, lump sums work better than money added to salary: you can do something with £500 but the equivalent £10 per week seems to disappear unnoticed into the melting pot.

Make the pay-out at useful times

It is nice to get a lump sum bonus at any time, of course, but if it is paid out at particularly useful times of the year, e.g. before the summer holidays or just before Christmas, it is so much more appreciated.

Tell the bad news straight

Prepare employee expectations right from the outset. Tell them that you will give them the bad news as well as the good news as it happens. Don't pussyfoot. If you are suffering in the market-place they have to know about the realities of life. At least you will all be in the same boat, and they will know that the solution is in your own hands, i.e. the only way to recover is for everyone to work at it together. Team-work is even more necessary in the difficult times.

Don't pay out when there isn't any money

Don't pay out bonuses for making smaller losses. Employees suspect then that there must be a second set of books, a secret pile from which the company can actually pay out bonuses. Promise to raise salaries perhaps from a certain point as performance improves, but don't pay bonuses. Employees cannot understand how any company can actually pay bonuses when they say they are still losing money. Similarly, don't pay out bonuses which have not been earned in order 'to keep people happy'. Again they suspect you are not telling all the truth and that there is a secret pile somewhere. Not only does it kill your credibility, it leads next time to their probing and questioning anything you say. Tell it all straight.

There are endless forms of profit-sharing formats and schemes. Rather than adopt some standard off-the-shelf arrangement, develop a form which suits your situation. The do's and don'ts above should be of some help. But profit-sharing certainly pays off both in terms of long-term company performance and developing positive employee attitudes.

REWARDING EMPLOYEES IMAGINATIVELY

There is no need for rewards to be on a company-wide scale, of course, to have an encouraging and motivating effect. However, using your imagination does help. Julian Richer runs a chain of specialist hi-fi shops around the UK, and very much believes in rewarding his employees. In fact, each month he gives his top performing branch the use of his Rolls Royce for a month as part of his incentive plan. 'The eighteen or nineteen-year-old who takes his mother or his girl-friend out for a drive in the Rolls thinks it is amazing,' he says. 'It's all part of making the job more fun'. Other staff may get the use of a Jaguar Sovereign, spend a few days at his holiday home in York, win gold-plated badges for 'service beyond the call of duty', or even have a private consultation with his Harley Street doctor.

Julian Richer believes in getting his people both interested and excited about their work, and shares out 15 per cent of the company's profits in a tiered bonus scheme involving all his employees. But it is not just sales that count: staff are also measured on customer complaints, promptness in answering the phone (he checks by phoning branches himself), punctuality and efficiency in maintaining stocks of popular lines. He even deducts 'idiocy marks' for omissions, like forgetting to empty the cash register on a Saturday evening. Every week he sends out a tape-recorded newsletter and includes a new code-word to make sure his staff actually listen. He also holds a regular dinner with each branch and insists that new recruits sit next to him at table. Staff find it a very lively company to work for. Unlike most of the retail business, staff turnover is small, and even through the 1990–1991 rececession in Britain, the company continued to grow strongly; in fact, in 1991 *Richer Sounds* won the Guinness Book of Records award for the highest sales per square foot of any retail outlet in the world!

GETTING EVERYONE TO SEARCH OUT EXCELLENCE

It does not have to be the boss who does all the rewarding: you can get employees themselves to identify the unsung heroes who regularly put themselves out to help their fellow employees, who 'go the extra mile' to do a superior job. At Avis, the car rental company, for instance, employees can be nominated by their colleagues for a *Double-Bagger* award. The name comes from the boys in supermarkets who help customers carry their heavy bags of groceries to their cars. If the contents of the plastic bags are too heavy items sometimes fall through the bottom but not with the Double-Bagger boys. They put one bag inside the other to make sure their customer's heavy purchases are safe. They are the type of people who take the trouble to do an *excellent* job for the customer.

At Avis, when an employee is nominated and their manager endorses the nomination, a certificate is then presented detailing just how they demonstrated super service. When employees accumulate three DB certificates, they get a bronze award, a silver badge and a cash award with six certificates, and a gold badge for nine. At that point their photograph and a description of their story appears in the company magazine, demonstrating to others just what the company values. Some managers tend to pooh-pooh the idea of badges, but when staff are doing a fairly repetitious, mundane job every day, they greatly appreciate the recognition and wear their badges with pride. And what a great idea to have every employee on the look-out for superior service: that's one good way to make excellence a way of life.

I love the idea they used at the Sheraton Hotel in St Louis,

Missouri, before it was decided to build a new sports stadium on their territory. They got their *customers* to search out examples of excellent service. When they arrived guests were given a booklet of coupons which said: 'As our customer you are very important. Would you mind taking this praising coupon book? When you see any of our staff doing something right or treating you well, would you get their name and present them with a praising coupon or turn it in to the front desk?' Instead of leaving guests just to make complaints they gave clients the opportunity to do the positive thing, that is, to actively praise the people who take extra trouble to serve them well. That makes an interesting turnaround.

The idea came as the result of suggestions from the hotel's Quality Committee. Employees were later able to redeem their coupons for cash or gifts like clock radios, Sheraton T-shirts, coffee mugs, etc. It created a lot of interest and a lot of fun. In fact, the idea worked so well they introduced 'back-of-the-house' praising coupons where, if a front-line employee like a waiter got outstanding service from a back-of-the-house person (like a kitchen porter, for example), the waiter could award him one of his praising coupons in the same way. They found a lot more people wanted to 'go the extra mile' to give outstanding customer service. That is the kind of reward system that changes habits in an organization, that changes their whole way of doing things.

THE POWER OF VISIBLE RECOGNITION

Napoleon said his great discovery was that 'men would lay down their lives for ribbons'. We do not want anyone to die in the service of their company, of course, but we do need to realize the power of visible recognition. The signs need not be costly, they only need to be endowed with *value*. The fact is, like Napoleon's foot soldiers, most employees lead ordinary, often humdrum, lives and many harbour a secret hunger for appreciation and distinction. Companies need to create opportunities to satisfy that hunger. Using tangible signs of recognition not only gives employees such opportunities but also helps encourage the cultural behaviour the company wants to see.

Four Square Catering, who run cafeterias and restaurants in industrial locations around the UK, very much recognized this factor. Catering daily for large numbers of diners who all want their meals within a short space of time can create hectic conditions for employees, and customers are much more likely to find reasons to complain than to give words of appreciation. It is one of the besetting problems of industrial catering. As part of Four Square's training for its employees in customer service, some years back they introduced a number of awards in the form of badges. Those who passed customer service knowledge tests and were nominated by their manager qualified for a bronze badge in the form of a rosette with a Four Square logo inside it. For further achievement, as staff earned bars to their badges, they could then graduate to a silver badge and eventually to a gold badge. As Terry Eccles, the company's Catering Manager says: 'It was not the cost of the badges that attracted people to qualify (even the gold badge only cost 45p). The badge was visible evidence of their worth and achievement'.

The system worked well. *Incentive Today* magazine awarded the company their 1987 prize for employee motivation. Even more important, Four Square's customers noticed the difference too. Staff organized special 'National Days' where they not only served special meals in Chinese, Hungarian or Polish style, they dressed up in the clothes of the country as well. Customers noticed the staff's badges (and bars) and started asking them questions about it all: they felt a great deal to be proud of. Complaints dropped to a trickle. Said one client's personnel manager: 'I always thought the best we would ever do with the cafeteria was to have our people "not unhappy". Now people are actually telling me how good they think the cafeteria is. That I never expected'.

PUBLISH AND MAKE HEROES

Publishing stories of employee exploits in serving the goals of the company is another way of giving staff tangible recognition. Not only do employees tend to cut out and preserve the article or photograph recording their moment of glory, the stories show other employees just what their company values most. That is a double benefit. The head librarian of an eastern US city asked his employees to search out stories of fellow employees who were doing that bit extra to advance the department's goals. Quite a few unsung heroes emerged. In no time they had unearthed 50 stories. The best were included in their new employee handbook just to show new employees, right from the beginning, what it takes to be valued in their team. The purchasing manager of a mid-west US city went a bit further. She placed an advertisement in the company newspaper asking for stories about her staff who had provided outstanding service. When she got them, the newsletter editor published the best for all to see, and later the manager awarded her heroes an 'Oscar' statue at a special lunch called in their honour. The fact is that the stories are there if you search them out. When you publish them and make a fuss of them, in no time at all the trickle becomes a constant stream.

Perhaps one of the biggest hero recognition ceremonies is that run by the Mary Kay cosmetics organization. They celebrate their heroes in the grand fashion. They invite as many as 25 000 people to their three-day conventions called Seminar in Dallas to laud and reward their top performers in sales, recruiting and unit performance. The top performers are invited up on stage to be feted and receive their awards, and later their photographs and names appear in a commemorative brochure and in the company's monthly magazine *Applause*, which has a circulation of some 200 000 copies. At Seminar they also have a Directors' March for all who have reached that elevated status, and a March for Team Managers and Future Directors. The directors with the top sales records get pink Cadillacs, and these are all lined up in a great impressive row outside the venue. They create quite a stir in Hong Kong, Paris, Hawaii or other similar destinations as they are taken on all-expenses trip with their spouses with first-class transport and accommodation all the way. At Seminar, the highlight is when they crown on stage superachievers by presenting several Mary Kay Queens with a satin sash, draping a mink coat over their shoulders, putting a diamond ring on their finger, placing a tiara on their head, and finally awarding them the 'crown jewel' of a diamond bumblebee.

You may think this is all a bit 'over the top.' Mary Kay Ash, the company founder, has often been told that awarding ribbons for reaching sales targets, printing photos and names in the house magazine, and feting special achievers before huge audiences may work with women but not with men. Her response is: 'I just smile when I hear such remarks. Did you ever notice the stars on a 6 foot 7 inch, 275-pound linebacker's helmet. Or the medals on a soldier's uniform? Men are willing to risk bodily injury and even their lives for praise and recognition'. Your rewards, praise and tokens of recognition may not take such an elaborate form, but they are some of the most powerful weapons in the management armoury to focus attention, encourage good habits and shape your culture.

CELEBRATE SUCCESS

When your company achieves some notable success, celebrate! Reward the behaviour you want to see repeated. In fact, make the whole company feel like winners. Make them feel so good about it that they will want to keep repeating the performance. When SAS, the Scandinavian airline, clocked up a $70 million profit from a $10 million loss the previous year, and simultaneously won the conveted title of *Airline of the Year* they had set out to achieve, they celebrated their success with all their employees in a big way. Every one of the 20 000 employees got a parcel in the post just before Christmas. In it was a gold watch with a seconds hand in the shape of an aeroplane, a memo announcing more liberal rules regarding free trips, and a letter from CEO Jan Carlzon, printed on parchment paper, thanking them all for the great job they had done. At the beginning of the year they had all received a little red book entitled *Let's Get in There and Fight,* and now in this parcel was a second little red book called *The Fight of the Century.* In addition, there was also an invitation to a great celebration party. Staff were delighted. One employee wrote: 'There I was, a grown-up, at the post office with my package, and I was so happy I was ready to cry. It was the first time in all my years at SAS that I had ever received a personal thank you for what I had done; and, best of all, I felt I deserved it'.

Why did Carlzon do it? It's hard delivering service with a smile every hour of the day week-in, week-out, he says. Often one's efforts go quite unrecognized. In fact, in many companies the only thing that gets attention are the mistakes. This was a way of saying a big thank you, of making everyone feel good about what they had achieved. That high self-esteem in employees is a key to their continuing to deliver superior customer service. Also, he wanted them all to feel part of the same team, albeit a very big team. That is where the party came in. Some 4000 people attended the Stockholm party alone: there were pilots, mechanics, loaders, secretaries, managers, office staff, salesmen, computer technicians, and the rest, all rubbing shoulders together, having fun, and recognizing that it takes a lot of different people to make an airline work. That is the kind of function that breaks down interdepartmental barriers and makes the whole business feel a collective success.

LOOK FOR OPPORTUNITIES TO CELEBRATE SUCCESS

Making dog and cat food is not the most exciting operation in the world, but at Pedigree Petfoods, part of the Mars Corporation in the UK, they present all their employees with 'milestone gifts'. For example, in the 1970s, when they hit £100 million sales, everyone was presented with a gold pen to mark the occasion. That was followed with a matching gold pencil for £200 million. At £300 million, ladies received a beautiful leather purse, and men a leather wallet, each suitably inscribed. What the company did not tell them, just by way of a surprise, was that inside each was a five-pound note. Pedigree also sends its pensioner employees a Christmas hamper every year as a mark of their appreciation. When recently the managing director was retiring and his replacement had been nominated, they decided to mark the occasion by sending a hamper to every employee. They displayed the hamper contents at each location for everyone to see, with a message of 'goodbye to Les, and hello to Heino'. One of the more cynical storemen stopped me on a visit at the time and said: 'I'm amazed. What other company would do a thing like that?' 'Yes,' I said, 'what other company would do a thing like that. . .?' No wonder Pedigree can count on its people to do whatever it takes to stay a front-rank company.

An essential part of the celebration process is getting people *feeling good as a team* about their accomplishments, feeling good to be part of their company. One UK Midlands engineering company, for instance, decided to celebrate their achievement of the BS 5750 qualification, the British Standards Institute quality accreditation. It took more than a year of hard work revising and documenting procedures, and getting everyone on board in implementing the new systems. However, they achieved the qualification on their first application. The company then invited every employee to a great party in a super hotel, and invited them all to bring their wives and partners to join in as well. The families were pleased to hear the MD congratulate his employees, and thank their families too for their behind-the-scenes support. The following week, to mark the fact that everyone had contributed, the whole workforce gathered outside the plant to have their photograph taken for the Group Magazine. Today, behind their reception desk, a great stained glass panel marks their 1990 achievement in permanent colour. It's the kind of public celebration that has the whole workforce saying: 'We're a great team, and proud of it too'.

DISTINCTIVE WAYS OF CELEBRATING SUCCESS

In companies where employees are involved in doing much the same thing every day, it can be difficult to maintain their enthusiasm unless there is something to be proud of, something to be pleased about. That is something that is well understood at Milliken, the international textile company headquartered in South Carolina, USA. Having introduced a Quality Through Participative Management programme in the early 1980s, chairman Roger Milliken became frustrated at the fact that good ideas from one plant were not immediately implemented in others; they suffered from a touch of the 'not invented here' syndrome. So they introduced Corporate Sharing Rallies, where every three months 100 or so teams voluntarily get the opportunity to present their ideas or success stories. At the end attendees vote on what are the best projects (not the best presentations necessarily) and these receive special awards. There are a few useful rules, such as: each idea or project has to be presented with a quantitative measure of its improvement value; ideas are judged on their quality, not on whether they are 'big' or 'small'; no criticism is allowed of any team's presentation; no complaints about lack of co-operation from whomever are permitted. Whether they win or not, every team who participates gets a framed certificate signed and presented personally by president Tom Malone or the chairman himself. People queue up to attend what are now called the Fabulous Bragging Sessions. That is where you get not only public credit for all your efforts and hard work, you learn a lot of very useful things as well!

At Domino's Pizza, the format may be different, but the intent is the same: to give all the people out there doing the everyday jobs of the company the chance to shine and show their skills. Domino hold annual 'Olympics', where employees compare their prowess on 14 areas of competition, ranging from vegetable slicing and dough-making to driving, loading and store delivery. Even service representatives, receptionists and accountants have their own contests. Judging panels, largely composed of the company's franchisee customers and suppliers, decide on the winners of each category, who receive prizes amounting to several thousand dollars. With an average employee age of around 30, the competitive idea of the 'Olympics' catches Domino's employees' imagination. They spend nearly all year 'training' for the event and, of course, that keeps their everyday skills very sharp.

MAKING PEOPLE FEEL GOOD ABOUT THEIR WORK

By holding Company 'Olympics', Domino Distribution President, Don Vleck, has in fact raised what might otherwise appear mundane skills into something to feel good and proud about. That ability may indeed be one of the key qualities of good leadership. Irwin Federman, President of Monolithic Memories in California, expressed it in this way: 'Our individual potential is a direct derivative of our self-esteem, which means we feel good about ourselves. If we come to regard ourselves more highly, then we come to expect more of ourselves. This business of making another person feel good in the unspectacular course of his daily comings and goings is, in my view, the very essence of leadership'.

Yet many employees just do not feel good about their work. Often they think they get nothing but brickbats. My company is involved in conducting employee attitude surveys, and the pleas employees record about lack of appreciation and recognition are often quite saddening. Typical of the comments that appear are:

'You only see management here when something goes
   wrong; you never get any thank you's.'
'You do not feel like a valued employee.'

—

'To management you are just a number, not a person.'
'I feel management treat us like schoolchildren. As an operator I feel I must not have any ideas of my own.'
'They always talk down to you, and never give us any credit.'

These views may not be the truth, of course. That does not matter: if that is how they perceive it, that is how they will behave.

For many managers it is not a natural tendency to praise and reward the behaviour they want to see every time they see it. Yet that has the power to shape employee behaviour and change the culture of the business. Skinner, whom we mentioned earlier in this chapter, became more and more convinced as time went on that new behaviour is best fostered by means of rewards alone, and not by punishment. He simply ignored the undesirable behaviour and concentrated exclusively on encouraging the positive behaviour. Yet most of us managers confess that we criticize and complain much more than we praise. We need to be actively spending time walking around deliberately *catching people doing something right*, and to keep on rewarding the behaviour we want to see.

Of course, by rewards we do not just mean money. There is actually an endless variety of non-financial rewards which managers can use. Like, for example, eye contact, a pat on the back (literally), a smile, a thumbs up sign, a delighted 'yes!', words of praise, a wink, giving public credit at communication meetings, listening to what employees say, implementing their suggestions, trusting them to do important little jobs, buying them a coffee, bringing in a few cream cakes to celebrate, and so on. There is no end to it . . . *if* you are looking for the opportunities. That is why it is important for managers in training sessions to be given just such simple examples to stimulate their imagination, to get them *thinking in rewarding terms*. They need to know that the time or occasions when they are praising and rewarding must outweigh the complaining time by at least a factor of two to one. That sort of manager is a pleasure to work for.

BACK TO THE FUNDAMENTALS

Employees do not respond just because there is financial reward at the end. The money is interesting, of course, because of the extra opportunity that it gives you to have material things you might want but the rewards of praise and genuine appreciation are fundamentally needed because of *how they make you feel.* When people have negative associations of their feelings at work, they come to work under sufferance. Then they only turn up because of the money, and do only as much as they have to. When their mental associations are of good feelings, they keep wanting to come back to the place which makes them feel good. And just what are these good feelings we are talking about? They are simple cherished things like:

- Feeling *valued*

Feeling the company needs not just any old pair of hands but *you* personally, and the experience and ideas you bring to the team.

- Feeling *important*

No one wants to feel they are an unimportant cog in the great business machine. When your manager makes you feel important to him, it gets easier to get out of bed in the morning.

- Feeling *recognized*

Badges of achievement may seem 'small beer' to some, but for many it is a sign of distinction in the crowd.

- Feeling *respected*

When you are treated like an adult, you want to act more like an adult.

- Feeling *needed*

When the boilerman knows the company actually needs him to get the company started in the morning, he will struggle through the snow to get there.

- Feeling *you belong*

It is hard to get that feeling in a lot of businesses, but when employees do, that is when they will do double back flips if necessary and leave you wondering at their dedication.

- Feeling *somebody cares*

It is one of the best feelings in the world. When the company cares about you, you care about the company.

KEY POINTS SUMMARY

- To change the habits and culture of a business you must reward and encourage the behaviour you want to see. *The behaviour which gets rewarded gets repeated.*
- When employees own a share in their business, serving the business well is then in the employees' own best interest. Ownership changes behaviour.
- Businesses who share profits with their employees do consistently better on every key measure than those who don't. The record shows it is good for the business and good for its employees.
- Observe commonsense rules on profit-sharing: make the scheme simple; publish performance regularly; pay everyone on the same basis; make the payout significant; do not pay out when there is no money.
- Use your imagination in the recognition you offer employees, like driving a Rolls Royce or even using 'praising coupons'. The possible variations are endless.
- Get both employees and customers to look out for superior performance. Make excellence into a way of life.
- For many otherwise repetitive and humdrum jobs, badges of achievement can be effective forms of distinction and recognition.
- Make heroes of those who contribute well to the company's goals. It shows what you value, and encourages the right behaviour.
- When you achieve some success, celebrate and enjoy the feeling. Make the whole team feel like winners.
- Create opportunities, like Fabulous Bragging Sessions or Company 'Olympics', where employees at all levels have a chance to feel success in your business.

- Reward the behaviour you want to see in your employees every time you see it. Keep rewarding it until it becomes your new way of life.
- Make your people feel valued, important, recognized and respected in your business. They will always want to do the best they can for the company that makes them feel good about themselves.

11

Getting started

THE DRASTIC APPROACH

In the 1950s and 1960s, Dunlop was a blue chip company by any standards. In its heyday the company employed over 100 000 people in the five continents of the world. Not only were they a household name in tyres, they also made tennis racquets, shoes and golf balls. The name was recognized by consumers everywhere. Investors and institutions bought their shares because they were a reliable, solid business.

Over the years, the company became complacent. Their huge market and continuing profits convinced senior management they were practically invulnerable. They developed a massive bureacracy operated from palatial headquarters in London which effectively stifled middle management and plant autonomy. With six or seven different Trade Unions in their plants, they were plagued by disputes and often made unwise concessions for the sake of peace and quiet. Their competitors started nibbling at their market and profits began to wobble. Top management, however, were locked into the old ways which had served them so well in the past. They felt that by sticking with the old formulae 'everything would come all right in the end'. It did not.

Even when the warning signs were writ large upon the wall, the paralysis at top level was such that in the end the only remedy was a complete change of ownership. The tyre company was finally bought over by Sumitomo in 1984. From employing some 25 000 people in the UK, the business now employs only 2500. The name of the company has changed to SP Tyres. Dunlop is now only a brand name.

With that complete change of ownership, employees might have expected some drastic action, but that has not been Sumitomo's approach. They have kept the same employees, and all the directors but one are long-serving Dunlop people. Instead they have set out on a programme of changing the whole culture of the business. The biggest difference now is that the company's commitment to quality is all-pervading. There is a fetish about good two-way communications throughout the business with special encouragement for quality groups and continuous improvement. The Japanese insist on a clean plant. When asked what was the biggest difference from Dunlop times, one long-serving middle manager said: 'You can eat your dinner off the floor now'. Status differences are disappearing. There is now only one dining room: six of the previous seven have been converted into training rooms with managers constantly engaged in training staff in Total Quality methods. The six different unions on the site now sit down together in one pay negotiation as they all realize their future is very much in their own hands. The company moved into profit in 1987 and continues to expand its business. 'There's actually nothing revolutionary about what we're doing here', says Director Ian Sloss, 'it's all just plain common sense. But we could not have done it under the old regime. It was just too bureaucratic.'

THE SYSTEMATIC APPROACH

In Dunlop's case it took a complete change of management to make the necessary changes happen. That is the drastic approach. The sensible thing to do is to start changing the habits of people throughout the business long before it collapses. There is no 'one best way' to do that, but it *does not* mean launching enthusiastically into the process just hoping for the best. Use a systematic approach. After all, you may have put up with how your business operates for years. It surely deserves a few months to plan your long-term future. That planning phase is something the Japanese take great care over. One of the British managers at Sumitomo said: 'The Japanese don't rush into things. They don't want to be associated with failure, so they take time to make sure everybody is on board before they start. They plan for the long-term interest of the business. Then they pay attention to the detail, to make sure they get things right'.

The systematic approach means that senior management first take the trouble to educate themselves, to investigate what other successful companies may have done. Also, if they want to achieve some kind of leading edge, they need to find out just what are the best practices around. Here are some of the ways to do that.

Conferences and seminars   Not only do you get up-to-date concepts and ideas at seminars, but often speakers are real, live managers who will tell you all about the difficult realities to counterbalance the seductive blandishments of professors and consultants. You also rub shoulders with other delegates who are in the same position as yourself, or who are a bit further down the path and can give you useful tips. In fact, you often pick up as many useful ideas from other delegates as you do from the people speaking at the conference. Also, the contacts may mean you can later arrange visits which may help open up a few closed minds.

Books and articles   These are easy to obtain and cheap for the ideas they produce. Your reading will be so much more intent, of course, with a clear purpose in view. It helps too if your colleague directors or managers are reading the same material. Then you can discuss together the relevance and practicality of the ideas for your particular company situation.

Consultants   Generally consultants have up-to-date concepts to put in front of you, otherwise why would you consult them? Also they tend to have worked out methodology and procedures available which can save you a lot of hard work and mistakes in remaking the wheel. However, they have to make a living, so if you invite them along, their primary purpose will be to sell you something. That is a pressure you have to live with. If you invite several consultant companies to come and present to you, you learn more and you see different approaches. The fact that you 'have other people coming to see you' also helps reduce the sales pressure, and seeing several consultants helps to choose who best suits your style and purpose.

Company visits   There is nothing more convincing than seeing for yourself, in going to see companies who are well ahead in the field in which you are interested. It opens minds, convinces doubters and generates enthusiasm. The process is sometimes called benchmarking: you choose to visit companies that you take to be the best in their field on some aspect of performance, and measure your own company performance against that benchmark. The companies need not necessarily be operating in your commercial field, they just need to be the best you can find. Send a good-sized delegation (including non-management people): the more you have a critical mass of convinced and enthusiastic people in the company the more you will develop an energy to succeed.

Management discussions   As reading, attending seminars and visiting goes on, top management in particular need to discuss what they are discovering. They need to talk through what ideas and approaches seem to meet their purposes best, which direction their thoughts are now taking them in (these will alter and develop as time goes on), how they might want to start, what the priorities are, etc. Showing appropriate videos, hearing reports on seminars and recent visits can all help in the process.

Often an outsider can help as a catalyst in the proceedings, to hold up a mirror as needed, or to neutralize situations where executives defend previous actions and get involved in unproductive points-scoring or intellectual fencing matches. He can also contribute some useful outside experience and add a bit of structure and discipline to the discussions. He might even rattle a few cages if necessary. The purpose of it all is gradually to *converge to agreement* about the direction the team wants to take, and the methodology they want to employ.

GETTING THE FACTS ON WHERE YOU ARE NOW

Whatever you think of your business now, what helps to get it all into perspective are some facts, some hard data. That means asking people who are closely connected with your business, who know how it really is, and getting their responses in some quantified and comparable form.

Customer surveys

If you ask the right questions, customer surveys often produce information which shatters illusions, and shows the scope for improvement. It helps if this is done face to face by independents using a structured questionnaire which produces quantified data as well as qualitative (i.e. including suggestions, comments and quotes). Customers are much more willing to be frank to people not employed by the company, especially if they know their comments will be anonymous. The questionnaires need to be well thought through. It is difficult to go back and ask the questions you discover you wanted to ask when you are halfway through your visit programme. The questions should be specific: about quality product by product, on-time delivery, invoicing, keeping promises, service quality item by item, speed of response to problems, how the company specifically compares with its competitors, etc. Interestingly enough, although managers will argue about details of the company's performance before a survey, they seldom challenge the figures when they appear. They tend to treat them as facts. That gives you a solid platform from which to start making improvements.

Supplier surveys

These can be just as informative. However, suppliers need to be assured that their commercial position will not be compromised by telling the truth. That is where the use of independent outsiders can again play a useful role in guaranteeing confidentiality. Typical of the output from supplier surveys are comments about wanting to do a good job but the short-term changing of schedules makes life difficult, about the lack of enough forward information on future plans, about getting little or inadequate feedback on their performance, etc. However, suppliers generally want to be helpful: their future business is tied to yours. If they think there are steps they can take which will help the business of both parties, generally they will want to take them. Of course, they know the facts about how you really are now, and will give you useful information about how the situation can be changed for the better, upstream of your business. Later, you may want to treat them as 'partners' in serving your own customers well, and getting that upstream end of the business right will be very important.

Employee surveys

Finally, surveys of employee opinions can be very revealing. Whatever management believe is true, employees will tell you how it really is. Their opinions may not be the truth, but it is on their *perceptions* that they will be acting and responding, so you need to know what these really are. The survey questions should focus particularly on the goals that you think are important.

- Are managers treating quality seriously?
- Are they helping you serve our customers well?

- Do they seek and use your suggestions for improvement?
- Do they take prompt action to get your problems resolved?
- Is co-operation between departments improving?

The data also should be collected in such a way that individual managers get the scores from their own departments. In that way it has more impact, and front-line managers are the people who can do most about it.

With these kinds of data, you know more clearly the difference between what you are and what you want to be. It helps convince sceptics of the need to change, it acts as a stimulus to action and – just as important – surveys taken later will show in a measurable way just how much real progress you have made towards your chosen goals.

MAKING THE COMPANY'S GOALS CLEAR AND SPECIFIC

Having educated themselves on the possibilities, and armed with useful data, top management in the company needs to take time to define their goals clearly, to decide what exactly they are going to commit themselves to in terms of changing the company's culture and style of operation. This is no flavour-of-the-year target, but a long-term commitment, a sea change for the business. As such, it deserves some serious *undisturbed time* to think about and discuss, away from the normal work situation. That may mean some *Awaydays Meetings*.

The structure of such top management strategy meetings can take many different forms, of course, but this is the format I prefer.

Pre-think brochure

Each team member receives a brochure in which a number of questions are posed pertinent to the company's preferred new direction. They are asked to compose their considered views on each. For example:

What exactly do you think the company's new vision or goals ought to be?

What new measures do you feel ought to be put in place to ensure focus and prove progress?

Should we change our reward systems to reflect the changes? How?

What better forms should our internal communications take?

What training is going to be needed for our various work groups?

How do we get all our managers on board?

Considered thinking on specific questions before the event materially improves the quality of the subsequent discussions, and can produce a great variety of ideas when everyone is given the air time during the Awaydays to express their views.

AWAYDAYS MEETING

Generally the meeting should start with a talk from the chief executive about what he wants to see the business achieve, and how he believes the style of operation should change. Thereafter there is a great variety of agenda items which can be used. Some Awaydays build in some 'outward bound' experiences like canoeing or mountain climbing, i.e. doing something novel and physical to relieve what otherwise might be rather long, hot-house discussion sessions. In any event, the meeting needs to get through the important agenda items on which the team members have all done some individual pre-thinking. Since we are talking about the long-term direction of the business here, it may take more than one session to do this adequately. The fundamental purpose is for the leaders of the business to develop a clear vision of the company's future. Without that, there is no chance at all of the rest of the company helping them to get there.

It is crucial that the team achieves shared views on specific goals without railroading people or shouting them down to suppress anxieties or dissent. If the price is not paid at the front in taking the time to persuade the whole team, or in modifying the specific wording of the goals to reflect the legitimate points of team members, the price will be paid later 'back at the ranch' when individuals make difficulties and show little commitment in practice to the company's objectives. In that respect we could learn from the Japanese: they take the time to get everyone's initial understanding and commitment, then go at implementation with a will. Culture change is no place for the Western tendency for quick-fix solutions; it needs genuine long-term commitment.

An experienced and respected facilitator is always an advantage at meetings of this significance. A good facilitator is actually much like a sheepdog. The sheepdog comes around his charges at the top of the hill and gets them gently started off in the right direction. Moving under their own power they may wander off the track a little, but with gentle steering they pass through the right gates. If they go widely astray, the dog applies more pressure, or may even give some animals a nip if they do not stay in the pack. If they go along nicely by themselves, the dog lies down and stays quiet. When they get into the fold, he lies outside panting after all his hard work. The sheep have actually arrived at their destination by themselves, but the dog knows they would not have got there so easily without him.

ACTION DOCUMENT

From the Awaydays an Action Document is composed listing the agreed conclusions of the team, which becomes the blueprint for action. Any specific actions proposed must have the full, unqualified support of team members and appear in the document with prime contractors and dates attached. The Awaydays decisions become the mainspring of the long process of culture change.

STEERING GROUP ROLE

When the process starts gathering momentum there can be a whole series of projects going on: new communications procedures introduced, appraisal and rewards systems being changed, training courses being implemented, and so on. Indigestion can easily occur, projects and changes can get out of sync with each other, and co-ordination becomes a great problem. One solution is to appoint a high-level Steering Group to make sure the change process stays on track, and to ensure that too much is not tackled at once.

The chairman should be the chief executive. After all, we are not simply changing one system in the company, we are intent on changing the whole culture of the business. If that is not chief executive work, what is? Furthermore, his presence will indicate to everyone in the business just how serious the work is. Other members should be those who have the power and authority to get things done, and whose continuing commitment is crucial to the process. The group should be big enough to cover the spectrum of the business, but not so large as to become unwieldy. Temporary members can be co-opted as necessary to deal with particular projects as they develop. Where new initiatives are planned, teams should present to the group the detail of their intentions for their approval.

The key functions of the Steering Group are to:

- *Give visible top-level support to the change programme.* That gives the whole process credibility and overt top-of-the-house commitment.
- *Set objectives and decide on priorities.* The Steering Group effectively decides the pace, shape and order of the process of change.

- *Allocate money, people and resources.* The Group must have the seniority and authority to sanction the resources that are needed to make things happen.
- *Receive reports on progress against objectives, and 'encourage' completion.* When project teams have to report on progress at the highest level, they tend to get things done.
- *Give continuity to the long-term change process.* Culture change takes time. The process can, and no doubt will, take years. Even when one key individual moves on, via the Steering Group the process will continue unabated.

GETTING MIDDLE MANAGEMENT COMMITMENT

Let us assume we now have clear, actionable company goals and heartfelt commitment by top management. How do you now get management throughout the company to sign on to the new goals? That is best achieved in my view by giving them real *ownership* of the departmental objectives they propose to pursue in support of the company's overall change programme.

A powerful way to do that is to conduct a series of cascading *Team Objectives Meetings*. These are conducted with people who normally work together every day: 'natural teams' who report to one boss. This is a critical factor. If training or reorientation of this kind is done with individuals selected from different departmental groups, they may go back to work full of enthusiasm, but because their colleagues do not yet know the 'new language' or understand the concepts they get little response or support. As a result, they are pressed into going back to the current ways of doing things 'in the meantime'. By the time the others have attended sessions, those who went before have lost all their initial enthusiasm, and the implementation of change becomes patchy and often perfunctory.

However, when a whole work team decides together on actions and objectives, the execution tends to be immediate and thorough.

TEAM OBJECTIVES MEETINGS

The agenda for the Team Objectives Meeting (TOM) varies, but often contains items such as the following:

- What objectives do you now intend to set if your team is to make its full contribution to the new goals of the business?
- What specific actions can you take
  – in the next week,
  – in the next three months,
  which will get you off to a positive start?
- How do you intend to measure your progress? How will you collect the information? Who will compose the information? How will this be fed back to the team? How will it be used to take further action?
- What obstacles are acting as hindrances to your making your full contribution to the company's goals? Detail what action you propose to take on each.
- Are there any relationship problems between your team and other departments which need to be improved? What specific actions do you intend to take on these?
- Have you any positive ideas which the company could adopt to further its chosen goals?
- Prepare a summary of your conclusions for presentation to your Super-boss as your team's contribution to the company's new goals.

My advice is to use an independent trained facilitator throughout. It materially improves the tone of the meetings and the business-like quality of the results. This is the sequence of events in the TOM process:

- A *seminar* is held with the team to explain the company's goals and change of direction. The format of the TOM programme is detailed. A meeting agenda with pre-think questions is distributed to each team member.
- There is an *interval* of seven to ten days' thinking time.

- The TOM itself is held off-site, undisturbed, for two or three days, depending on the content.
- At the end of the meeting, the team makes a formal presentation to their *Super-boss* (i.e. their boss's boss) about their objectives and how they propose to support the company's change of direction specifically in their area.
- The actions and objectives agreed are produced in a typed-up *Action Document* which then acts as the team's bible for the next year or so. Copies can be passed on to other departments for their benefit.
- The team sets up a process of *self-management* by putting in place regular team review sessions to make sure they deliver on their commitments.

CASCADING DOWN THE ORGANIZATION

The cascading TOM process is shown diagrammatically in Fig. 11.1. This is how it works. Team A first conduct a Team Objectives Meeting and publish their resulting *Action Document*. This is available to Team B before they hold their TOM. Their boss, Ms B, fully understands the music behind the decisions taken by the top team at their TOM, because she was there. When she conducts her meeting with her own team, she can use that first-hand knowledge to make sure any objectives they set truly support the company's intentions. At the end of the TOM, Manager A comes along as *Super-boss* to hear a presentation on their proposals, and give them his direct endorsement. Later, Manager B will act as Super-boss in turn to Team C when they hold their TOM. So, step by step, the process cascades in a practical and controlled fashion down the organization.

The outcome from such a series of TOMs is:

- Every team finishes with a list of agreed actions with specific responsibilities and deadlines attached.

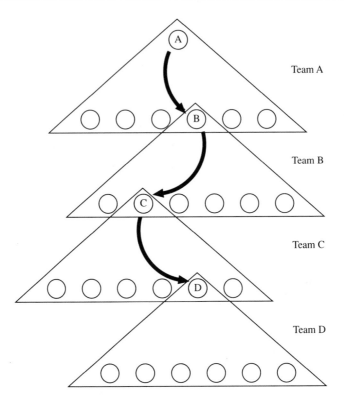

Figure 11.1   Cascading team objectives meetings

- All the actions are in support of the company's goals, and carry the explicit approval of the team's Super-boss.
- Since each of the teams' members are the *owners* of the proposed actions, they feel that much more committed to their implementation.

Team Objectives Meetings have a habit of generating a great deal of energy and enthusiasm, and as such team members are usually impatient to get into action as soon as they get back to work. Before long there are actions taking place all over the business, all with the ultimate intent of implementing the new cultural and operational thrust of the company. Not every team produces magical results and converts, but the exercise does get teams mobilized and focused on the company's key goals. With strong and consistent follow-up, the process often develops a momentum which becomes quite unstoppable.

MAKING STRUCTURAL CHANGES

Organizations are sometimes so entrenched in old ways, however, that major *structural* change is what is necessary to set the company off in a new direction. That was the conclusion Kodak came to when they lost the contract for the 1984 Los Angeles Olympics to Fuji. Peter Ueberroth, who masterminded the organization and marketing of the Games, said: 'They were so arrogant . . .'.

Kodak realized they had to make some serious structural changes in how the business operated. It certainly sent a cold wind whistling through the business when the company ended its lifetime employment policy and for the first time parted company with thousands of staff. One of the most significant changes, however, was their move to decentralize the decision-making process by creating 17 new business units. Covering about 80 per cent of the company's products, the new units became responsible for their own marketing, product development, growth and financial performance. That meant new responsibilities and a whole new set of reporting relationships at the most senior levels. A structural change of this magnitude produces for a short time a period of *flux* in the patterns of behaviour which, if well used, can move the whole company into a new operating mode. Of course, Kodak has to get a lot of other things right to outdo the competition, but that is the kind of organizational shift that helps to move mind-sets. Behaviour is virtually forced to alter because the rules of the game just are not the same any more.

An obvious example of this can be seen in the 'structure' changes to the UK industrial scene which took place during the 1980s. The rules of the game were altered by some fundamental political decisions made by the government and produced some remarkable changes in behaviour. For example, trade unions were required to conduct ballots of their members before official strikes could be called, they were deprived of their former immunity from legal prosecution and, as a result, their funds were open to sequestration for breaches of the law. There was, as expected, a great deal of initial turbulence, but gradually industrial relations settled into a much more stable pattern to the point where in 1991 days lost through strikes in the UK were the lowest recorded for 100 years.

The government also embarked on an extensive programme of privatization of some large nationalized businesses. They were no longer prepared to allow the taxpayer to subsidize their huge annual losses, and by selling them off effectively forced them to stand on their own two feet. And some truly dramatic turnarounds in performance resulted. British Steel, for example, whom we mentioned earlier, moved from a mega loss of more than £1780 million in 1979 to a profit of some £730 million in a very competitive market in 1989. They greatly increased their productivity too: in 1979 they turned out 12.5 million tonnes of finished steel with 186 000 employees, while in 1989 the company was able to produce 13 million tonnes with only 52 000 people. In fact they have become one of the most cost-effective steel producers in the world. British Gas is another case in point. They have thrown off their Victorian image to become a robust commercial organization producing the fuel which most domestic users prefer. Despite having to peg their prices to three points below the annual rate of inflation, they are remarkably profitable: £1.6 billion on £9.5 billion sales in 1991. Also they do not confine their business to the UK any more; they have now become a global player with interests in more than 40 other countries, including the USA, South America and the Middle East. Commercial independence and changes in the political circumstances have quite transformed the culture of these businesses.

BREAKING WITH THE PAST

In other circumstances, high-profile action by a company's chief executive may be what it takes to show the company is making a clear break with the past. When Robert Townsend (of *Up The Organization* fame) took over as Chief Executive of Avis in 1962, it had never made a profit in its 13 years of life. Among other things he discovered that Avis' financial reporting was in a mess. Townsend strongly believed that a financial controller's job is to 'provide an honest notation system by which managers can take responsible action toward their chosen goals and measure their progress'. That was precisely what he thought he was not getting. So he moved the controller aside, and despite protests from the rest of his board, moved into the controller's office and took over the function himself. He stayed there for several months. The message that action sent round the business was loud and clear: we have to know the numbers, and we need to do whatever it takes to turn this business into a financial success. That abrupt sharpening of focus certainly had its effect. With their new *We try harder* slogan and a whole programme of new activities, Avis turned in successive profits of $3, $5 and $9 million during the next three years.

That kind of dramatic action can help shake people out of their lethargy, and make the point that this is not another fad or flavour of the year, but a permanent change of era. It can also be done by the slow burn method, of course, and that causes less heartache and upset. The advantage of the 'kick-in-the-pants' action is that it gets the whole change process off to a flying start. There is no pat formula to adopt: you just have to have the courage and conviction to do it. If enough people round the organization feel it is about time *somebody* took some action you will soon have an enthusiastic band of supporters. There is a risk, however: if you don't get it right, you may not be there very long.

—

MULTIDISCIPLINARY PROJECT TEAMS

Changing the whole direction of a business also means some tough and painstaking work has to be done. This is where project teams drawn from a variety of disciplines and departments have a crucial role to play. Teams should focus on key issues and be given challenging forward-looking briefs which take the company energetically down the path it wants to go. Here are a few examples.

- Reduce the production lead times on our top three selling products by 50 per cent within nine months. Get the agreement of all the necessary parties to the actions that have to be taken to make this happen. Plan how the changes proposed will be communicated and implemented. Keep the costs of implementation low. (*Machine tools company*)

- Cut company stockholding – raw materials, work in progress and finished goods – by 50 per cent within a year, without damaging customer service or production performance. Propose practical check systems for use in each area of the company which keeps stocks at these levels. Visit other companies who have successfully cut stockholding and build into your plans the lessons gained. Propose further steps to cut stocks by a further 50 per cent in year two. (*Consumer durables manufacturer*)

- Review our entire pay and rewards scheme to:
  — ensure they line up with our new company goals;
  — reward achievement and team-work;
  — avoid inconsistency and invidious comparisons between departments.
  Keep it simple. Propose how the changes can be introduced and welcomed. (*Hotel chain*)

- Revise our employee communications system so that it:
  — gets management meeting information down to the lowest level in the business within 48 hours maximum;
  — allows any employee to speak to anyone in the business to resolve any customer problem quickly, at worst within 24 hours;

   — obtains, and rapidly implements, employee job improvement suggestions. (*Insurance company*)

● Propose steps whereby waiting time for patients is minimized in every area of the hospital (15 mins max). Suggest procedures within which each department will set standards and measure performance. Propose signs which allow even older patients to find any department easily and without fail. (*Hospital*)

All of these projects could result in actions which set completely new standards for the organization. They have the potential to move the company a quantum leap forward, to cause significant shifts in the old behaviour and habits of the business.

BENEFITS OF PROJECT TEAMS

The reason I favour cross-departmental teams so strongly is that they offer such a telling list of benefits.

Practical, workable proposals

The most important outcome. If team members are drawn from the departments most affected by the proposed changes, they will want to make changes of the type they can live with and make happen. Eccentricities of any one department's ideas are soon 'trimmed' by the needs and demands of other departments to make the whole chain of events practical and workable.

Learning about the business

Team members learn about the wider business picture. They begin to understand the work and problems of other departments first-hand and to act more like *businessmen* rather than accountants, buyers or production people.

Breaking down interdepartmental barriers

Departmentalism and parochial attitudes can be the bane of effecting change in any organization. Multidisciplined teams overtly demonstrate that better outcomes can result from cross-department co-operation. In addition, when the project team has finished its work, the relationships remain. It loosens up inter-department co-ordination as team members feel more inclined to go and consult former team colleagues on other issues.

Getting big issues dealt with

Issues given to one senior manager to mastermind can often founder simply because of the difficulty of getting full co-operation from all the departments involved in making the necessary changes, i.e. one voice against the whole company culture. Eight convinced people in a project team, who are from different departments and own their proposed solution, have a much better chance of making things happen in practice. If their proposals also have clear top man backing, so much the better.

Manager development

Taking part in a successful project team can provide one of the most important formative influences for developing managers round the business.

Innovation and teamwork becomes a habit

Interdisciplinary project teams, working together to solve problems or take quantum leap initiatives, become just part of 'how we do things round here'. That can keep the business constantly fresh and developing. It becomes a habit to keep setting new challenges . . . and to keep meeting them.

RULES FOR PROJECT TEAMS

Some rules born of experience will help in setting up and using interdisciplinary project teams:

1 The brief needs to be simple, challenging and unambiguous. Do not hedge it round with qualifications and obscurities. Wherever possible, express the objective of the project in the form of a clear, measurable goal where team members will know clearly when they have passed the winning post.

2 The members of the team should be chosen from each department which has a material influence on the outcome, and whose commitment or expertise is needed to make any agreed solution work in practice.

3 Two or three of the team members should be *full-time*, the others only part-time or co-opted as necessary. Simply giving managers a project to do along with their current work means they constantly have to fight the pressure of different priorities. If you want well researched and robust proposals you need to give them the undisturbed time to do it. Always use your very best people, preferably those you cannot afford to release!

4 Team members must have the authority to take decisions in the team which will be commitments on their department's behalf. If they cannot do that, the team member should be a person who can. In practice, if it comes to a big commitment, the team member will indicate that it is something he will need to confirm, but it is no good having someone who has to check everything like a messenger boy.

5 Make it a rule that any recommendations or proposals made must have the 100 per cent agreement of the team. Otherwise, the dissenting departments will simply drag their feet and effectively kill off the proposals in practice. With the 100 per cent agreement rule, the team has to produce solutions which deal effectively with the legitimate points brought up by members from different departments. That does two things: it produces more robust solutions and it demonstrates that

departmental barriers are an irrelevance in getting things done.

6 The project team should make their recommendations direct to the top management team in the company. The project team then treat the whole issue as of the first importance. You get much more commitment when they know they have to stand up and be counted in front of the most important executives in the business.

7 Give the project a realistic but definite timescale. If it is relatively long, e.g. three to six months, ask them to report on progress every month. Fix the dates firmly in everybody's diary: and do not put them off, otherwise you give the (true) impression the subject is really of secondary importance. Insist on substantial progress every month and do not accept excuses.

8 Insist that they keep their proposals simple. If they produce good but complex recommendations, send them back with the brief: 'Now see how simple you can make it'. Once they know they have your support, they can often get surprisingly ingenious at the process of simplification.

9 Do not set too many teams going at once. That can cause confusion and disruption. Go for the priorities first.

KEY POINTS SUMMARY

- No one pattern of business behaviour is good for ever. Keep on developing. Do not wait till drastic medicine is the only thing that will work.

- Start by finding out who is doing it best today. Use conferences, seminars, books, articles, consultants and company visits to get mind-opening ideas which will shape your thinking.

- Get the facts on where you are now. Get some hard data on how your customers, suppliers and your own employees see you.

- Changing your company culture is for the long-term. Do not rush it. Top management must take the necessary time out to become clear and specific about their future goals.

- Use a high-level Steering Group to energize, authorize and control the whole business change process.
- Giving middle management the opportunity to take *owner-ship* of the objectives they want to achieve in support of the change process will help get that all-important *critical mass* in favour of the changes.
- A cascade of Team Objectives Meetings will take the message and the energy down through the organization.
- Structural changes, or attention-grabbing moves by top management, may be needed to give the process a no-going-back character.
- If major cross-company issues need to be tackled, multi-disciplinary project teams with challenging briefs can achieve remarkable results.

12

Involving the whole organization

GETTING THE REST OF THE COMPANY ON BOARD

The vision is clear, the goals have been agreed by top management, a series of team objectives meetings has cascaded down through the management organization, cross-departmental teams are addressing some key business issues, the foundations have been laid. Now all that remains is to persuade the other 85 per cent of the people in the business to come on board. Of course it is possible to communicate the good news that the business is now embarking on a path of continuous improvement, total quality, 100 per cent customer satisfaction, or whatever, but you do not want employees simply to look on from the sidelines as 'the company' gets on with it. You need all those who make the products and deliver the service face to face to be personally engaged in the process of helping make the goals come true on a daily basis. In this respect they *are* the company, and they each need to be thoroughly involved right from the start. First of all though, you need to get their attention.

CREATE IMPACT WITH A LAUNCH EVENT

This is where a launch event can be a great help to make employees sit up and take notice. The event needs to be something unusual. It needs to take employees out of their normal work and put them in a situation they have never been in before. That immediately creates interest. Ideally, it should touch every person in the business, leave nobody out, in order to emphasize that, in changing the practices and culture of the business, every employee has a definite contribution to make. The event needs to grab employees' attention and create enthusiasm for the 'new way'. When staff return to their workplace, they should all be talking about it. If everyone has shared the same experience they will all begin to feel part of the same process. That initial wave of enthusiasm is vital.

National Westminster Bank started their drive for superior customer service with just such a series of events. They were already one of the biggest banks in the UK, but to stay on top they felt they had to deliver the kind of service which would set new standards for the industry. A daunting task, especially as they have some 3 000 branches and 70 000 employees spread across 21 regions of the country. However, they were determined to press ahead. To make the whole experience memorable and demonstrate how serious they were, they decided not to use existing hotels, but to build seven purpose-designed auditoria (very much like domed marquees) equipped with presentation theatres, television screens and syndicate rooms. Each was set in the grounds of a beautiful country location like the Hurlingham Club, Ripley Castle and Loseley Manor. This was 'Class 1' treatment: exactly the kind of treatment they wanted their staff to give their customers.

Each event, attended by 150 staff representing a cross-section from top management to trainees, lasted one day. The chairman, the directors and general managers all participated. The sessions were held on Tuesdays, Wednesdays and Thursdays (Mondays and Fridays are busy days in the banking business) with no more than 15 per cent of staff away from any branch at any one time. Despite the huge logistics problems, some 60 000 of the staff attended One Day Events in the six months from October 1987 to April 1988. The programme for the day was delivered entirely by the bank's own staff, both to demonstrate the commitment inside the business and to brand the day very much as *NatWest*. First they showed staff their market research findings of what customers really wanted, explained the objectives of their Quality Service Programme – to deliver service which would set a standard for the industry – and emphasized the need for their help in achieving it. The pace of the day was kept deliberately lively, with both thought-provoking presentations and working syndicate sessions. These dealt with customer and staff behaviour, banking skills, the value of team-work and ended with brainstorming sessions on what they could all do to help back at the branches.

It cost NatWest around £100 per head to stage the events, but they felt it was both necessary and worth the effort for the momentum it put behind their Quality Service Programme. Back at work, having been introduced to a six-step problem-solving procedure at the One Day Events, staff immediately became involved in their branches in Quality Service Action Teams (QSATs). This brings us to two important points about initial launch events.

- Staff should all be able to attend the launch event within a relatively short timescale, certainly within each work location, otherwise enthusiasm is patchy and the initial momentum is damaged. When the events get underway, everyone should know when *they* will be going, even if that is two or three months on. Everyone should be included: otherwise people feel left out and then simply act as a drag on those who want to get on and do things.
- Secondly, participants should have something to take action on as soon as they get back to work. That is the purpose of it all, i.e. getting employees to help you change the style of the business, getting people everywhere taking actions which will change behaviour in the chosen new direction. So, after the event, managers have to be ready to channel that initial enthusiasm in practical ways as soon as staff get back to work. That gets the whole programme off and running.

GET EMPLOYEES INVOLVED IN PROBLEM-SOLVING

British Telecom, the UK telecommunications giant, was privatized in 1984. As a nationalized company, they were not highly regarded by the British public either for their service or their charges. They were regularly chastised for the number of public telephones out of order, the number of missed connections, how long it took to install a new telephone, how long it took to get repairs done, etc. Recently, BT has become a much improved performer. Among other things, it has become the world's most profitable telephone company, reaching over £3 billion profit on £13 billion sales in 1991, despite being under a government edict to keep overall price increases to 6.25 points below the annual rate of inflation. BT has also made real improvements their customers can see: over 95 per cent of public telephones are now working at any one time; less than 1 in 200 calls fails to connect because of faults or congestion; 95 per cent of new phones are installed on the day agreed with the customer (in less than eight days); and 97 per cent of faults are now cleared within two working days, with some 90 per cent in one day.

Figures like these are not achieved by accident: it takes systematic forms of problem-solving and attention to detail to make it happen . . . and to keep it there. Roy Banks, BT's Manager of Quality Programmes, says it owes much to the company's eight-step problem-solving cycle, now used widely throughout the business. The elements in the BT cycle are shown in Fig. 12.1. There is nothing magical about the process but it does give staff a routine to follow. It encourages them to analyse causes and consider options rather than jump immediately into quick-fix, off-the-top-of-the-head solutions. Also it presumes the problem-solving will be done in teams, where everyone can both contribute ideas and take ownership for the decisions. Of course, there do not have to be eight steps; NatWest had a six-step process, for example. The British Telecom procedure is perfectly all right, but after their step

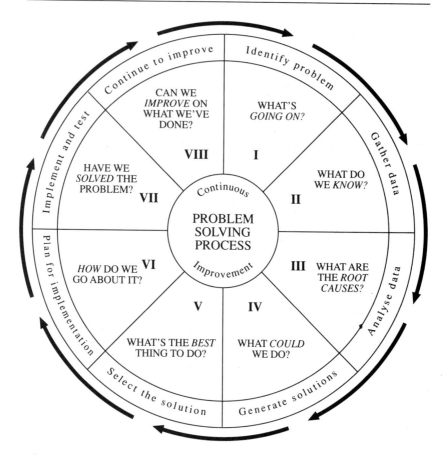

Figure 12.1 Problem-solving circle
© British Telecommunications plc
Reproduced by kind permission

VII, 'Implement and test', I would build in one important step, i.e. 'How do we make it a *permafix* solution?' When a solution has been identified, it is important for the problem-solvers to think in terms of how to make the process *fail-safe*, to resolve the problem *permanently* so that it does not come back again. There will be plenty of new problems, so make sure those you do solve do not come back. That saves you continuously remaking the wheel.

Having a simple problem-solving process gives staff a common language, a routine to follow. Employees in a company as vast as BT (220 000 employees in 1991) begin to feel part of the same team when they recognize the problem-solving cycle in every area of the business. In effect, the company provides the process, but the employees own the problems, the ideas and the solutions. That way you help employees to help you, you make it easy to do the right thing. Once they get into the routine, it simply becomes second nature, just part of 'how we do things around here now'.

ENCOURAGE EMPLOYEE SUGGESTIONS

AIB, Ireland's biggest bank, took a different approach to get all of their employees involved in their Marketing Action Programme. The bank now has outlets in the UK, USA and Europe as well as Ireland, and has ambitious plans for further growth. The basis of their Marketing Action Programme, started in 1986, was 'a long-term commitment to making the transition to being the best in tomorrow's market-place'. Part of that programme was to 'include all our people, to harness the interest, dedication and skills of everyone to the task of becoming the best'. When the bank's Chief Executive, Gerry Scanlan, saw an employee suggestions scheme in operation on a visit to the USA, he decided it was just what he needed to give his own programme a boost.

Their suggestions programme, christened *Superthought*, started in October 1987 and ran for a period of 12 weeks. In a video shown to staff throughout the company Scanlan himself explained the purpose of the scheme, and described some of the prizes that could be won. The programme was operated on a work-team basis at both branches and in the various bank departments. Staff met for one hour a week to discuss their ideas, but often this spread over into their own time. Ideas were submitted in two categories: cost-saving, and enhanced customer service. All 9000 of the bank's employees were involved, with every idea submitted awarded credits depending on its savings or benefits potential. The credits were then exchangeable for gifts at local department stores, while everyone taking part became eligible for a Grand Draw in which the star prize was a brand new car. That certainly generated some interest.

Some 1200 teams were formed, with each of the team leaders having been trained by the bank in how to brainstorm for ideas, and how to present the best of these on the specially designed forms. About 264 part-time evaluators, helped by more than 200 support staff, examined the suggestions and fed back quickly to the teams concerned. The bank expected about 4000 ideas from the programme: they actually got 11 000. The 1800 approved for implementation resulted in a bottom-line contribution of some £12 million. That made the programme worth while by itself. But the excitement the scheme created for three months involved everyone and got them all thinking about their jobs and how they could do them better. That is just the kind of attitude that makes the difference between one bank and another.

CREATE VISIBLE 'NEW ERA' SIGNALS

There are cynics in every business. They have seen it all before, they are the 'I'll believe it when I see it' merchants. They only start to give you credit when they see the signals with their own eyes, when there is visible evidence which touches them in their everyday work. The more these signals line up with each other, making a consistent pattern, the more convinced they become. That is when they jump on board to help you, and the whole drive gathers momentum. The signals need to show in the practical ways outlined in earlier chapters. For example:

Company communications
Your house magazine and notice-boards start carrying items showing the goals in action, celebrating the 'heroes' who show

the flag and set the example. You may have introduced new start-of-the-day meetings where front-line managers get together with their teams to sort out the day's work and where they listen more to employees' points and take prompt action on them. Senior managers may be seen more around front-line areas, listening, conversing, taking interest. Company stationery may carry the new company slogan, knowing that the daily subliminal effect will help support all the other actions being taken across the business.

Training

Remember, you have to answer the employees' question: 'What should I now do differently to what I was doing before?' The answer has to be specific to the job-holder. No one should be beyond training: the refocus of mind-set should affect everyone in the business, from top to bottom. Then when employees see even top management getting into training, they will begin to feel the company is really serious.

Trust

One of the most convincing signals of change for employees is when they are given more genuine responsibility, they are trusted to verify their own product quality, their views are listened to, they are treated like adults, their word is accepted. That kind of change affects them every day, and they start to change their view both about themselves and the company.

Measurement

As we know, companies not only measure what is important, what they start to measure *becomes* important. If the measures are pursued daily, weekly, monthly, employees begin to give the items more attention. That changes habits. If the measures are publicly visible (posted on department walls) that not only raises their profile but urges continuous, steady improvement. If rewards are based on the outcomes of the measures, then of course that reinforces their importance even more.

Rewards

Keep rewarding the behaviour you want to see until it becomes the new habit. Being able to share in the company's financial success is a powerful motivator, but just as important are the non-financial rewards managers use every day, what they regularly stroke and encourage. You will start getting through to the vast majority of the company's employees when front-line managers spend time catching their people doing things right. Step up the volume of things that encourage employees and make them feel good: congratulations letters from the boss, seeing their name in print, awards for achievement, badges of recognition, success celebration parties, using the boss's Rolls Royce. If you use your imagination the list is endless.

Signs of respect

Employees know what you think of them by how you treat them. Don't send them to toilets you would not use yourself, or persuade them to eat or take their breaks in cafeterias you would rather not visit, or work in areas you would never work in or park their cars miles from work. Giving employees daily reminders of your lack of concern does not make them want to be concerned about what is important to you. One of the quick ways to get employees to take notice is to refurbish their toilets, or paint their cafeterias: they will perk up and pay attention long enough for you to start some more fundamental things going.

FOSTER CHAMPIONS

Employees are forever reading the signs of what goes on, of what is valued and rewarded in the business. One useful way of sending messages about what is valued is to foster the champions of the new era, those who carry the message about the new way.

The point was illustrated quite graphically for me when talking to one of the managers in what was formerly Dunlop. The managers there are still the same, but the tyre company is now owned by Sumitomo who are dedicated to the concept of total quality. Mick Sidwell, an Export Manager there, was introduced to the concepts of 'right first time', clean workplace and statistical process control. He could understand all that, it was just common sense, but transferring responsibility to ordinary front-line workers, trusting them to check their own quality, for example, he found much more difficult. He realized it would mean a major style shift in his way of managing. He says he struggled for three months with the changes, and the mental conflict spilled over to his home life. Looking back he now feels 'I was actually guilty of not allowing my people to enjoy their job'.

Then, as he got into running a quality improvement group with his team, be began to enjoy it. He was asked to become a TQ trainer. 'Me? I've never been asked to do anything like this before.' 'Well, now we're asking', said the company. Having to teach the subject to other people is a great way to reinforce commitment, as Sidwell found. He became one of the technique's strongest advocates, and relishes talking about the successes he experienced. 'It has just changed my life,' he says, 'I wasn't even allowed to go and talk to people in other departments under the old regime. Now I'm encouraged to get on and do things.' He says his wife and family have noticed too. 'No one would have asked me to do things like this before, and I wouldn't have had the confidence either. Now I talk to people like you, I stand up in front of audiences, I really look forward to coming to work every day.' When you see the zeal in his eyes, you know he is not kidding. For him the whole thing has been a great turn-on. With enough champions like him around, the rest of the company begins to get pulled along in their wake.

At the beginning champions may be hard to find, of course. It can be like pulling teeth. People seem actively resistant to change. My advice is to start with those who are willing. Give the pioneers every support to make their initial attempts into successes. One or two obvious successes will then do more to convince sceptics than any amount of verbal persuasion. When the onlookers see some managers getting treated like heroes, they will want a slice of the action too. With enough people looking forward to coming to work, and the challenge and excitement it provides, the company will soon be on its way.

ISSUE A CHALLENGE OR TWO

What else can you do to get employees involved? How about setting a challenge or two? Not only does it stimulate employee interest but often produces surprising results. As part of their drive towards excellent customer service, Joshua Tetley, the long-established British brewer, wanted to encourage staff to use customers' names. They created a 100 Club for all those who could both remember the names of 100 customers on sight, and some pertinent facts about them. It is nice to be recognized in your local pub, the company thought, it is the sort of thing that makes customers choose one pub in preference to another. Employees who achieved the feat, and had the fact verified by their manager, were awarded a 100 Club badge. At the last count over 1000 staff in Tetley's 400 pubs had qualified for a 100 badge. But they did not stop there. The company had to go on to produce badges for 250, 500 and 1000 customers personally remembered. One bright lady even managed 2000 names! A pint of Joshua Tetley beer is always very nice, but how much better it tastes in a pub where people actually recognize who you are.

A different type of challenge was thrown down by the MD of a Japanese car company. While on a visit to Volkswagen in West Germany, he discovered that set-ups on their Schiller 1000 ton press took two hours. The process on the same machine in his company was then taking four hours. When he got back to Japan, he immediately challenged his managers to get the die change time down to a figure lower than the Germans. With the help of Shigeo Shingo, formerly Chief Industrial Engineer with Toyota, they managed after six months of trials and hard work to get the time down to an hour and a half. Everyone was happy.

Shingo was astonished when, three months later, the manager of the department phoned him to say the MD had told them he now wanted the changeover time down to three minutes! This is crazy, they thought, it has taken us six months to get it down to an hour and a half. But Shingo was fascinated by the challenge. Could they *really* get it down to three minutes? They realized they could not do it using the old methods – it was going to take quite new concepts to achieve it. Incredibly, though, within a further three months they had done it. The fundamental new concept was to *externalize* as much of the changeover work as possible, so that the amount of work left to do during the machine stoppage time was cut to a minimum. By preparing dies in advance, simplifying bolt clamping mechanisms, introducing stop limits so that the die would automatically be lined up accurately when offered up to the machine, having all the tools and materials close to hand they managed to get the change time down to just three minutes. Quite a feat. Now Shingo's SMED concepts (Single Minute Exchange of Die) are used all over the world.

The MD of the car company explained his approach. 'I always like to cut things in half,' he said. His technique was, for instance, to give instructions for production time to be cut in half. People were taken aback at first, but even so would come up with new ideas and work at them. He would constantly visit the shop and ask how things were going. Progress initially would be slow, but eventually someone would come up with a really great idea, the pace would start to hot up, and sure enough production time would be cut in half. At that point he would thank everyone for their efforts, but three months or so later he would give instructions for the production time to be cut in half again. Despite that being a much more difficult task, eventually they would succeed in cutting the time in half yet again. 'It's funny,' he said, 'people don't think of cutting an hour and a half to an hour as much of a goal, but if you tell them to cut the time to three minutes, then you put them in a desperate state and they come out with real resourcefulness.' It is amazing what a well-placed challenge can do.

CREATE SOME PRESIDENTIAL IMPORTANCE

Different employees are switched on by different tactics, and it is fascinating how many people start taking an interest when they know the president of the company is involved. An Wang, the founder of Wang Laboratories, the international computer business, is well aware of the syndrome. 'The motto "Find a need and fill it" has guided the company for almost all of its history,' he says. 'It's a principle that every employee can understand – you don't need to go to the CEO to have it explained.' Dr Wang does not want any good product idea to get lost somewhere in the hierarchy of the company. So he invented a hotline with which any employee with a good idea can bypass his or her immediate superior, if necessary, and communicate it directly to him. Employees know that the President himself will examine any idea they think is important enough to commit to paper. Dr Wang says modestly: 'The hotline also fosters sensitivity in the way supervisors deal with subordinates.' I'll bet it does.

Another way to send a message round the company, and to get enthusiastic volunteers at the same time, is for the chief executive to put pet projects 'on offer'. One airline chief asked publicly for volunteers to work with him to improve their service versus their competition. He offered no extra inducements or payment but nearly 1 in 10 of the airline's staff immediately offered themselves for the job. Task forces were set up in every area to introduce practical changes which would help them achieve their ambition of being voted best businessman's airline.

Even with many other projects going on at the same time, they achieved their objective within two years. There is nothing to beat the dedication of enthusiastic volunteers, especially if the chief executive is supporting them.

One large petroleum company used a similar technique to staff their task forces. Members of the company were invited to submit ideas to the Directors' Steering Group for new projects which would help the company move towards its new goals. When the directors approved, the proposer would either become project leader or nominate someone else for the job. The leader would then send out a memo describing the project and requesting volunteers with the appropriate skills or experience to take part. The volunteers, having discussed the details with the project leader, would then 'negotiate' with their own manager to make suitable arrangements to take part. The approach has several advantages. The Directors' Steering Group co-ordinates the number of initiatives being undertaken. Their high-level support helps smooth the way to get things done. You identify the champions around the company, the enthusiasts who are your most ardent supporters. Useful interdepartmental relationships are struck up. Project team members learn while solving real problems. Volunteers plus presidential level support: it makes a powerful formula.

LEARN FROM OUTSIDE THE COMPANY

Managers who have worked in the same organization for 20 years or more tend to do the things they have always done. It is all they have known. That is where learning from companies *outside* the organization can have a powerful effect in getting managers to adopt a whole new outlook.

Several years ago, Roger Paine was a Chief Executive in local government in the county of Shropshire in the UK. He relates how he used to lie awake at night and think: 'Why can my employees not eat, sleep and breathe the value of the products we offer like they do in Marks and Spencer?' He decided to get in touch directly with Lord Sieff, who agreed to have one of Paine's senior managers working with them for twelve months in a series of blocks. When the manager came back to talk to the top team about what he had found, they were fascinated, the meetings would go on for hours. They discovered some interesting things. Marks and Spencer do not make their systems and procedures complicated, they keep things nice and simple. They have no great order of information technology, no endless high tech and, above all, they treat their employees with respect and dignity, they make them feel important. All that translates into staff who want to do their best for their customers, every day of the week.

Paine started implementing some of the lessons they learned straight away. With his senior executives behind his efforts, the local authority surveyed their customers for their opinions, they introduced more careful induction of new employees and better training, they promoted 'secondments' where staff could spend time in other departments to broaden their experience. With a group of staff from across the authority they agreed on what were to be their most important values: quality, caring and fairness. To help the transition process along, Paine discouraged memos in favour of people talking directly to each other, and every Monday morning he spent time facing real customers on the council's reception desk. Soon the council's customers began to see the difference: it was not the same place at all. That is how some mind-opening visits to companies you respect can help your change process get off to an energetic start.

LEARN FROM INSIDE THE COMPANY

Motorola, the multinational electronics business, has set itself some taxing product quality objectives, like six sigma quality (less than four defects per million parts produced) by 1992. One of the ways they help themselves reach such far-out objectives is to learn from whoever is doing it best in their own plants, wherever they are in the world. For example, the Motorola plant in Scotland, engaged in the production of microprocessors and silicon chips, exchanges information on cycle time, scrap, yield, and productivity with sister plants elsewhere in the world. Having identified the best performance, their operations managers then meet together every three months or so to pass on how they do it. Motorola have learned one invaluable lesson: not all the great ideas are outside the business; they are right there in your own patch if you just look and learn. The learning is not only cheap, it is directly relevant to your own operations. Once managers start meeting to swop information and learn from each other, that debilitating 'not invented here' syndrome soon becomes irrelevant.

The learning from sister companies is something that the Mars Group has tapped into for some years now. Virtually every function in the business – manufacturing, purchasing, personnel, marketing, research – meet at world-wide and regional conferences to talk and exchange ideas. Some plants have extended the process down to their shop-floor operators. For example, Pedigree Petfoods recently sent 35 manufacturing operators from the UK to their sister units in Germany and France. Naturally, the language barriers were an initial problem, but left to their own devices 'it was amazing', said Manufacturing Director Roger Chatterton, 'how quickly communications were flowing. Operators found they were facing common problems and learning how they each tackled them. When they came back they were eager to try out some of the new ideas.' It creates a bit of excitement when operators get the chance to visit other company operations. Giving operators the task of looking for good ideas while they are there means they get more interested in the job and come back with practical improvements they can apply straight away.

CONGRATULATE AND CELEBRATE

If it feels good to take part, employees will soon want to get involved. That is the message of 'congratulate and celebrate'.

Initially some may disdain badges of recognition from the company, but when they see others being made a fuss of, and wearing their badges with pride, they will soon want one too. As at Four Square, the catering company, they will not only start sporting their badges, complete with bars, but silver ones and gold ones too. It makes people feel good to see their name on the notice-board or their photograph in the company magazine. When people with the Mary Kay organization see the spotlight shining on top performers at their lavish 'Seminar' jamborees, it makes them want to have some of the limelight too. When you take part in a huge celebration party like SAS held when they became Best Airline, the whole company begins to feel like winners.

That is just the feeling one food industry chief wants his employees to have when he throws his theme parties at the end of a successful year. He uses the parties both to thank his employees for all their efforts and to bring them together with executives and staff from the companies they serve. For one party, guests were told to appear in 'Caribbean Dress Only'. As they arrived on a cold, grey evening they found themselves ushered through the entrance of a huge marquee into the atmosphere of a luscious, sweet-smelling tropical island. Asked to remove their overcoats and shoes as they came in, guests found themselves walking on warm white sand while rivulets of water cascaded over mossy rocks into pools filled with beautiful tropical fish. Cocktails were served in coconut shells and scooped out fruit 'cups' from a native hut covered with banana leaves. Jungle sounds could be heard through the luxuriant foliage all around as they sipped their drinks next to flower-covered plants. A steel band played gentle, rhythmic music, and in the warm scented atmosphere guests danced the whole night away. It was a completely different world.

Liz Moberly of *RSVP Events* of London organizes many such parties and insists that you must get the details right. 'It's not enough for the environment just to look right,' she says, 'it must smell and feel right too. It's really got to beat their expectations, blow their minds if you like. They have to be saying ooh! and aah! as often as possible. That is what gives people good feelings and makes the whole thing memorable.' As one marketing manager put it: 'Anything you do – even a staff party – must be a reflection of how you, as a company, do things. If management expect the staff to show attention to detail, they must put the same effort and the same attention to detail into entertaining them.' You don't have to spend the earth, but if you are going to do it, do it in style.

BRINGING PEOPLE TOGETHER

In fact, a party can be useful not just to celebrate success, but to 'unfreeze' a situation where it is proving difficult to get things going. When British Airways took over British Caledonian Airways, who operated out of Gatwick Airport rather than Heathrow, there was a turbulent time trying to merge the two companies together when morale fell to a low ebb. To help give staff confidence in the new company's future, BA decided to throw a series of 18 Christmas parties involving every member of staff and all their partners, some 7000 people in all. Guests were bussed to a secret destination (actually a disused hangar at Gatwick old heliport), entering first through a science fiction walkway into a large geodesic dome. There, video screens hung from the roof showed a film of Gatwick's history, and only moved from black and white into full colour at the point when BA and Caledonian merged. Having moved into the large auditorium next door, there was a half-hour presentation from senior management on the problems they were all facing and the solutions they were planning. Then suddenly the atmosphere and lighting changed and the huge stage revolved to reveal a spectacular night-club setting. A twenty-piece orchestra appeared, there was a cabaret show, and a song and dance group sang the party's theme for the evening, *Celebration.*

All guests were then treated to a great slap-up meal, and just as they thought the evening was coming to an end, the General

Manager announced,: 'You ain't seen nothin' yet!' As a finale everyone stopped dancing to join in singing Christmas songs together, while snow cascaded down from the roof and a 45-foot Christmas tree rose up through the dance floor. It was quite spectacular, and quite touching. The event certainly left its mark. 'A great morale-booster', said one member of the staff as she left. 'It was incredible. I just feel uplifted,' said another. It is difficult not to be friends with your neighbours when you are having great fun together, when you have your arms round shoulders singing carols. There is no doubt that the event helped set BA at Gatwick on their way. *Imagination*, the London company who conceived the event for BA, say you do not have to spend huge sums of money to get the right effects. The food company boss, who arranged the Caribbean party for his people and some of their customers, says: 'The difference in cost between giving a good ordinary party and a good theme party is not so enormous. If it is done properly it creates great excitement and the mood is totally different. If people really have fun together it is extremely helpful over a very long period.'

SOME FINAL WORDS OF ADVICE

Not everything is going to work

Not everyone will be turned on by the same things. You have to expect disappointments. Attitudes which have grown up over years can be notoriously difficult to shift. Just keep going, keep trying, and eventually you will get there.

Do not attempt too many things at once

There are so many things you could do – and the ideas given in this chapter are by no means exhaustive – that it is tempting to set off too many initiatives in a wave of initial enthusiasm. Going suddenly from nothing to an all-singing, all-dancing programme may come as a shock to the system to many. The sheer volume can cause serious indigestion, so take it step by step.

Aim for early success

It is very important that the first few things you introduce are seen to succeed. In the minds of employees that early success will help to convince them that the new ideas are 'a good thing', and give them the confidence to join in. For example, if a pilot scheme is tried in one area, is given a lot of management attention and is seen to succeed, those in adjacent departments will soon be asking when they can take part too. Remember that willing volunteers to the cause are worth a lot more than conscripts.

Do the simple things first

Do not give yourself more chances of failing by biting off more than you can chew: that will simply convince people that 'it is never going to work here'. Plan it all out, in detail, and know in advance what you will do if this happens or that happens. When you succeed with the first initiatives, you will then get a lot more support.

Start with those who are committed

Not only do they give you the best chance of success, they will be your walking advertisements in the offices, the cafeteria, in meetings, and in the car going to and from work. Leave the sceptics and the cynics till later when you have solid evidence of success.

Support your champions

When you see a beautiful plant growing, nurture it, water it, feed it and protect it. Soon there will be plants like it growing all over the garden.

Keep some good shots for the next phase

Initial enthusiasm fades, so you will need to bring on another initiative to keep the momentum going. Each new wave will help to drive the message deeper and convince employees that the new way is here to stay. Also, some are early joiners, some are late joiners. Different concepts switch on different people. Keep going till you have convinced them all.

KEY POINTS SUMMARY

- In most businesses 85 per cent or more of employees are non-managers. Only when the habits and behaviour of that majority are affected, culture change really begins to take hold.
- Create impact with a launch event. Make it unusual, attention-grabbing and fun. Give participants something active to do as soon as they get back to work.
- Get employees involved in problem-solving. Give them a step by step routine they can follow. With company support, they will take on ownership for problems in their own area . . . and get them solved.
- Encourage employees' suggestions. Evaluate their ideas quickly, and give credit where it is due.
- To convince employees, signals of the 'new era' have to show through in every aspect of the business: in your communications, your training courses, the delegating of real responsibility, in what you measure, what you reward and in the respect you show your employees.
- Foster your champions. They are walking, talking advertisements for the new era.
- Issue a challenge or two: make them think. Quantum leap challenges can often plumb depths of resourcefulness that employees themselves did not know were there.
- Create some presidential importance. Projects take on a different meaning when they are seen to be close to the president's heart.
- Learn from outside the company. Open up minds by sending both managers and staff out to see how it is done elsewhere.
- There are lessons to be learned right in your own backyard.

Set up mechanisms to make it easy for staff to learn from each other.

- When employees achieve some success, congratulate them. Use celebrations to say thank you, to bring people together, to make the whole company feel like winners.
- Start with the simple things and succeed the first time round. Begin with those who are enthusiastic and leave the sceptics till later. Keep some shots in your locker for the next wave. Changing culture is a long journey.

13

The most likely reasons for failure–and the antidotes

There are always going to be problems in implementing culture change, always things to go wrong. It is rather like a voyage of discovery: it involves vision, risk and determination. You have to think of yourself rather like Christopher Columbus. You are deliberately sailing off on an exciting journey; you may well reach places no one has ever been before – indeed, that is exactly what you are hoping for. You can anticipate there will be hazards, rocks to avoid, winds to blow you off course, but despite it all, you are determined to press ahead. A few people will wonder why you are doing it; they may think you are a bit mad even to start. But there is no excitement in doing what you have always done, no sense of achievement. You can take advice from other experienced sailors, but even then you know you will be sailing sometimes in uncharted waters, and meeting situations you have never encountered before. However, the prize is such that you are prepared to take the risk.

I can help a little on this management journey, but even with that advice there will be situations you did not bargain for. I cannot list everything that could go wrong, but I can warn you of some of the worst hazards. And to a great extent, forewarned is forearmed . . . .

LOOKING FOR QUICK-FIX ANSWERS

There are no quick-fix answers. Don't let anyone persuade you that there are. You may solve a problem with a campaign, or create an awareness with a training programme, but that is not changing the culture of the business in a widespread and permanent way. Real culture change takes time.

At Motorola's Scottish plant in East Kilbride, Dominic Reilly is the manager of the Six Sigma programme, the vehicle of the company's culture shift world-wide, designed to take them to record levels of quality performance. The programme started there around 1988. 'One thing you have to learn in the business of getting culture change is patience,' says Dominic. 'I got very frustrated at first, I couldn't seem to get anything rolling. Anyone who says they can do it in a year just hasn't been there.' They first set up a Steering Group with the heads of every department in the company and agreed on their overall programme goals. Each department then set itself specific targets as their first steps on the road to achieving six sigma performance. They developed lists of action items and had periodic reviews of results. They set up some fifty Area Improvement Teams around the business. Despite all that work, Reilly reckons it took 18 months before he started to see real evidence of the programme taking hold, of departments taking the *spirit* of the changes to heart and becoming self-starters in the change process.

ANTIDOTE

Do not expect overnight success. Have patience. Figure 13.1 shows what Reilly thinks happens in the change process.

Some departments take to the changes very quickly and soon start introducing improvements. Others take time or appear to drag their feet. Continuing operational priorities tend to crowd out managers' attention to the programme objectives because there is still a lot of rushing around, doing all the things they

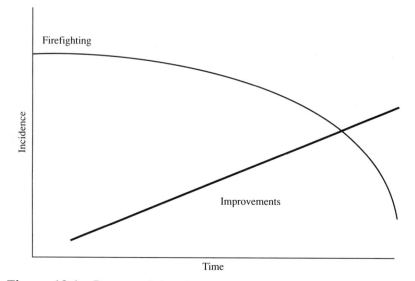

Figure 13.1 Pattern of the change process

did before. The urgent defeats the important. You begin to despair that the necessary attitude changes will ever take hold. But as you foster the early champions and publicize the successes, gradually more and more areas come on board. The whole thing begins to dig in. Eventually the planned improvement process takes over from the firefighting, and the old kick and rush syndrome begins to recede. That is when you know the new systems are becoming routine, just part of 'how we do things round here'.

GOAL-SETTING PROBLEMS

Of course, the obvious and worst problem is not setting any goals. Therafter, the most common problems are: setting too many, choosing goals which are not actionable by all employees, and lack of constancy.

Setting too many

The greatest temptation when setting out to change attitudes and the culture of the business is wanting to put everything right at once. That simply guarantees dissipation of your efforts. The fundamentally important point here is that the task is not to cover all the bases, or to make it look good on paper, but to change behaviour, to change the outlook and habits of everyone in the organization. That demands *concentration*, single-mindedness of purpose, long-term commitment. You may choose to please corporate head office with your 'mission statement', to include points which will charm the chairman, but that does not change employee behaviour. The more long-winded you become, the less chance you have of succeeding.

ANTIDOTE

Go for one key goal. It is hard, but try. With everyone in the organization putting their collective weight behind it, movement will *definitely* take place. Limit yourself to three goals at the most: clearly the more you spread your effort, the less likely you are to achieve remarkable results. And that is the goal of the culture change: remarkable results. Don't worry about all the other possible objectives you have to leave out. Work will continue on these anyway. It is important that when the pressure is on, everyone knows where the priority lies.

Not actionable by all employees

If only managers feel themselves activated by the goals of the business, then they are going to have to shove the other 90 per cent of employees into taking part. That weight of inertia and indifference is just too great to move. The goals need to be understood and supported by all employees so that they can do something active towards them every day they are at work. The crucial factor that makes any group of people into a team is a shared goal. Without that shared goal they can never be a team.

ANTIDOTE

Only establish culture change goals where you know every employee will be able to make their personal contribution towards it every day.

Lack of constancy

Moving the goalposts seems to be a favourite management pastime. If one initiative does not work, they get impatient and try another . . . or they are seduced by the sweet talk of the latest group of consultants they speak to. 'What next?' employees say, 'Not another flavour of the month. We've seen it all before.' As a result, employees hold off with their commitment until they see management is actually going to stay with it.

ANTIDOTE

If you cannot see yourself still doing it three years from now, just don't start. Employees will become supporters only when management demonstrates constancy of purpose.

PROBLEMS AT TOP MANAGEMENT LEVEL

Lack of Commitment

The fatal flaw. This kills more change programmes than any other factor. 'If big boss is not committed, why should we be?' say employees. Commitment in this case means showing enthusiasm, talking incessantly about the goals dear to your heart, not being discouraged by the inevitable problems and setbacks, sticking with it through thick and thin. Employees do not listen as much to the words that you say, as watch what you do. It is not the words that count, it is *the example*.

ANTIDOTE

Don't be persuaded to start with something you do not truly believe in because your people will find you out.

No follow-up

On a recent visit to a manufacturing company, I spoke to a machine operator who was not very happy. 'Management has been going on at us about the need for good quality. In fact, I went to a training course on this SPC,' he said, 'I thought it was a good idea. But I've filled in this chart for weeks now and nobody has ever asked me anything about it. They just don't seem to be serious.' That kind of experience is poison to any new programme. Naturally he will tell his mates, and very soon they will conclude that it is all just for show.

ANTIDOTE

Follow up religiously. What convinces employees it is really important to the company, is that management at all levels are seen to be devoting their time, their effort, their attention and their money to it. You do not need to shout and preach, just follow up.

Expecting instant results

Let's face it, the pressure on many managements to concentrate on the next quarter's results inevitably makes them think short-term. They might not be there for long if they don't. The culture message is: we do not want results next year, we want them *now*. But culture change is not about baking an instant cake. It is about growing a plant, and it takes preparation, the right conditions, and careful nurture to get it to flower. But we have to make money too. So, how do we balance the two?

ANTIDOTE

Write longer-term goals about where exactly you want to be, say, in three years' time. Make the goals specific, and measurable. Then agree specific milestone targets for the intervening years, so that if you have to accommodate short-term needs, the steps you take will all be in the right direction. Initially, it will feel like the graph shown in Fig. 13.1, with lots of the old behaviour and firefighting still going on. But, be patient. Gradually, as the improvements you introduce take hold, so the firefighting will subside, and a new and calmer culture will develop. Certainly, it will not all be sweetness and light, but it will definitely be a world you prefer.

Conflicting management priorities

No single thing is the most important all the time – not even your culture change programme. Priorities change from day to day. However, if you have spent effort and money on a high-profile launch, it is important to treat any initial related projects with the highest priority. One British company who launched a Just-In-Time programme, for example, set up several high-level project teams to examine their purchasing systems and inventory control. Having put in several months of hard work, the first team to report to the board had some novel ideas to propose. They were all keyed up and ready to go, but after spending most of the day hanging around outside the board room, their presentation was eventually deferred. They were quite deflated. Having earlier been told their project was of vital importance to the business, the board were now obviously saying: 'We have more important business to attend to'. Another date was fixed up, of course, but unfortunately that day a bubble burst: their work was important, but not *that* important.

ANTIDOTE

It is hard enough to generate enthusiasm in employees for new ways of operating, so do not kill it when you've got it. If the company has declared a new 'highest priority', it has to be seen to be treating it that way, especially at the beginning. Rekindling enthusiasm is like reheated food – it is never as good.

LACK OF TOP MANAGEMENT CONTROL

If the authority and control of top management is not applied to the change programme, things can go badly awry. Here are some of the more common problems that can occur.

Inconsistent management action

One large UK manufacturing company attempted very seriously to introduce a team-work culture within its business. Indeed, as a launch programme, each department in the business was given time off-site as a work group to come up with a set of *team* objectives, which would be their measurable contribution to the company's drive for improved performance. Action lists for every department were approved directly by the MD and published. At the same time, personnel department had been conducting a staff job evaluation programme, and also had plans to introduce a new appraisal system. Under pressure from personnel at corporate head office, both were put into effect. The new job-evaluated grades upset a lot of people: indeed appeals were lodged by staff in every department. The new appraisal system had money awards attached, but they were related to *individual* rather than *team* performance, and extra pay awards were confined to only the 'top 20 per cent' in every area. Naturally, the other 80 per cent were not too pleased. 'Where is all this team-work now?' they asked. It just looked as if the right hand did not know what the left hand was doing.

Be careful that when you first start out in your chosen new direction, that other changes do not go ahead which effectively contradict your new goals or alienate the very people you need to have on your side. It may seem obvious, even ridiculous, but believe me it does happen. Life elsewhere in the business goes on and you need to make sure your special efforts are not sabotaged before you get off the ground.

Delegating too far

Often with the best of intentions senior management will establish a new full-time position, e.g. total quality manager, or customer service programme manager, to raise the profile of the new drive, and indicate their degree of seriousness. However, in too many cases this becomes a way for managing directors to get the responsibility off their desk, to be relieved of any feelings of guilt on the subject so that they can get back to doing what they have always done (i.e. the really important things). If things do not go particularly well, they can always blame the programme manager for the lack of progress. That scenario is a disaster for any change programme.

About a year ago, for example, I visited a company who had recently succeeded in qualifying for the British Standards Institute 5750 certification. It is not a particularly easy qualification to get. To succeed, companies have to document all their quality procedures in detail and satisfy the Institute's auditors in 19 different sections of examination. The company had made special efforts to qualify, but now their quality manager was in despair. Behind his head, lined up on clipboards on his office wall, were the lists of quality faults which had been reported to each division, but on which no remedial action had been taken. Faults that were still unattended to after second promises were highlighted in luminous pen. 'I'm tearing my hair out here,' said the Manager, 'no one is paying any attention. If the auditor visited us now we'd be thrown out immediately.'

ANTIDOTE

You cannot simply endow some middle manager with a new title and leave it at that. People round the business then give the matter mere lip service, and treat the new drive with disdain. The urge and commitment has to start – *and remain* – at the top of the business. Otherwise, it just does not work. As one company boss, who is right in the middle of a very successful change programme, told me: 'The biggest lesson I have learned is that the champions of change have to be the top team. If you've not got it there, you've not got it.'

Lack of top-level power behind the programme

If there is no senior body to report to, or to co-ordinate the whole drive, efforts to change become patchy and unco-ordinated, and the programme often ends up as a frustrating mess.

ANTIDOTE

From the start, establish a top-level Steering Group, preferably with the chief executive as chairman. Major project teams should report there to show their work has behind it the highest authority in the business. Team members should *tingle* before they present, because it is seen as that important, that serious. The Steering Group needs to have the authority to say 'yes' to proposals, to make things happen. They need to oversee all that is going on, to plan the change calendar, and to say 'no' to the things that do not fit. This is not a mere training programme, it is a drive to change the habits and character of the whole business.

MIDDLE MANAGEMENT RESISTANCE

Middle managers, who know the ropes, have ways of frustrating even the most straightforward initiatives. One large British utility visited IBM to get their advice on how they could use communications to help change attitudes within their company. As a result of the IBM inputs, the company decided to make a video programme which would explain to all employees the thinking behind their new objectives. They were very surprised after several weeks of showing throughout the business that the video appeared to be creating no impact at all. Middle managers, who had been told to show the video to all employees, had decided it would have to be viewed by staff after work, in their own time. As a result, less than 10 per cent had actually seen it. The first reaction of managers who feel vulnerable is to dilute the effect of anything that might upset the *status quo*, to preserve the old world which they know and love. You need to show the managers how they can succeed in the new world as well as the old.

ANTIDOTE

- Spell out exactly with managers how you see their role needs to change. Generally, they want to help. Show them exactly how.
- Early in the process get them to work out specific actions which they and their team can take to advance the company's new goals. Any resistance will diminish as soon as they take on a sense of ownership for the changes.
- Involve them in multidisciplined project groups, where they actually propose actions to implement the 'new way'.
- Use the evidence of personal survey feedback (as described in Chapter 6) to reveal their own attitudes and encourage change.

EMPLOYEE RESISTANCE

A traditional British industry with dyed-in-the-wool attitudes, and multi-trade unions is a daunting prospect for any manager bent on change. That is the way it was in one large plant of a UK metal products manufacturer. They decided to use a drive to create a just-in-time manufacturing process as a vehicle for change. Some employee groups were downright truculent: they certainly were not going to change. Others used the opportunity to press for more money: 'What is it going to be worth if we co-operate?' they said. These kinds of responses can make you want to give up before you start.

Companies should realize, however, that the overwhelming feeling created among employees faced with major change is *insecurity*. Will I have to start learning new skills at my age? Will I be any good? Can I really cope with all this computerized stuff? Will I be demoted, lose money? Will I lose my job even? These feelings often preoccupy their minds so much that they cannot even listen to what is being proposed; it is almost as if they do not want to listen. This is the time for sensitivity, understanding, and step by step progress.

ANTIDOTE

- Offer an undertaking of no compulsory redundancy as a result of internal changes introduced by the company. Remove their worst fears right up front. You may have to institute a programme of *voluntary* separation so that those who do choose to go leave with a sweet taste in their mouth. You do not want feelings of resentment and aggression clouding the start of your programme. Make the first associations positive.
- Start simple, with those who are willing. Do not bite off some major project to start with, and fail. That serves to convince everyone that the initiative is 'never going to work here'. Early success is absolutely crucial, so only start with

something you know has at least an 80 per cent chance of success. That gives you something solid to build on, and helps to give everyone confidence.

- Use colleagues to persuade others. As one mechanic from the company mentioned above said: 'There was a lot of resistance at first here. When I started to take part, some said: "Look at that creep". But when we started to score some goals, then everybody wanted to play.'
- Publish successes, celebrate heroes.
- Train, encourage and reward, assiduously.

LACK OF 'STRUCTURE SHIFT'

Training is useful to impart new knowledge, to open employees' eyes to how they can be more effective in the job. Yet if all the systems and procedures in use in the business remain unchanged (i.e. the systems that produced the behaviour you have now), then gradually employee behaviour will revert to the old ways. To make the initial behaviour change permanent, you need *structure shift*. By structure shift I mean changes, for example, in:

- The organization structure (new reporting relationships, new responsibilities, new job titles)
- Procedures (new steps to follow, new charts to fill in)
- Documentation (different documents, different information formats)
- Measures (new data to collect, to be fed back, and followed up)
- Rewards system (different job evaluation categories, new appraisal system, bonus arrangements attached to perform-ance measures)

By themselves, the effects of training, will gradually fade. But there are antidotes. To help *permanize* the effects, implement structure shifts which will make it easy to adopt the new style, make the new behaviour automatic.

ANTIDOTES

- Change the organization and reporting relationships. At can-maker CMB Aerosols in the UK Midlands, the company removed two layers of middle management as a way of streamlining their operation and pushing more decision-making responsibility down to the shop-floor. Team leaders were trained before the event, but the major reason front-line employees started taking more on-the-spot operational decisions is that there were simply no layers above to consult. They just had to get on with it. Now the company is getting record productivity and quality from the plant.
- Transfer responsibility – completely. If you want operators to make it right first time for the customer, get rid of the quality checkers. Trust them to do the whole job right first time. If you want front-line managers to make to schedule, get rid of the progress chasers. Ask the managers to sign off the schedule at the beginning of the week and then make meeting schedule the key part of the job.
- Make procedures changes. Give production operators statistical process control charts to complete on their own operations, to keep up quality. Get production teams to fill in their own output charts and publish them on the wall.
- Introduce new measures which focus attention. Avis has been 'trying harder' for decades, but their recently introduced customer service measures certainly sharpened up their performance.
- Change the rewards system. Rank Xerox altered management thinking dramatically by making management bonuses directly dependent on their customer survey satisfaction scores.

TRAINING PROBLEMS

Skimping

It all seems so short-sighted, but it happens a lot. Top management go off for several 'working weekends' at a nice hotel, but front-line employees have to use one end of the cafeteria, or the corner of the safety training room. 'We cannot afford to spend all that money. Things are very tight at the moment', they say. Initially, NatWest Bank spent about £100 per head training their people and getting them into making early changes. If it is not worth that to you then don't start, you are just not serious. You may save yourself some money, but you will not change behaviour much.

ANTIDOTE

Treat the training not as a cost but as an *investment*. Combined with the other steps laid out in this book, the pay-off will simply swamp any initial costs. If you are going to do it, do it well. By all means make sure you get every last drop of benefit out of the spending, but don't skimp.

Poor planning

If trainees are just taken from any department willing to send them, it may take months for everyone in any department to be trained. By that time early trainees will have lost their initial enthusiasm, and the whole thing will become haphazard and ineffective.

ANTIDOTE

Do the training area by area in a systematic fashion. Ensure that *everyone*, including the manager, is covered in any department within a defined and short space of time. Make sure other departments know exactly where they come in the planned training calendar – that will prevent them fretting in the meantime.

No follow-up

The faults that occur most often here are: trainees do not have specific actions to take in connection with the training as soon as they get back to work; or their managers have not been primed to use their training as soon as they return.

ANTIDOTE

Build in post-event action steps to all the training you give. Also, one-shot training will get you off the ground, but it is hardly enough. You will almost certainly have to give further training injections over time, so plan, at least in outline, your possible second or third training modules.

PROBLEMS OF COMPANY SIZE

There is no question that the bigger the company, and the longer established, the harder it is to change the culture. Huge utilities in the UK like British Telecom, the Post Office, and British Rail have all found it a daunting task to move their companies' well-established cultural habits. Sir Leonard Peach, IBM's UK Personnel Director, has a favourite response when visitors to his company ask him what is the most important factor in developing a culture like theirs. 'Start thirty years ago,' he says. Yes, it takes time, but do not let that be a reason for not starting at all. At first, it can be very frustrating. You may see little or no effect from spending a lot of time, effort and money. You begin to think it is going to be impossible to move the habits of a lifetime. But stay with it, eventually the big ship will begin to turn. And when it does, it will travel just as strongly as before in the new direction.

ANTIDOTES

- Start with a pilot area, with someone who is already an enthusiast. Give the group's efforts every possible support. Make sure you get an early success. Talk about them, publicize their achievements, reward their success, but do not shove it down everybody else's throat by insisting they do the same.
- Rather set a few challenges: 'Think you can do better than that?' Some will definitely rise to the challenge, and produce a 'We'll show them!' performance. Again talk about them, publicize them, show what is valued around the company.
- Transfer ownership. Ask every department to meet and decide what they are going to do specifically to advance the company's new goals in their area. Get them to articulate their commitments to an authoritative group, e.g. a Steering Group. Do not accept half-hearted suggestions. If you are not happy, send them back to 'think again'.
- Follow up. Conduct regular reviews of where each team has got to. Make sure the reviews are 'high-status'. Do not put up with half-hearted efforts.
- Use a new common language or system. It does not matter whether this is Total Quality, Computer-Integrated Manufacturing, Putting Customers First, Just-In-Time, or whatever: it depends on what is appropriate for your business. The important points here are that it is *new* (it causes the adoption of new behaviour, a new culture) and it is *common* (the new language promotes common cause and understanding across the company).
- Measure, and publish. Introduce measures with feedback of results to every department. Keep asking about them, follow up.
- Conduct successive waves of activity. You will not change a large company's culture with one big blast; it is anything from a 3- to 10-year task. So assume there will be successive waves of training, further sophistication of your

originally modest systems, improving performance with experience and breakthroughs from time to time on which you can build. Add some excitement with a relaunch, a high-profile competition, a Quality 'Olympics' or similar event.

- Communicate, communicate, communicate. Keep the issue in employee minds via house publications, notice-boards, team meetings, videos, senior management visits, projects, etc. Treat your programme like a new consumer product: keep singing your product's praises, and keep it constantly in the pubic eye until it gets substantial market share.

LACK OF PERSISTENCE

After lack of genuine management commitment, this is the element that causes most culture change programmes to fail. The tendency to expect instant results, to give up and move on to something else before you have exhausted the first initiative is both strong and widespread. There is always some seductive new idea to tempt one, some new fad which will make you look up to date and 'with it'. If it happens to fit, *integrate* it into your efforts, but do not let it redirect the whole company. If it does not fit, kick it firmly into touch.

There will be obstacles, prophets of doom and corporate nit-pickers. 'Do you see what they are doing at ABC plant? They could do with a bit more old-fashioned discipline instead of all these arty training courses, if you ask me.' 'Well they tried this over in XYZ company, and it didn't work there.' 'Never Mind all this stuff about attitudes and culture: keep your eyes on the numbers, boy, that's what you're getting paid for.' There will be all of that, and more. That is why you have got to be convinced about the path you have taken, because when people are talking about you and casting aspersions at head office your resolve will be severely tested. The results will come through if you stick with it, but they are guaranteed not to come through if you give up.

ANTIDOTE

Don't launch out till you know your chosen new direction is what you really want to do, what you are convinced about and what you are going to stick with. 'Hose down' those with unreasonable early expectations, especially those at head office. If anything, underclaim and overdeliver. Go for modest but early success, and build gradually and steadily on that. Remind yourself, when you do get the moans, groans or disappointments, that you did expect that. Take it all as just part of the game, and keep going. Columbus had to weather a few storms getting to his destination. So will you.

KEY POINTS SUMMARY

- There are no quick-fix answers. Don't let anyone persuade you that there are. There is no magic key either. If there were, we would all use it. Real culture change involves vision, risk, determination and time.
- Avoid setting too many goals, making them only actionable by managers, and falling prey to moving the goalposts every year. Clear focus and constancy of purpose will get employees joining you in support.
- Lack of genuine commitment and follow-up by top management is the most common and serious deficiency in creating culture change. Only start out if you have true, heart-felt conviction. Do not expect instant results, take at least a three-year view. Do not let the urgent eclipse the important long-term projects.
- Top management have to stay very much in control of the change programme. Inconsistent management actions in the business may simply convince employees you have not got your act together. Project leaders should report to the top team. A 'programme manager' without top management authority will not have the power to make things happen.

- Middle management can help or hinder the initiatives. Spell out their new role, and get them actively engaged in the process.
- Employee resistance will largely stem from feelings of insecurity. Address these worries directly. Start with those employees who are most willing, and build on early successes.
- Consciously, step by step, introduce 'structure shift', i.e. changes in your organization, procedures, documentation, measures and reward systems which will make old habits inappropriate and encourage the new behaviours you most want to see.
- Skimping on training is just false economy. Plan it systematically, and follow up all training with post-event action steps.
- The older and bigger the company, the longer it takes to bring about culture change. The following then become even more important: have a clear goal, use a common language, set challenges, transfer ownership, measure constantly, and follow up. Assume you will need successive waves of activity over several years, and communicate constantly.
- It is not easy. It takes clear vision and persistence. But remember Columbus. He changed everyone's view of the world. On a smaller scale, you can do the same in your company.

14

What it is like in companies who know their goals

One always hesitates to proffer examples of companies who are doing it well, for fear that readers will mistake them somehow as paradigms of perfection. They are not perfect. The people who work there would be the first to say so. They know from the inside all their little foibles and imperfections. Certainly they are 'excellent', in the original Latin root sense of the word of 'flying above', in the dictionary sense of 'surpassing others', and they work hard at staying that way. From that point of view they are worth observing, worth emulating as they show characteristics from which we all can learn.

Although there are other organizations that could qualify to appear here, I have chosen three particular companies. They are: Kwik-Fit, Mars Confectionery and Linn Products. They are all quite different in their style of operation, and in the products and services they offer yet they all display similar characteristics.

THE DISTINGUISHING FACTORS

Firstly, they have all *got their act together*. They know how they are, what they are and why they are. The fabric of their culture is 'all of a piece'; it all fits together. The people in the business talk about it as if it is all quite understandable, like it all makes sense. They may get slightly embarrassed if you talk about some anomaly or other, but it does not stop their understanding of the dominant character of the place. It is just like Blackpool rock: the message you get at the top is the message you get all the way through.

Secondly, they are quite *distinctive*. They are very much themselves, they haven't slavishly copied anyone else. That does not mean to say they do not learn from anyone else, quite the contrary. They learn and develop all the time, but they do it very much in their own style. Linn Products, for example, where staff wear all kinds of casual dress, would not want to copy Mars Confectionery who provide white workwear for all their people. It would not fit their style. But they are both very effective at what they do. And of course not everyone takes to these styles. Some new starts at Linn have left after only a few days and some executive types have refused to join Mars when the company insisted that they had to clock in like everybody else. But the companies don't worry unduly about that, they don't try to be all things to all men. They just say: 'He wasn't a Mars-type person'. They think it is important to take on people who will fit the culture.

Thirdly, they *believe in themselves*. Employees are not pussyfooting or apologetic when talking about their company's policies. They have no trouble defending them because fundamentally they think they are right. You have no doubt when you talk to Tom Farmer of Kwik-Fit that he is wholly committed to the aim of '100 per cent customer satisfaction'. He believes in it. Staff at Linn know there is a Linn way of doing things, and they not only defend it, they rejoice in it.

Fourthly, *their beliefs shape their behaviour*. Mars *think* single status. They would never think of introducing a policy or benefit which could not apply on an equal basis to all its people. That is the way it is at Mars, that is how they do things. Kwik-Fit would never think of introducing new products or services to the company if they did not think they could regularly deliver '100 per cent customer satisfaction'. It is just too important for their reputation with their customers and their own self-esteem.

Fifthly, their culture *stands the test of time*. Founders and chief executives come and go, but the culture lives on. That is because it proves its worth in the good times and the bad. It acts like an anchor in the stormy times, and it fills the sails when the weather is favourable. This is no flavour-of-the-month fad, it is part of the permanent character of the company. It influences both thought and action from top to bottom in the organization.

Now to the companies themselves.

KWIK-FIT

Kwik-Fit, which operates a chain of tyre and exhaust fitting centres, is now the biggest company of its kind in Europe. It has expanded from some 213 outlets in 1981 to around 600 in 1991. These are spread throughout the UK and Ireland, with about 120 located in Holland and Belgium. Sales during that time have risen from £27 million to £229 million, corresponding profits from £4 million to £24 million. The company also includes in its services the fitting of batteries, radiators and shock absorbers, and is expanding its activities with 'menu priced' brake replacement and other car servicing items.

The early days

Tom Farmer, the current Chairman and founder, started his first tyre replacement business way back in 1964, in a corner shop in Edinburgh. There he early learned the value of good publicity. Because he was selling at a discount, the bigger boys were making it difficult for him to get tyres. He confided to a journalist who promptly wrote up his story in a national Sunday newspaper. When he turned up at his shop after church that Sunday to see if there was anyone around, a queue of 42 cars was waiting for him to open. The company was on its way. In fact, it did so well, Farmer sold out to Albany Tyres for some £400 000 in 1968. After two years as a director with the company, Farmer decided to leave with his family for America.

Having settled in San Francisco, Farmer played the part of leisured retiree, but the style did not suit him. One evening his wife sat him down and persuaded him he needed some future purpose to his life, and as often happens when your partner tells you some home truths, he realized she was right. They returned to Scotland after only six months. In the meantime, of course, Tom had added to his own knowledge by observing customer service US-style, in particular their advertising, their quick service offers, their guarantees, their catchy names and the rest. As he was prevented by contract for a period from setting up a rival tyre replacement company back in the UK, he set up Kwik-Fit to carry out exhaust replacements, and recruited several of his old staff to help him. Many of them are still with him today.

Company philosophy

It was back in 1972 that Tom Farmer wrote:

> At Kwik-Fit the most important person is the customer and it must be the aim of us all to give 100 per cent customer satisfaction 100 per cent of the time. Our continued success depends on the loyalty of our customers. We are committed to offering them the best value for money with a fast, courteous and professional service. We offer the highest quality products and guarantees.
>
> We at Kwik-Fit realize that our people are our most valuable asset. The Kwik-Fit people at our centres are the all-important contact with the customers and they are the key to the success of the Kwik-Fit Group.

Today these philosophies still drive the company. Their slogan 'Our aim is 100 per cent customer satisfaction' is seen everywhere in the company: it is plastered all over their depots, written on every invoice, it appears at the top of the company's headed paper, and in their annual report. It pervades the business. And both staff and customers know the company means it. Tom Farmer looks down from posters in every depot telling them so and offering to put right any problem. Attached to every invoice is a postage paid, tear-off card asking customers for their comments on the service they received, with Farmer's Edinburgh address on the back. No depot wants to hear about a customer complaint from Tom Farmer.

John Clark, Director of Operations, tells a story which sums up the company's attitude to its customers. He once received a complaint letter written on a brown paper bag. It came from a miner who said he was losing money by not getting to work on time as a result of dud batteries supplied by the company. John travelled up to Glenrothes to see the man, and the address led him to a row of miners' cottages. He could see no car outside but knocked on the door anyway. A man in his fifties appeared dressed only in his long underwear, who, when he heard why Clark had come, invited him in. The house was in a terribly untidy state. Above the cooker the wallpaper had gone crumpled and dark brown, while coal spilled out of a hall cupboard. The man shoved the dog off the couch to let his visitor sit down, and offered him a cup of tea in an old mug. Clark learned the man's wife had died and his children had emigrated. He now lived all on his own. When they later went outside to examine the car, he discovered it was a three-wheeled Reliant Robin kept in a small shed close to the house. Clark took the battery away, and discovered it *was* dud – the test equipment at the depot was faulty. He not only fitted a new battery, he gave the man his card and told him to phone him direct if he had any further problems. The man still uses their depot today. By putting himself about, Clark had in fact turned a customer, however humble, into a walking advert for the company.

Advertising and marketing

The company recognizes the value of good advertising. When in 1985 TV adverts for the company showed fitters in blue overalls performing little dances and singing 'You can't get better than a Kwik-Fit fitter', the jingle took a trick with the public. In surveys not only did more than 90 per cent of the public recognize the slogan, comedians started using it in their routines too. Now fitters carry the words on the back of their overalls, a daily reminder of their key role in making good their reputation.

Kwik-Fit realize that no one wakes up in the morning and says: 'What a lovely day, I must buy myself a new exhaust system'. It is a 'distress purchase', as they say. So, in an industry which has had a reputation for poor service and workmanship, Kwik-Fit not only undertakes to beat any competitive price, they try to make the experience as trouble free as possible. Peter Holmes, the company's Marketing Director, says the important factors for customers are: the product price, convenience of depots, immediate availability of stock, good service and guarantees. Of some 220 000 jobs completed each month, some 350 or so customers forward queries and complaints, which are quickly followed up. They also conduct regular customer telephone surveys to test their quality. To reinforce their own reputation the company has now introduced own brand products, 'Centaur', on which they offer extra guarantees and 'no quibble' money-back undertakings.

Clear rules, clear procedures

The company realizes that it is their people out in the centres who make or break their reputation. As a result, they do not call their office in Edinburgh Head Office but *Support Office*. 'Our job is to support our people in the field,' says Farmer. That is also why they give a lot of attention to training, both in their two specialist training centres in northern England and Edinburgh, and on the job. New employees are encouraged to learn new skills in tyre fitting, exhaust replacement, shock absorber exchange, brake fitting, and the rest. Staff can take tests laid out in manuals at the fitting centres to become successively one, two, three or four star fitters. Since it entitles them to more bonus, most of them do.

In addition, they have a clear Code of Practice, shown to customers, which they are all expected to follow. This is it:

Kwik-Fit fitters are expected to be prompt, helpful and courteous at all times. In particular, they must always:

- Treat your vehicle with care and fit protective seat covers.
- Examine your vehicle with you and give an honest appraisal of the work required.
- Give, on request, a binding quotation before the work commences.
- Ensure that all work is carried out in accordance with the Company's laid down procedures.
- Inform you immediately of any complications or delays.
- Examine all finished work with you before the vehicle leaves the premises.
- Have available for you all parts removed from your vehicle.

The company is not tolerant of staff who do not follow procedure. They expect it. They treat centre managers as some of the most important people in the business, but equally they expect them to know their stock, achieve their targets, explain any extra discounts given, submit their data correctly and bank their cash and cheques every night without fail. Everyone knows they are expected to do whatever it takes to get problems resolved and their goals achieved.

Rewarding performance

Part of Kwik-Fit's company culture is their built-in system of rewards and recognition. For example, at each depot the volume of sales achieved automatically generates a predetermined bonus pool, which is shared by all staff every month. A one-star fitter gets one share, a two-star fitter gets two shares, and so on up to supervisor who gets five shares. If they beat their monthly target their bonus pool is increased by 25 per cent, if they exceed the target by 10 per cent the bonus pool is made 50 per cent larger, and a 20 per cent excess achievement doubles the pool. Staff are urged never to push a sale, but naturally the whole team is interested to see sales volume increase.

Via tests and performance staff can graduate through the 'star' system to become a supervisor, then a master manager (in charge of a depot), then a partner (in charge of three depots), with profit-share increasing at each level. After three years' service all staff are allocated shares in the company and can buy more through a special sharesave scheme. At depot level, awards are made when depots achieve zero customer complaints: a bronze award after three months complaint-free, silver after six months, and gold after nine months (well-deserved since even one complaint puts the depot back to square one).

Strong information flow

One of the undoubted keys to Kwik-Fit's success is its computerized operations information system. They could not cope with manual systems as they got bigger, and in 1982 installed computer terminals, called management action terminals, at every depot. They were specially made to be understandable to any fitter, to withstand grease, dirt and even coffee being spilled over them. When they were installed reams of paperwork were abolished. In addition, by 7 am each day directors in Edinburgh have complete print-out information showing the previous day's sales by region and depot, margins achieved on every product category, and comparisons of yesterday with the week before, and this month with the previous month. Their fingers are very much on the pulse of the business.

The computer also records employee time and attendance, stock movements in and out, credit card transactions, banking and cash reconciliation. Based on the day's sales it automatically reorders stock for the various centres, and pays the invoices electronically when deliveries match up. On the other hand, if

Kwik-Fit's own prices change, these are updated centrally and appear automatically in depot managers' lists the following morning in time for opening. The whole behaviour of the business, whether at Edinburgh or the depots, is very much focused on keeping close to the numbers.

Summing up

Kwik-Fit's managers know how their business is performing every day, but the theme that shapes their behaviour most of all is their commitment, from the top of the house to the front-line staff, to customer service. A vice-president of the Bank of America in England, who quietly visited a Kwit-Fit depot to see if their commitment to service was really shared by their staff, later wrote to Tom Farmer:

> 'I have to say that he [the manager] is truly an excellent ambassador for your company who really believes in every-thing you stand for, both in terms of customer service and innovation.
>
> Having witnessed Dean's enthusiasm and commitment, I can only say how much it has helped me to realize that the only way to achieve success is through the culture of the organization. You just cannot achieve it without living and breathing the virtues you are trying to extol.'

I couldn't put it better myself.

MARS CONFECTIONERY

Mars Confectionery was established by Forrest Mars senior in 1932 in Slough, England, where he first made and sold the Mars bar. Since then, the company has become a key player in the UK and European confectionery markets. Now their products include brands such as Mars, Twix, Snickers, Bounty, M & M's, Maltesers and Galaxy chocolate, virtually all household names. With some 25 per cent of the UK confectionery market, the company now also sells ice cream under similar brand names, and since launch in 1986 has already gained a 20 per cent share of the wrapped ice cream market in the UK. Total company sales in 1991 were around £600 million.

Company philosophy

Mars operates its business according to *The Five Principles*. In every Mars plant and office round the globe the principles are visible in summary for all to see. They are:

- *Quality*   The consumer is our boss, quality is our work, and value for money is our goal.
- *Responsibility*   As individuals, we demand total responsibility for ourselves; as associates, we support the responsibilities of others.
- *Mutuality*   A mutual benefit is a shared benefit, a shared benefit will endure.
- *Efficiency*   We use resources to the full, waste nothing and do only what we can do best.
- *Freedom*   We need freedom to shape our future, we need profit to remain free.

The principles translate into various actions in practice. For example, in relation to *quality* and value for money, Mars is the only company I know where, even when the company could take a bigger margin, they will deliberately build in more visible value (cost) to the product to ensure the consumer gets the best deal they can manage. That partly stemmed from Forrest Mars' conviction about *mutuality*. He used to say that if the customer did not keep perceiving good value in your products, you soon would not have a business. Similarly, even if you could squeeze a lower price out of your supplier on materials, you had to end up with a price which was seen as a good deal by both parties. Otherwise, you simply could not build productive long-term relationships. Mars commitment to *efficiency* means the company very much sticks to the core business it knows; although their volumes could justify it, they still do not make any of their own packaging or do any of their own transport.

Consumer and market led

The company is very strongly market-orientated. They constantly watch their market share numbers and analyse them every which way. They continuously conduct market research and hold focus groups with customers to find out what they think first-hand. They are forever involved in merchandising their products, conducting in-store promotions, introducing special deals, and advertising. Mars are permanently among the top ten TV advertisers in Britain, and their 'A Mars a day helps you work, rest and play' slogan is one of the best-known in the country. They repeatedly come up with new ideas to tempt their consumers: fun-size, snack-size, king-size, twin-pack, multi-pack, etc. They continually introduce new products and although they are not always successful, some of the notable recent successes have been Mars Milk (milk with a Mars bar taste) and a whole new range of ice creams.

The longer-term development of the company's brands is a separate function from sales in Mars. Brand managers decide on the brand's positioning, initiate the research and development work on the products, oversee product quality, meet legislation requirements on product claims and wording, and organize the advertising. Sales people call on the stores and shops, visit the big chain store buyers, work to get acceptance of their latest product promotions, and fight to get as much shelf space as possible. Every four weeks sales growth against plan is published on notice boards for all to see. By any standards it is a company which constantly thinks about its customers and its market.

People policies

Another key factor in the Mars culture is its people policies. Ever since the business was founded by Forrest Mars in 1932, it has sought to attract and retain above average people who in turn would produce above average performance. As a result, the company conducts extensive pay and benefit surveys every year and deliberately pays its people whatever is necessary to keep them significantly above the average. Mars have very low staff turnover, and some very good people. Associates have an annual appraisal with their boss which may lead to additional rewards. To emphasize the importance of team-work in the business, there is a company-wide bonus scheme linked to meeting planned growth and profit targets. As milestones are reached during the year, this triggers payment of several days' pay on the same basis to everyone in the business, from managing director to shop floor operator. Mars' package of pay and benefits makes them among the best paid people in the country.

The company has always been single status. In Mars all employees are called 'associates' and the title is not just skin keep. For example, everyone (including the MD) clocks in, and they all get 10 per cent more pay every day when they clock in on time. Everyone is paid weekly, by cheque. The same non-contributory pension and life assurance arrangements apply to all, and whatever level you are in the business the holiday entitlement is identical. Throughout the business everyone is addressed by their first name – what makes it easy is that they all have their names on their work garments or on their desks. There are no special car parking spaces for senior managers; if the MD arrives late he just has to walk further to his office.

There are no special dining rooms or toilets either. You see, Forrest Mars reckoned that if the cafeteria and the toilets were good enough for the MD to use, they would be good enough for everyone else. And they are.

Easy communications

Mars make it easy for associates to communicate by having no office walls. In fact, there are no personal offices at all. The MD sits at his desk in the middle of their large open-plan office with his fellow directors at desks in a kind of cart-wheel lay-out around him. Radiating out behind the directors are their divisional staff, with the divisions who most work with each other placed closest together. Meetings or confidential discussions take place in well-equipped meeting rooms round the perimeter of the office. There is no way one division does not know what the other is doing, and that is because they meet and talk to each other every day.

Mars are open with their information too. Everyone knows what everyone else is earning, and associates can see what is in their own personal files at any time. Board meetings are held every week, and the outcome is immediately cascaded down to the lowest levels in the business. Managers get regular prepared briefs for communicating to their people. Similarly, associates can talk to anyone else in the business they need to without anyone getting upset. If they have a grievance, they can choose whether they talk to their manager or someone in personnel. If it is not resolved, it will get to MD level within 48 hours. Of course, the system is not perfect, but the company takes pains to make its communications work.

Concern for people

Although it is a commercial and market-orientated environment, there is very much a family feeling at Mars. Fathers, mothers, brothers and sisters all work there. Associates stay a long time, turnover is low. Says Shassin Mohammed, one of the company's machine operators: 'We have a very good atmosphere. It is like a family here in the bay. We are all very good friends. We like to help one another.' Even when they retire, associates join the Marsters Club to stay in contact. Mars Confectionery is not the kind of company to lay people off. They have had their business difficulties in their near 60 years of operation, but in all that time they have never declared anyone redundant.

However, it is the stories that people relate that tell how it is in the company. For example, on one occasion one of the company's associates fell ill with cancer. He had come back to work briefly, but then went absent again. To help lighten his life his wife took him on holiday to Greece. Unfortunately, his condition suddenly deteriorated and he was admitted to hospital. However, patients have to arrange their own doctors and nurses there, and the complications and worry were making his wife quite distraught. The company decided to send one of its own nursing staff over to Greece to help and a few days later brought the family back in a specially chartered plane. The company gave the event no publicity, but naturally people heard the story. They felt it was just 'typical' of Mars.

Commercially sharp, financially aware

Mars is one of the biggest buyers of cocoa in the world. The price at which they buy can have a major effect on the profitability of their business. They not only watch prices in the commodity market every day, their buyers make trips to Africa and other producing countries to make bean counts as the plants are growing. They never want to be taken by surprise. On the production side, the company operates its manufacturing assets 24 hours a day, 7 days a week. Plant associates work a four-shift system to turn out the company's products in volume, for example three million Mars bars every day. Mars sales per associate figure of £260 000 is way above the manufacturing industry norm.

The company produces a rolling five-year plan every May, and by November each year has an approved short-term plan, i.e. for the following year. The financial year is divided not into months but into 13 four-week periods. Detailed financial figures are available showing period variances against plan seven days after each period end. Sales, cost and profit figures are all examined, but one key figure which drives the Mars business is ROTA (return on total assets). They set specific ROTA targets at the beginning of each year. This has several important effects. The company tends to get rid of assets which show on the books but which are not earning their corn: that keeps the asset figure lean. Secondly, because assets are valued at today's replacement cost, they tend to use the latest equipment, as new equipment shows no higher in the books when they get it. Thirdly, everyone's pay from shop-floor to director is tied to the level of ROTA achieved and that makes it in everyone's interest to keep the figure healthy.

Summing up

Like other companies Mars have had their brand failures from time to time, but all their competitors see them as very strong players in their market-place. Sales and marketing people trained in Mars are keenly sought by other consumer-oriented companies. The company operates planning and financial controls which the Office of Fair Trading once described as 'of a kind exceptional in this country'. For many, though, what makes Mars stand out are its people policies. In his 1989 book *The Hundred Best Companies to Work For in the UK*, Bob Reynolds gave Mars the highest marks of any organization. 'Mars is one of the most perfectly balanced enterprises we have encountered. It believes that its attitude to its people should be as important as its commercial activity,' he said. 'For too long Mars has kept quiet about its superb employee relations. It is a story which deserves to be better known.'

LINN PRODUCTS

Linn Products is a relatively small company – 120 employees and sales turnover of around £11 million in 1990 – but a very distinctive one. The company designs, manufactures and sells top-of-the-market hi-fi equipment. Almost everything about Linn is unusual if not unique: their philosophy, their products, their computer system, their manufacturing system, their building. As Jerry Ubysz, in charge of the company's computer systems says: 'Of course it's typical of us to do the opposite of what everyone else is doing on principle.' He exaggerates. The company pays very conventional attention to its financial numbers, and has been growing steadily and profitably ever since its foundation in 1973.

Influence of the leader

The founder, boss and driving force behind Linn is Ivor Tiefenbrun. Born in 1946 of Jewish parents, his father ran a successful precision engineering business in Glasgow. Ivor was interested in hi-fi. In fact, when he got married in 1969 he bought a bed, borrowed a wardrobe, rented a £5 two-ring gas cooker, and paid out £650 on a hi-fi system. 'That would have bought you a very nice car then,' says Ivor. 'My wife went hysterical. I said, "wait till you listen to it." To me, a hi-fi changes a house into a home.' Today his zeal for hi-fi is undiminished: you only have to talk to him to know it. He loves his products, and he wants them to be the best. Many of those in the industry who know think they are: 'Probably the best turntables and speakers in the world,' says Trevor Butler, news editor of *Hi-Fi News*.

Using his own time and his father's facilities, Tiefenbrun produced in 1972 what has now become the industry standard for turntables, the Sondek LP12. He reckoned then that no amplifier could eliminate rumbles or vibration picked up from the turntable, or put back any information missed by the cartridge stylus. It would never be right at the loudspeaker end unless you made it right at all the stages before. These stages have now become known as the hi-fi *hierarchy*, the sequence in which you should choose (or put right) a hi-fi system: turntable, tonearm, cartridge, amplier and speakers, in that order. Enthusiasts are convinced enough about the Linn approach now to buy the equipment in 30 different countries, including Japan.

Ivor is an unusual character. He is serious about his business, but hates bureaucracy and formality. He dresses casually (jeans, trainers and open-necked shirt) and so do all his people. The office environment is completely open-plan, with his own desk visible to all at one end of the office. 'Everybody knows everything here,' he says. 'They know every day the company is on the line, and we can only succeed if we are all pulling together.' He expects great things of his people, that they should use their brains as well as their hands, to take initiatives to get things done. Says Jackie Ward, who has grown from office junior to customer liaison manager: 'If you want something done, you just get in there and do it. We don't have to refer to anyone. We know what to do.' He also believes in a continuous search for the best. Every year they spend about 6 per cent of sales on research and development, and their researchers just assume they are shooting to be the best. When asked if a new amplifier he was developing was going to beat the competition, one of his R & D managers retorted: 'Of course, otherwise there would be no point in doing it, would there?'

Company philosophy

Every employee gets a copy of the company's philosophy statement. Composed by Tiefenbrun, a few extracts will illustrate how it is at Linn.

Everyone should clearly perceive our objective and understand what we want to do and achieve. **We want to make better hi-fi for more people**.

The more clearly we define our objectives the more simply we can conduct our affairs. The more simply we express our goals and conduct our affairs the more effectively we can concentrate our efforts. Bureaucracy is the machinery of security and so stifles opportunity and prohibits success. Whilst we have to administer and cope with complexity we must avoid unnecessary complication. Unnecessary effort or complication squanders our resources.

In this company we have employed great people because good people are not good enough. Great people can produce great ideas and perform great deeds . . . People have ideas about the things they do, the things they know about, and above all the things they are interested in. So the scope for ideas is distributed throughout all the people in the company . . . The company must encourage and exploit the participation and suggestions of all employees.

The function of management is to support the person doing the job, it must never be the other way around. Senior and middle management in most companies are the biggest barrier to new ideas because they are often divorced from the job. The only way to judge management is to look at the performance, output and morale of the people they serve. Indeed, managers are most effectively judged by the people they manage.

We want the best. We do not want to make 'also-ran' products . . . I often think the object of life is to prove everyone else wrong, but I mean our competitors not the people I work with . . . We do not want just to beat our competitors, we want to get them to admit they are beaten. In other words we do not want an arguable advantage, we want an enormous one . . .

We want a thrilled customer, not just a happy one.

Radical thinking

This radical approach, this constant search for the exceptional solution, shows all round the business. For example, before deciding on the form of a new manufacturing facility in 1983, the company visited some of the world's best designed factories in Japan, Europe and the USA. They then appointed as their architect Richard Rogers, designer of the Pompidou Centre in Paris and the Lloyd's Insurance building in London. Set amidst green fields near the village of Eaglesham, some eight miles from Glasgow, the building was designed to allow a quadrupling of output with only a 50 per cent increase in people (so far they are on track). Full of natural light, the building allows great flexibility of use. For example, the space within the building can be reconfigured to handle change of use, extra office accommodation could be hung from the roof trusses, or additional modules attached to two sides of the factory.

A computerized 18-metre high warehouse at the back of the plant with 2.5 kilometres of racking holds all parts, materials and finished products. Automatic guided vehicles (AGVs) trundle constantly round the plant and can fetch anything for operators within 10 minutes of request. The shop-floor is simply a grid of spaces each serviced by the AGVs and each provided with electric power, compressed air, a computer data line and test facilities. As a result, any product can be made anywhere in the plant. Linn's faith in its own future was tested when the project cost some £4 million at a time when company sales turnover was only £3.7 million. But they got the kind of facility they needed and it gave the company the leading-edge image it wanted. They also won the Royal Institution of British Architects' 1988 National Award for Architectural Excellence.

During the 1980s Linn also developed a unique computer system. Functions like production management, stock control, machine shop scheduling, accounts, financial forecasting, office administration had all been computerized piece by piece. When the automated warehouse came along, the company decided it needed a completely new system which would handle that facility and integrate all the other functions on one central database. However, they found that getting a system with a secure, common data store could not be written in conventional programming languages. So they called in computer expert David Harland from Glasgow University to help. The solution was a new computer language called Lingo. When this would not run fast enough on conventional computer machines, they found they had to build a completely new machine. The machine, called the *Rekursiv*, allows more than one person access to the same data at the same time, it prevents system crashes, and makes all of Linn's systems compatible. Already the Department of Trade and Industry have bought 15 machines for use in colleges and universities.

Single-stage build

A key element in the running of the Linn factory is the concept of single-stage build. Some years ago, when frustrated by productivity and quality failures, Tiefenbrun asked one of his operators to build one of their best-selling products complete by herself. Against a conventional production-line time of 27 minutes, the lady took only 17 minutes. That was the start of Linn's present production system where products are all built from start to finish by one operator. The system has quite far-reaching effects. For example, parts are stored on pallets in the warehouse in complete kits from which operators can build a whole product. The AGVs deliver the pallets, which may in practice have wall-boards hung with parts bins, on to waist-high racks throughout the factory. The pallet top acts as the work surface for the operator. All the required services (electricity, compressed air) are already piped to each work station.

When assembly is complete, the operator calls up the central computer. The computer pulls out the appropriate test procedure from its central files, and runs the specified tests automatically on the newly assembled product. Watching a TV set at the work station as it does so, the operator can pinpoint any defects and put them right. The operator then puts her (or his) name on the product before calling on the AGV to take the finished item to store. There is no service department at Linn.

Products with problems in the field go right back to the operator who made them. Very few products come back.

Flexibility in the plant is very much encouraged. For example, staff in the machine shop are trained to operate every machine tool. After two years in the company, product builders are capable of assembling every product the company makes. The single-stage build system is also more adapted to the building of prototypes and the testing of new products. It effectively means there is virtually no work-in-progress. And it allows the company to respond to customers with what they call 'real time manufacturing', i.e. delivering what the customer wants, when they want it. Linn prides itself that if an order for a product is received by three o'clock on any day, the right product can be taken out of store, assembled, tested and delivered by noon the following day.

Summing up

Linn is a company with a tendency to think radically whether it is about their building, computer system, manufacturing processes or their products. They are willing to take risks to gain a quantum leap advantage, and they have the tenacity to stay with their beliefs until they make their systems work. Not all new employees take easily to the Linn system, but those who do stay a long time. They know they are responsible for their own quality and for taking initiatives to get things done. They talk about being the best and staying that way. With excellent products, continuous innovation and an enthusiastic work force, they will remain a hard company to beat.

KEY POINTS SUMMARY

There are a number of companies whose way of doing things, whose *culture*, helps them stay ahead of the pack, helps them stay at the top of the league in their chosen field. They show some key characteristics:

- They have 'got their act together'; their culture is all of a piece.
- They are distinctive. They learn from others, but they are very much themselves. They are proud of what they are.
- They believe in what they are doing. They do not change their behaviour under pressure or for convenience. They stick with their commitments.
- Their beliefs shape their behaviour. Whatever initiative or policy they introduce, it fits with their existing beliefs.
- Their culture is no passing fad, it is permanent. It sees them through the good times and the bad. It stands the test of time.

Index